Gillian Le

CW00524395

From Head to Tail
With Love

From Head to Tail
With Love

by

Gillian Leonard

Acknowledgements

Sovereign Photography, New Barnet
Carol, Practice Manager, Wood St. Hospital
Cousin Eileen for her help proof-reading

First published 2005
Leonard Publishers
Leonard House
190 Bramley Road, London, N14 4HX
Copyright © Gillian Leonard 2005

Printed in Great Britain by
Arrowsmith, Bristol

ISBN 0-9550392-0-7

Dedicated to the Memory
of Mark Winwood BVSc. MRCVS.

PREFACE

It is New Years Eve 2000. Outside the snow lies several inches deep and frozen solid, while inside the coal affect fire lends a warm glow to the drawing room with it's Christmas tree shimmering with tinsel and coloured lights. A Father Christmas face smiles down from the top of the tree watching the contended scene before him.

The three goldfish swim around their hexagonal tank diving this way and that, chasing each other in play.

Blackie lies full length on the sofa blissfully asleep with a tummy full of dog food liberally endowed with ham and garlic sausage while Miffy, equally contended, stretches out upside down across the seat of one of the armchairs.

Rocking gently in my chair by the fire, I survey my family with a deep feeling of love and gratitude.

This Christmas could so easily have been very different. The beginning of the third week in December Blackie, once again, had been urgently admitted to Wood Street Veterinary Hospital in a state of collapse with a temperature of 105°. In desperation I telephoned and spoke with Olive, the kindly receptionist returned from retirement to help out over the Christmas period. Hearing of Blackie's condition, without hesitation, she told me to bring him in straight away, Mr Winwood would see him as soon as we arrived.

For three days Blackie lay in a hospital cage connected to a life saving saline drip, being cared for day and night by the dedicated nurses and staff under Mr Winwood's direction.

It had been touch and go for a while but then a few days before Christmas Blackie recovered sufficiently to be allowed home.

Miffy danced along the top of the car seats with excitement when she saw Blackie coming out of the hospital gate, walking with me towards the car. She had missed him while he had been away but joy of joys he was back with us again now!

We all spent a wonderful Christmas in the company of our friend Audrey, who lives across the road. Miffy and Blackie enjoyed their numerous presents of doggie treats from the tree and their special Christmas Dinner of roast beef in gravy.

Now, as the year draws to it's close Blackie and Miffy are happily in the midst of their small but devoted family.

Since 1927 when our parents had acquired their first dog, Paddy, an Airedale/Irish Wolf Hound cross, the family had enjoyed the love, tears, laughter and company of a succession of animals all of whom had been – and still are – very much part of our family. Very much loved and always remembered.

Chapter I

Towards the end of January 1961 my brother Tony, who had recently returned home after seven and a half years in the Royal Marines, finally succeeded in persuading our parents to allow him to have a dog.

Thirty four years earlier our parents had been given a six month old, chocolate brown Airedale Irish Wolfhound puppy for a wedding present. Paddy had been a great joy and much loved. He shared many happy holidays over the years and, travelling in the family car had covered best part of the British Isles. His great love was to sit with his head hanging out of the car window barking with the sheer joy of life. In those days the roads were empty and one could travel many miles without sight or sound of another vehicle. When in the country, should Paddy spot a rabbit or other creature foolish enough to provide a moving target, he would be over our Father's shoulder, out of the car and away across the fields before anyone could stop him.

In the early days of their marriage Mother and Father lived in an average size semi-detached house in Sudbury in Middlesex, which in the late 1920s was still virtually open country. Their house backed onto open fields providing a paradise for Paddy. At that time Mother ran a Brownie pack, also Guide and Ranger companies in Bayswater. When she was ready to leave for London if Paddy was nowhere to be seen she had no need to worry knowing he would not be too far away. Sure enough, on her return home about 11 o'clock at night Paddy would be sitting on the doorstep waiting for her.

Paddy had two distinct sides to his character. In the home he was the most gentle, placid of animals, devoted to his master and mistress.

In those days Father was Junior Partner in a Bond Street firm of milliners and was often away from home for up to six weeks at a time touring the country. Each morning while he was away, Paddy would rush downstairs at the sound of the postman, sniff out Father's letter from the post on the mat then take it upstairs to Mother while wagging his tail like mad with excited pleasure.

Within a year Paddy and our parents moved to a very large upstairs flat overlooking the park in Wembley which, though developing fast, was still comparatively rural. So close was the link between master and dog that on many occasions, though not expecting his return for several days, Mother would know Father was on his way home because Paddy would stand on the settee with his front paws resting on the back, looking out of the large bay window waiting for the car to come into sight. All afternoon he wondered backwards and forwards to the window watching, waiting. Eventually on his arrival Father would tell how he had suddenly decided to turn the car around and head for home.

Sure enough the time he made his decision coincided with Paddy's first trip to the window.

Our Mother too enjoyed Paddy's devotion and never more so than when she was confined to bed for six weeks when she first contracted nyphritis in January 1930. Our Father engaged a nurse to look after Mother during the this period. She arrived each morning at 9am and stayed until 5pm when, having made our Mother comfortable she would say goodnight and walk across the park home.

The day she arrived Nurse made it quite clear she would not allow an animal in the sick room and banished Paddy to the kitchen. Undaunted and determined to stay as near as possible to his beloved mistress, Paddy watched his opportunity. When Nurse headed in the direction of Mother's room, he crept silently down the passage behind her, in through the door and slid noiselessly under the bed detected only by his mistress. There he stayed all day without a sound until, having taken leave of her patient, Nurse descended the stairs and Paddy heard the front door close firmly behind her. With the coast clear he emerged from his hiding place, greeted his mistress then curled up on the rug in front of the bedroom fire.

After a day or two Nurse must have realised what was going on but, either in recognition of his obvious devotion or because of his excellent behaviour, she choose to turn a blind eye to Paddy's artfully concealed presence. In return Paddy showed his appreciation of her "blindness". When Nurse left the room after saying goodnight, he would creep from under the bed, slide out of the door behind her then appear as if from nowhere and escort her down the stairs, out of the house, across the park to the far end of the alley leading to the road in which she lived. There he would stand watching until Nurse was safely through her front door when he would turn and make his way back across the park to his own fireside, gaining entrance to the house by scratching on the front door with his paw until the tenant in the ground floor flat, who at this time was busy preparing her husband's evening meal, let him in.

So developed a mutual feeling of trust, friendship and respect between Paddy and Nurse while dog and mistress remained together undisturbed.

The front door of the flat was directly opposite the park gates and Paddy never missed an opportunity when the door was open to dash down the steps, across the road and into the park. One day the inevitable happened and Paddy crawled home obviously injured and looking very sorry for himself. Father, being home, immediately took him to a veterinary surgeon in Stonebridge Park who confirmed Paddy had been hit by a car and would need to be "hospitalized" for a while. A week later, after dedicated nursing, Paddy was declared well enough to go home. A very thankful Father went along to collect him but before Paddy would leave the surgery he showed his appreciation of the care and attention he had received by going up to the veterinary surgeon, wagging his tail vigorously and as the man bent down to stroke him, giving him a grateful lick on the face. Paddy never forgot the surgeon's kindness and ever-after whenever they met whether in the surgery or in the street, Paddy always gave him a special welcome.

Although Paddy generally enjoyed good health he had a tendency to suffer with a touch of rheumatism in his front legs. When he was in pain he would approach Mother, sit in front of her and give her first one paw then the other to have them gently rubbed. Her efforts were always rewarded with an endearing nuzzle accompanied by a loving lick.

In 1934, when my eldest brother Anthony – better known as Tony – was born Paddy's loyalty and devotion engulfed the new arrival as warmly as his parents, he would sit next to the pram in the garden hour after hour guarding the infant.

As I have already said, there were two sides to Paddy's nature. In complete contrast to the gentle loving home dog, in the street he became a compulsive and cunning fighter. The bigger the dog the more eager Paddy was to attack and he could never resist the challenge of an approaching alsatian. He would saunter up to his victim as though passing by uninterested then suddenly turn and hit the unfortunate animal broadside. Several times Mother arrived home after one of Paddy's escapades, covered in blood, on one occasion whilst wearing a brand new pale lemon dress. Twice our parents were summoned and had to appear in court as a result of Paddy's fighting. Each time they were fined £1 – a not insignificant amount in those days. Try as they may they could find no way of curbing his antagonism towards other dogs.

Paddy lived a full, happy life and then, when our parents were forced to move temporarily into a rented property on the outskirts of Sudbury, the landlord refused to allow them to bring Paddy with them so he was looked after by Mrs Spiller, the ground floor tenant in their previous residence and an animal lover.

Our Father visited Paddy regularly and took him for long walks trying hard to retain as much of their former life as possible during this period. Then our parents had to go away for a week on business and were unable to take Paddy with them. While they were absent Mrs Spiller's husband was admitted into hospital with a minor ailment and she decided she couldn't cope with Paddy as well as visiting the hospital. So, without making any attempt to contact our parents, she took Paddy to the vet and had him put to sleep. Such a wicked and cruel act from a woman purporting to love all animals. An act which tore our parents' hearts to shreds and for which, though now long dead herself, she has never been forgiven by any or us.

Chapter II

As time passed their growing son confined Mother more to the home. Dearly wanting another pet but realising Tony would need most of her attention, instead of having another dog Mother acquired a very large tabby tom cat for company and called him Tiger.

Tony and Tiger grew up together forming a bond so strong that when Tony was old enough to go to Sudbury Junior School, about three quarters of a mile away across the busy Harrow Road, Tiger always walked with him. He waited at the school gate while Tony went into the playground then turned round and walked home again. More often than not the elderly auxiliary policeman at the crossing would wait for Tiger to come back then see him safely across the main road before leaving his post.

Towards the middle of 1941 Mother discovered she was expecting another child. There had recently been reports in the newspapers of two cases where a baby had been smothered by a cat sitting on the infants face. Worried by this previously unconsidered danger Mother reluctantly decided she had to find a good home for Tiger.

By the time I was born in March of the following year Tiger was happily settled with a loving family living less than a mile away. Tony was extremely sensible and though missing Tiger sadly, once Mother explained the dangers to the new baby he understood the necessity for her actions.

Not living too far way, from time to time, Tony still saw Tiger who never forgot him and was always delighted to see his young friend again.

Chapter III

During the ensuing years various pets including rabbits, goldfish, cats, a guinea pig and chickens were kept by our family. Then, in the mid 1950's, Father brought home a young golden labrador puppy for me. One of Father's colleagues was trying to find good homes for several puppies after her bitch had produced and weaned a litter. Father had always wanted another dog but circumstances had not permitted until now. Also taken into consideration was the fact Tony was away serving 7½ years in the Royal Marine Commandos so a dog would be good company for me.

Without question the new arrival was named Paddy. Like all puppies Paddy was adorable, he had a lovely temperament endearing him to everyone he met. He had the most gentle eyes imaginable, set in a soft serene face. Although Paddy was officially mine in no time we all grew to love him dearly. Even at such a young age Paddy was very intelligent. He was quickly house-trained and learnt to walk on the lead without too much trouble. In fact he both learnt and grew very quickly.

Unfortunately this presented a problem. Before he was a year old Paddy was so strong Mother, who was very petite, could no longer hold on to him when on the lead. When he stood up he could put his paws on her shoulders and on two occasions he unintentionally knocked her over. I was still only a child and Father was out at work all day thus it fell to Mother to exercise Paddy. She persevered for several months but eventually had to acknowledge, for Paddy's sake, she would have to find a more suitable home for him. One where he could receive all the exercise he really needed.

At this time Mother was undertaking voluntary work in the local baby clinic and it was one of the attending mothers, a great animal lover, who lived backing onto Oak Hill Park in East Barnet, who gave Paddy a loving home.

Choking back the tears, Paddy was handed over to Mrs Tandy. It was heartbreaking having to give him up but he would – and did – have a wonderful life with his new family who adored him. A gate at the bottom of their garden led straight in the park which became Paddy's personal "garden".

A year or so later, while out with friends on our bikes, I met Paddy on the edge of the park and our joy at seeing each other again was over-whelming. Paddy had not forgotten me – nor as the years passed did he, as his spiritual visits to me proved. Paddy is still very much loved by us all.

Chapter IV

In 1956, World Refuge Year, I brought home a beautiful young tortoiseshell kitten.

At Southaw Girls School we had all been raising money in various ways to help refugees. As one of the girls was trying to find good homes for several kittens I eagerly offered to take one, at the same time making a donation to the Fund.

It would be wonderful to have a kitten. To watch it grew day by day. To love it, play with it, cuddle it.

The little ones would not be ready to leave their mother for another two weeks – it seemed an eternity. At last the day arrived and the kittens were finally ready to leave the "nest". The girl lived only a short distance from the school so, full of excitement, I knocked at her door on the way home and collected our little bundle of fluff. Tucking her safely and warmly inside my jacket I set off to cycle home across Oak Hill Park, talking softly all the way to the kitten to reassure her.

In keeping with the our previous two cats, this little girl was named Billy. She was the personification of perfection in feline form. Petite, pretty and with the sweetest nature, she quickly became a much loved member of the family. Though she loved us all she was particularly attached to Mother, sleeping on her bed every night.

For four years Billy was the epicentre of our family's love. Then we noticed she was beginning to sit in a very awkward position – her front legs crouched down while her hind legs were high in the air behind her. After witnessing Billy in this posture on several occasions we took her to Mr Holmes, our vet in Totteridge, where she was diagnosed as having a tumour. Quite possibly she had been born with it.

We were devastated. Sadly there was nothing that could be done for her, she could only get worse. So, to eliminate further suffering for our dear Billy, one Saturday morning she was peacefully put to sleep in her own home on the sofa she loved to curl up on. We were all terribly upset but it would not have been kind to let her continue as she was.

Billy did not leave us though. Each night for many years to come, Mother felt her jump on her bed at night where she stayed until morning – just as she had always done. We continued to give her our love and often we would hear her meow around the house. While this was quite natural to us, the parents of a friend of mine, who were visiting us one afternoon, were greatly alarmed at the sound of an "invisible" cat meowing and made a hasty retreat as soon as they had finished their tea. They did not return!

Chapter V

It was not until Tony's persistent plea in 1961 did our family again experience the joy of becoming dog "owners". This time it was decided to adopt a rescue dog, a homeless animal, probably one that had been ill-treated and was in need of the love and security we were able to give.

One Saturday afternoon with this in mind, Tony and a friend drove to the Dogs Home in Battersea, better known as Battersea Dogs Home, in South London. However, this first trip proved fruitless for, though there were many dogs available Tony simply could not make up his mind which of the appealing faces to accept.

Three weeks later he returned to Battersea and this time there was no hesitation. Half an hour before their arrival a two year old black and tan Manchester Terrier cross by the name of Trixie had been brought in. The story given to the Home was that the owners were moving into a council flat and were unable to keep her. In my brother's words, he looked at her, she looked at him and that was it.

I shall never forget the first time I saw Trixie. I was working for the British School of Motoring in Muswell Hill at the time and as had become the practice, one of the last instructors to leave the office at the end of the day gave me a lift home – a journey of some eight or nine miles. Trixie must have heard the key in the lock. As I opened the front door she came trotting out of the lounge, down the hall to greet me, wagging her curly tail and emitting a wealth of warmth and affection. Like the other members of my family I fell in love with her immediately. Trixie's coat was primarily black with white blazoned across her lower chest and down her tummy, merging with golden tan to colour her legs. Her tail, upper most black with tan underside, curled up into a large circle on her back. All three colours painting her expressive and endearing face.

Prior to his setting out for Battersea, Mother had given Tony strict instructions to bring a dog rather than a bitch but though initially annoyed by his direct disobedience, within a very few minutes she was won over by Trixies captivating nature.

During the nine years that followed we came to know and love Trixie above all else and she returned that love and understanding without limit or reservation.

Though she took to us straight away and knew we all adored her, it was obvious her previous experiences in life and change of circumstances which, not unnaturally, had had an affect on Trixie and for the first three months she was with us she made no attempt to bark. When therefore she did eventually surprise both us and herself with a single whoof, she received plenty of hugs, fuss, praise and encouragement.

One day at the beginning of March our Mother said she was sure that she had seen movement within Trixie's abdomen and was convinced she was whelping. So Trixie was duly taken along to Mr Holme's practice in Totteridge, where she was seen by Miss Corsain, a London born lady with a brash vocabulary but a heart of gold, utterly devoted to her work and the well-being of animals.

After examining Trixie, Miss Corsain roared with laughter and said "Yes, any day now" warning Mother we would have to sit with Trixie, 'hold her paw' through the births and then clear up afterwards.

7

Obviously this was the true reason behind Trixie's abandonment to Battersea, her previous owners must have known of her predicament and not wanting the bother of dealing with a whelping bitch and litter of puppies, taken the easy way out. How callous people can be and how glad we were Trixie had come to us where she would receive the love and attention she needed.

It so happened at this time my brother was in Barnet General Hospital undergoing an operation for hernia and our Father, who held a highly confidential post in the Cabinet Office, was working night duty for a spell of five nights. Consequently Mother and I were alone from about 9pm onwards. On the evening of Sunday the 19th March Mother declared she had a feeling Trixie's time was very near so before retiring we put newspaper down in the hall, made sure Trixie was comfortable in her basket by the kitchen fire, left all the doors wide open and went up to bed to sleep – with one ear alert.

Next morning I was awoken by an excited cry from Mother who had risen early and gone down to make the tea. I jumped out of bed and dashed downstairs. There was our dear Trixie in her basket surrounded by five little black bundles. We had not heard a sound and there was absolutely nothing to be 'cleared up'. Everywhere was as clean as a new pin. Bless her heart she had given birth and cleaned herself and the puppies completely unaided. As we approached her basket Trixie looked up at us with an expression of deep concern and eyes full of anxiety which seemed to say "are you going to be cross with me, what are you going to do to me?". Our hearts went out to her all over again as we knelt by her bed reassuring her. From that moment on Trixie knew without doubt how much she was loved and cherished and gave us her complete, unwaivering trust – a trust that in years to come was to save her life. We made such a fuss of her, telling her what a good, clever girl she was and admired her very beautiful babies. She was so pleased, the anxiety went from her eyes and after visiting the back garden, she settled down again into her bed with an air of contentment while Mother and I washed, dressed and breakfasted.

Mother then telephoned the surgery to report the happy event, asking Miss Corsain to call and make sure all was well with Mother and puppies. I had to leave for work at 8 o'clock and Miss Corsain arrived not long after. The puppies again received great admiration and Trixie was told how proud Miss Corsain was of her for coping so magnificently on her own. She then suggested to Mother that Trixie be taken into the garden to "spend a penny" while she took two of the puppies away. She assured Mother Trixie would not miss them as she could not count. Three would be quite enough for her to look after.

When our Father returned home he was as enthralled with the new arrivals as we were and when Tony heard of the additions to our family he could hardly wait to be discharged from hospital.

Chapter VI

Trixie proved herself a natural and first class mother, she kept herself, the puppies and everything connected with them spotlessly clean at all times. There were two boys and a girl all with similar markings. Black back, neck and head with golden tummy and four golden paws. All three had light tan eyebrows and cheeks set in otherwise black faces which gave them a constant look of cheeky surprise.

In addition to caring for and training her offspring Trixie religiously kept us informed of their progress. Our Father, who had made all our childhood toys from dolls house and pram to a complete replica of Sudbury Town Station, now set to work to make a very special bed for Trixie and her new family. Raised 4 or 5 inches from the ground the soft wood structure was enclosed on three sides giving support and protection from unwanted draughts then finally was lined with clean paper. The new bed was large enough to accommodate Mum and puppies comfortably. As soon as Father brought it into the house, placed it in front of the drawing room fire and told Trixie it was for her, she carefully picked up her puppies one at a time, placed them firmly on the paper, climbed in with them then looked up at us as if to say "Thank you – it's lovely".

One day not long after this Mother was in the kitchen preparing the vegetables for dinner when a very excited Trixie came running in to her, tail wagging, nose wrinkling. She ran first to Mother and then back to the door asking as plainly as she knew how for Mother to follow her. The first of her babies had opened their eyes! Mother was as pleased as Trixie was proud and made such a fuss of them all.

When in due course the rest of us arrived home we were all greeted by an excited Trixie followed by Mother relating the days great news. This touching episode was repeated each time another puppy took its first look at the world around it.

Another great step forward was achieved the day the puppies discovered they could clamber out of the bed unaided. Little front legs plonked down onto the carpet as bundles of animated fur accompanied by two trailing back legs and tail followed helplessly. They had arrived – there was much to be explored but which way to go first? Whichever direction the puppies took it was not long before Mum picked them up by the scruff of the neck and returned them to the safety of their bed.

Were they never to find out what was beyond their immediate vision? Though to be truthful the clamber from the bed and first exploration of the world outside **had** been rather exhausting – maybe a short nap would be a good idea!

When the puppies were a few weeks old we became aware of a sweet, sickly smell emanating from their direction but were at a total loss to discover the cause. Then we noticed their fur was loosing it's glossy appearance and beginning to look tackie and matted. At the same time the sickly aroma became quite over-powering, so out went a plea for help to Miss Corsain who, in no time at all, was able to diagnose the problem. Trixie's milk was too plentiful and too rich for her babies so when feeding they were inadvertently rolling in the residue which clung to their fur, dried, thus producing this sickly smell and matted look.

The remedy was simple if time consuming. Every two hours Mother and Tony, who was home on sick leave, had to brush and comb each puppy to remove the tangles then comb in a white remedial powder. Each session took almost an hour to complete giving only the same amount of time before the process had to be started all over again. Gradually the rich odour was eradicated and the puppies' coats began to regain their silky mien.

The weeks passed and the puppies gave much pleasure both to their Mum and to us as they grew from wriggling velvet bundles into active puppies each with their own endearing personality.

With the onset of the warmer weather the maternal bed was put outside in the sunshine on the small paved patio so Mum and puppies could enjoy the fresh air. One of us always sat with them to ensure they did not come to any harm while romping around although as always Trixie kept a very careful eye on them.

The time came when it was decided the new family could safely be taken out for a walk with their Mum so down to the pet shop went Tony to purchase three small harnesses and leads. Such excitement! The puppies could not make out what these new toys were nor why they were getting so tangled up in them? What good was a plaything if it was wound round your tummy and legs? Eventually, with Trixie watching every movement, the puppies were ready for their great adventure.

What was happening? They were being picked up and taken in a different direction to the garden where they usually played! Out through a big hole in the wall and oh! so much space, which way to look first? Up the path, this time to a metal wall which was also opened and – oh dear, we are going down to ground level again – help, where is Mum?! There she is. Now what? Best stand still and see what happens. Oh, surely they do not expect us to walk with this funny thing wound round us? Oh, they do and gosh Mum is nuzzling us. Does *she* want us to move too? Oh well, let's humour them just a little. Hey, this is quite good, each time we take a step forward we are made a fuss of by the humans and Mum is pleased with us too – maybe this is worth doing!

So the puppies took their first, if short, walk which from then on became part of their daily routine.

Chapter VII

Much as we would have loved to have been able to keep all the puppies it was simply not possible and to be honest, Trixie was beginning to find, as they grow bigger, they were just a little too much to cope with. They would not allow her to rest so when they were about two months old Trixie was allowed upstairs to sleep while her energetic family were tucked up safe and warm together in their bed downstairs. On the first occasion this happened Trixie looked up at us with love and gratitude in her eyes as if to say "Thank you! I do love them all but, oh dear, they can be very tiring. Thank you for understanding my need".

The BSM branch where I worked had only been open 12 months. Naturally the chaps with whom I worked knew all about the puppies and had followed their progress with keen interest. Three of the instructors expressed the wish to give a puppy a good home and knowing the boys well, I was satisfied they would all provide a loving and secure environment.

So it was when the puppies were about four months of age they left the maternal home to begin their own independent lives. The little girl was given the name Sue and went to live with an instructor who worked at Finsbury Park Branch. The two boys were taken by Johnny Bebb and Freddie Pearse from our own branch and both having children in the 8–12 age group. All three puppies settled down well and seeing their new "dads" each day meant I was able to keep in touch with them.

Eventually Sue's "dad" left BSM so we heard no more of her. However by this time we were all happy in the knowledge she was well established in and cherished by her new family.

Johnny unfortunately ran into domestic strife and very reluctantly had to part with his puppy but found an excellent home for him with a friend of his who both lived and worked in one of Enfield's many large, natural parks. So puppy number two enjoyed a loving home and a full and happy life.

Number three was named, because of his markings which gave him the facial expression, "Cheeky". Freddie and Ann Pearse lived in those days in a prefab on the outskirts of Wood Green in North London and as Freddie had been instrumental in helping me pass my Driving Test we developed what was to become a life long friendship. Freddie would bring Cheeky round to the branch from time to time and I was amazed to see how large he was growing. I began to wonder what breed of dog his father could be – an alsatian, great dane?! What-ever his origins Cheeky was an extremely handsome dog. At home he seemed to almost fill the little prefab lounge but he also was very much loved by all members of the family. Regrettably Freddie developed cancer and was consequently at home for many months prior to his passing, during which time Cheeky was his constant and devoted companion.

A year or two after Freddie's death Ann was re-housed, moving into a high-rise block of flats not far from Bounds Green and, because he was an established member of the family, Ann was permitted – much to her relief – to keep Cheeky with her. Though by no means the most suitable dwelling for a large dog, Cheeky was happy just to be with his Mum who took him each day to a nearby park for a good run to compensate.

Ann had a sister living in Beccles who for many years had cared for their disabled brother until she herself became seriously ill and eventually passed over. Subsequently Ann left London, going to live in Suffolk to continue her late sister's role of house-keeper and nurse to their brother. Unfortunately, for one reason or another, it was not possible for Cheeky to move into the tiny Beccles house. Never-the-less Ann would not betray him. Not far from where she now lived Ann found a small though caring kennels and rest home for dogs. Cheeky was willingly accepted and soon made friends with the other residents, settling down to a secure, happy environment. Though managing on a very low income Ann paid Cheeky's fees for the rest of his life visiting him at least two or three times a week, giving him lots of love, treats and extra walks. When he eventually passed to spirit Cheeky had reached the ripe old age of 17 years, six and a half months. Later we were to learn he was the last of the puppies to pass over and with his arrival Trixie was finally content having all her family around her.

Chapter VIII

The house seemed strangely quiet at first without the constant activity of the puppies. However, Trixie was able to relax more and began to develop her own character as part of our family, something time had not permitted before the birth of her little ones.

It soon became clear Trixie was a very strong personality, extremely gentle and loving, eternally grateful for all that was done for her. She was also very obedient although at the same time she possessed the ability to think for herself and, in the nicest possible way, had a mind of her own. For example, she was very self-conscious regarding her toilet and would not even "spend a penny" if she thought anyone was looking at her. Should she be about to stoop and catch sight of a pair of eyes in her direction she would immediately rise, turn to face the onlooker and give them an indignant stare as if to say "do you mind – this is personal!"

Her road sense was excellent, consequently in those day of little traffic Trixie was rarely if ever on a lead. She would walk to heel or trot along in front as the fancy took her, always waiting at the kerb until told to cross and escorted to the other side. Totally trustworthy she often sat at the front gate quietly taking in the world around her while one of us was working in the garden or on the cars. Our house was approximately 50 yards from the end of the road, a junction diagonally supporting a small parade of shops on one corner leading away round the bend onto a large roundabout. Mother sometimes popped across to the these shops while Trixie sat patiently outside the gate waiting for her to return across the roads then call to her to come when she would wriggle – run down the pavement tail wagging, nose wriggling in sheer delight to welcome her Mum. Over the years only on one occasion did she leave the gate before being called and then she simply trotted down the pavement to our corner and sat waiting for Mother to come into view, when she danced on the spot until Mum safely crossed over to her giving her a pat and a stroke for being a good girl.

Somewhere in her past Trixie had obviously suffered at the hands of children for it soon became apparent she possessed an inherent mistrust of young humans. Rather than come into contact with them she would make a large detour around the pavement, room or area in which they existed. However, one young man, although only 4 years of age, possessed a genuine love for the animal kingdom and his sincerity quickly won him Trixie's confidence. Johnny, who lived facing us with his parents and sister frequently pestered his mother to bring him over to see Trix.

Every life form possess an aura of magnetic power or energy surrounding and radiating from it. When a human is afraid of an animal even though they may try to hide their fear it manifests itself in the form of a turgid brown colour in their aura which is both repugnant and an irritation to animals, stimulating in them anger coupled with a desire to attack. However, when the reverse is the case an animal lover will emit an orange coloured radiation generating a warm soothing ray which breathes a calming, pleasurable sense of security and well being attracting the animals like a magnet inspiring trust and confidence.

In true animal vein, Trixie bathed in and returned Johnny's love many times over with the result they became the firmest of friends. One day while stroking her tummy Johnny wanted to know what "these are for". Smiling, Mrs Ryder explained they were her "buttons", immediately Johnny wanted to know if he could have a new coat with buttons on like Trixies!

Animals themselves very often possess a love for their fellow creatures and our Trixie certainly was no exception. Oftimes she would come running up to one of the family agitating for them to follow her into the garden where she would lead the way to a bird, hedgehog or other life form in need of help. She would stand by her find protecting it and looking up with a pleading expression which said "Please help, I have found them but I need you to take over now". Many is the little animal who has been taken indoors as a result of Trixie's intervention and nursed either back to health or until they passed to spirit when they were given a humane burial in the leafy dell under the beech trees in the dell at the bottom of our garden.

On one occasion however she must have ventured too close to a Mother bird and her young. Hearing a commotion outside we rushed into the garden to see Trixie running up the path towards the house with a bird chasing after her, flying about a foot above her and only veering away when they were within 10 feet or so of the patio.

Chapter IX

In the late 1940's our Father had spent twelve months in Norfolk where he was responsible for opening the local branch offices of the MNI. Based in Wells he lodged with a local garage owner, "Bunny" Warren, his wife and children who treated him as one of the family. Consequently, come summer we spent a memorable holiday with him in this sleepy country village beside the sea where, being from a Norfolk family ourselves – our Great Grandfather came down to London at the beginning of the 20th century – we felt so much at home we tried, unsuccessfully, to find a property to purchase enabling us to move back to our native county. So when, in 1961 an instructor from BSM Palmers Green told me he had rented a cottage in Wells and enthusiastically described his holiday there, it was with great excitement that we wrote to Mr & Mrs Longstaff and booked two weeks for June the following year.

This was to be Trixie's first holiday with us and as the day approached with preparations under way she became increasingly excited even though she obviously had no idea where we were going nor probably what was actually happening. Finally the great day arrived. With the car loaded and all aboard, we set off for Norfolk. Trixie was as good as gold sitting happily between Mother and Tony on the back seat, keenly observing the strange new scenes of both town and country passing by outside. The refreshment stops provided special interest, offering many new and exciting smells to be investigated in woodlands, fields and hedgerows. Alas, all too soon, it was time to climb back into the car and continue on our way.

Mid afternoon we arrived on the outskirts of Wells and without too much difficulty located "Settina", our cottage for the duration. While we unpacked and settled ourselves in Trixie thoroughly enjoyed herself exploring the natural garden and land surrounding the cottage. Before long we were visited by a chocolate coloured mongrel dog whom we later discovered belonged to Mr & Mrs Longstaff and young daughter Sue. Despite the new arrival's keen interest in our Trixie, having sniffed a "good afternoon" she decided that was enough and totally ignored his further attentions until at last, accepting his failure to impress, he trotted back to his own domain.

The beautiful sandy beach at Wells, being approximately one mile from the quay and town, is approached via a narrow footpath running along the top of a steep embankment bordering on one side the sea and on the other a 50 ft grassy slope leading to the alternative route, a two lane road running parallel to the path.

Having reached the terminus of either the causeway or road it is necessary to climb up and over a high bank of sand dunes which hide the golden beach and from where the view is breathtaking, transporting the onlooker momentarily to a dream desert island in the South Pacific. Tapering into the dunes from the coastline to the left are the pine woods which suffered so badly during the floods in the early 1950's when many of the trees were swept away and many more left in such a dangerously precarious condition they had to be felled. After the floods the area behind the dunes on the landside had been cleared and with the advent of the growing age of the motorist, grassed over to form a car park sporting a small brick souvenir shop in one corner.

Turning from the top of the dunes down towards the sea and stretching along the beach for almost a mile stands a line of sturdy, well equipped huts accessed from the sand up half a dozen wooden steps. Number 134 belonged to Mr and Mrs Longstaff and was available for hire by holiday makers renting "Settina". Though overnight stays were not official permitted, the huts contained everything necessary with which to cook, eat and relax in comfort during daylight hours.

Needless to say we took advantage of this facility and spent our days during the ensuing two weeks enjoying the comforts of home combined with the idealic setting of sand, sea and sun. The weather was kind so our days were divided between lazing on the beach, frolicking in the sea and taking long walks through the pine woods, all of which Trixie enthusiastically joined in.

During these rambles we discovered Trixie's strong herding instinct. Woebetide anyone who straggled behind. They were quickly rounded up and returned to the family "herd"!

All too soon the holiday drew to a close and on the last evening Father offered to take us all to the village local for an "end of holiday drink". Naturally Trixie came too and to our astonishment she walked straight in and settled herself down under the table, quite at home. Obviously whoever she had lived with previously had been in the habit of frequenting public houses and taking Trix with them!

The following summer we returned to "Settina" and again hired the hut on the beach where we had spent such a pleasurable time the previous year. Having driven down the causeway and parked the car, we opened the door, immediately Trixie jumped out and was away across the park, up over the dunes before any of us realised what was happening. Knowing her loyalty and common sense no one was unduly worried. To our amazement on reaching the beach hut we found Trixie sitting on the top step waiting for us wrinkling her nose with laughter as if to say "see, I remember, I got here first". What a fantastic sense of humour and memory!

Chapter X

Trixies intelligence and ability to understand and respond to a situation became increasingly evident as time went by. She loved to be part of our family always enjoying a game or a joke. Whether on the beach or in the garden she adored a game of ball and would enter into the fun with all her energies. Often she would wrinkle up her nose, imitate a sneeze then laugh when one of us was playing with her or when she had done something she thought was amusing. To hide behind a tree, a wall or similar place of concealment then jump out at us was enormous fun, a huge joke!

At home Trixie slept in the front lounge of our through room either on the sofa or in one of the armchairs by the fire depending on where her fancy took her or the time of year. In winter a chair was pulled up close to the Parkray to keep her warm during the long cold nights while in the daytime she curled up on the end of the sofa to either snooze or relax while keeping a watchful eye on the goings-on. This was definitely her domain.

When, as happened from time to time, the number of visiting guests outnumbered the spare beds Father would sleep on the sofa which could be made up into one double or two single beds. On such occasions Trixie would be obliged to sleep in the chair regardless of her fancy. Each morning between 6.30 and 7am Trixie would jump out of the chair, go over to stand by Father and stare at him with a look that said "come on, time to get up and make the tea, you are on my daybed and I am waiting to take your place as soon as you move". Affable as ever Father would smile at her and say "Oh alright old lady I know, you want me to get up". The instant he moved and cleared the bedding Trix was up like a shot sitting on the sofa end radiating proud satisfaction on attaining her rightful place once more. Having achieved her objective, within half an hour the household was enjoying an early morning cuppa!

Devoted to all of us Trixie had a special understanding with Father who, though a very strong, down to earth person, is wise, learned and full of genuine deep compassion towards all lifeforms. A great one for his allotment, Father would rise early and set off down the road about 7am on a Sunday morning, pushing his handmade wheelbarrow and tools while Trixie trotted happily along at his side. The site entrance being situated only a couple of hundred yards from our house and on the same side of the road the journey took a mere five minutes. While Father worked the soil and tended his vegetables Trixie, in seventh heaven, roamed around sniffing, exploring the surrounding open spaces, investigating the undergrowth and inner depths of the tall grasses. About mid-morning she would decide she had had enough. She would then go over to Father, stand in front of him and look up at him as if telling him she was going. "Alright" he would smile and say "you are off now are you old lady? Go straight home theres a good girl" With a wag of her tail Trixie would trot over to the exit and keeping to the pavement all the way take herself home. Through the front gate left open for her, round to the back garden where she knew the kitchen door would be ajar.

Now, sometime since the birth and departure of her puppies, Trixie began to experience female problems with the result Miss Corsain decided it would be beneficial if she were spayed. The appointment for the operation, involving a two day stay in hospital, was booked. On the elected day a very anxious Mother, Father, Tony and Gillian took Trix along to the surgery in Totteridge Lane. The first time we had been separated from her since she became a much loved member of our family.

After two harrowing days and several telephone enquires, at last the hour came to collect Trix. Father was working so Mother and I accompanied Tony in the Austin 8 to Totteridge. What a wonderful welcome we received. Wrinkling nose, laughing eyes and wagging tail in between which was a tummy completely hidden by white bandages – an alarming sight!

Miss Corsain assured us the operation had gone smoothly, all was well. Trixie had been a very good girl however, now coming home she must be kept quiet to ensure her stitches did not break open. Although presumably she had spent a penny before being brought into Reception to greet us, on the way home she made it patently clear in her usual manner, by barking at us, that she wanted to "go" again please. Driving past Oak Hill Park in East Barnet Village Tony took the opportunity to pull over to one side and take Trix onto the grass. The first thing she did, as soon as she gained her freedom, was race across the field thus pulling apart the bandages and bursting open her stitches!

Apart from this first natural exuberance after her enforced confinement Trixie was as good as gold. She didn't complain, she tried to co-operate when having her bandage adjusted or wound inspected and showed her appreciation of all that was done for you.

The following week Trixie had to return to Miss Corsain for a check up also to have the bandages removed. We were delighted to learn all was well. No further visits were necessary.

Chapter XI

Come Christmas Trixie always had her share of parcels on the tree. She could not contain her excitement as each package was taken down, given to her and unwrapped. She danced around and around wriggling her body from side to side. Wrinkling her nose until the contents were exposed when she sniffed it all over, took it gently from the offering hands and either ate or played with it according to its purpose.

One year she had just been presented with a packet of Good Boy Choc Drops when the box was accidently knocked over, the contents spilling across the floor in front of her. Bless her heart, although she knew they were hers she made no attempt to touch them, just sat there looking from the chocolates to us and back again with an "Oh dear, look what's happened" expression on her face. Needless to say she was praised, patted and given a handful!.

Even more than doggie chocs, Trixie loved Polo Mints. If allowed to, she would eat a whole roll at a time. She only had to hear the word "Polo" and where-ever she was, what-ever she was doing, she stopped immediately, come running over to sit at your feet looking up "Yes please" written all over her face which embodied two sparkling eyes full of anticipation of the treat about to be received.

Unlike Polos, dinner was not always gobbled up quickly, creating the need for a game of 'I'm going to have your dinner' played on all fours with a human nose closely inspecting Trixie's food bowl. Such antics usually produced the right affect initiating a deep growl followed by the rapid disappearance of the meal!

Fortunately Trixie enjoyed comparatively good health due in part to a good loving home, nutritious diet, regular thrice daily exercise and a warm navy blue wool coat with red binding to wear in the cold weather. Her wardrobe additionally included a smart cheery red rain-coat for wet days or as was her delight, for frolicking in the snow. Back in those days snow frequently fell in winter settling anything up to a couple of feet deep. At this depth Trixie was naturally unable to cope easily so had to wade or jump across the frozen ground. However, great fun was had by all especially when the deepness allowed for a splendid game of chase to take place in the back garden.

Other amusements for both in and outdoors included play with a red tug-of-war toy, a sawbow ball and most of all a wonderful squeaky lamp-post created in white and red rubber.

Humans and dogs are not the only ones to enjoy a game. The tall beech trees at the bottom of our garden were home to many grey/brown squir-rels who, contrary to common opinion, do not hibernate. Even during the winter days when snow lay on the ground the squirrels would run all over the garden chasing each other up, down, round and about the rose trees or by way of a change across the toolshed roof before springing back onto the nearest branches, then leaping through the trees with a grace and elegance unequaled by anything man is capable of achieving.

During the mid 1960's we were saddened to learn of the death of Mr Holmes and, because his son did not wish to follow in his father's footsteps, the sale of the veterinary practice in Totteridge Lane. Miss Corsain left the area and returned to work in London.

My friend and near-neighbour Valerie Mainwaring suggested a Mr Stockman of Wood Street, Barnet who, with his wife, had joined the practice, established in the 1880's by a Mr Wallis later succeeded by his son-in-law Mr Pickup, in the 1950's. Valerie had been a client of the practice for several years and found Mr Stockman a pleasant, conscientious veterinary surgeon, so had no hesitation in recommending him.

As Trixie's vaccination booster became due we registered with Mr Stockman beginning what was to become a very long and happy relationship with a wonderful team of people totally dedicated to the welfare of animals.

Chapter XII

We did not return to Wells-Next-Sea for a holiday again. Our Mothers Aunty Winnie and Uncle Fred had retired in 1950, moving from their large detached home in Hinchley Wood to a delightful double-fronted bungalow in Aldwick Bay, five miles outside Bognor Regis, in West Sussex. The area was still open country then and the shingle beach but a short five minute gentle stroll across a cornfield from "St Davids", which was renown locally for it's magnificent display of red roses bordering either side of the front path connecting the wide grass verge with the bungalow's main entrance.

Aunty Winnie and Uncle Fred never had an animal of their own. However a beautiful white mongrel dog with a black patch over his left eye came to live in the bungalow next door. Patch had been born on board ship where he had stayed for the first few months of his life until being adopted by the family who moved into the RAF owned property next to St Davids. Whether as a result of his early puppyhood or whether it was just his nature, Patch suffered with a strong wander lust. Consequently he spent his days roaming the lanes, fields and beaches. He was known by literally everyone living in or around the villages of Pagham, Nyetimber and Aldwyck. Where-ever he roamed he was made welcome, more often than not receiving tasty tip-bits, a gentle stroke or pat on the head accompanied by kindly words.

Naturally he visited Aunty Winnie and Uncle Fred who came to adore him and he them, making their fireside, their armchairs in fact their home – his.

When, as a child I visited Aunty Winnie with Mother, Patch accompanied me everywhere I went. Very often I sat on the deserted beach for two or three hours just watching the sea, wondering at it's beauty, mystery and strength. Always Patch sat patiently beside me. If I wondered through the fields Patch strolled with me, guarding and protecting me.

During one visit Patch was unwell. He had caught his undercarriage on a wire fence resulting in a nasty wound. Never-the-less, when I went to the pillar box on the corner of Kings Drive, although it was only about a hundred yards from St Davids and Patch was really under-the-weather, he dragged himself to the front verge where he lay watching me while I walked to the box, posted the letter and returned. Never once did he take his eyes off me. Such loyal devotion. Patch was truly a wonderful dog – deeply missed by everyone in the area when he left us, but never forgotten and loved till this day by those who knew him.

Uncle Fred died in his sleep in November 1961 so, as our Mother and Aunty Winnie had always been very close, our parents took it upon themselves to take her under their wing. She frequently visited us for up to three weeks at a time. One or other of us would drive the 98 miles to collect her taking her home again at the end of her stay.

Large though "St Davids" was, it was not big enough for the whole family to stay with Aunty Winnie for a two week holiday without getting in each others way. Therefore, as self-catering accommodation on the beach was becoming available we rented a bungalow named "Crows Nest", owned by a Mr Harrison – who ironically originated from within a few miles of our own home.

Come the first week of September we loaded the car and with Trixie on the back seat as usual, set of for the sea stopping once or twice for refreshment and "wow-woz".

I should explain the meaning of wow-woz. Many years ago when our Mother was a little girl she was taken with the Sunday School on annual outings. Before boarding the train the School Superintendent would line the children up along the platform then, walking up and down the ranks, enquire whether anyone wished to do wow-woz before they began their journey. This was his way of expressing "to spend a penny". Thus over the years the word "wow-woz" had become an integral part of our everyday vocabulary. Trixie therefore had naturally be taught to "go and do wow-woz" prior to going to bed, setting off on a journey or similar event requiring such precautionary action to be taken.

Having arrived at "Crows Nest" we unloaded "Gertie", our 1948 black Austin 8, then began sorting our belongings into the various rooms and cupboards while Trixie enjoyed herself first sniffing around the bungalow then exploring both the shingle beach in front of us and the sandy, grass wasteland behind.

In truth it is difficult to say which is the front and which the rear of the dwellings on the beach. They are each constructed from two parallel old Great Western Railway carriages approximately 14 ft apart connected by a timber and mineral felt pitched roof creating a living room/kitchen below. The several hundred bungalows along this stretch of coast were condemned prior to the 1939–45 War, a directive which 60 years later has not been rescinded. However, the order is unlikely to be enforced now as owners have spent many thousands of pounds renovating their residence thus creating a market value equal to any purpose built property.

The dead-end track from Pagham runs behind the bungalows, whose gardens and front doors overlook the scrublands and are used by the postman, milkman, delivery men etc. At the same time, french doors on the other side of the properties face the sea, lead up two or three steps directly onto the beach and are in constant use by visitors and owners alike.

The September weather was always hot and sunny consequently most of the days from early morning until darkness fell, were spent on the beach or in the sea. Aunty Winnie being literally five minutes walk across the grasslands, we were able to both visit her and bring her onto the beach to share our enjoyment.

Trixie loved her holidays on the beach despite finding the pebbles rather difficult to negotiate. In an attempt to alleviate her suffering she walked with careful precision settling down as quickly as possible amongst our deckchairs and paraphernalia. We had purchased two tartan travelling rugs for her from Halfords at a cost of 42/6d (£2.22½p) each. One of these was placed folded on the beach for her to lie on.

Trixie did not go into the sea, she would come down to the water's edge with us then sit patiently watching, waiting until we came out again. One day however, while Tony and I were enjoying a swim and a game of ball about 20 yards or so from the shore, a large dog bounded along the beach making a beeline for Trix. Suddenly frightened by his huge size and boisterousness she sprang into life, dived into the sea and swam as fast as she could out to us, arriving with an expression on her face of utter astonishment at what she had just done. Praising her achievement, we re-assured and fussed her before accompanying her back to the shore where the offending monster had scampered off after his master.

Occasionally we walked along the shoreline for half an hour or so indulging in the peace and tranquillity while inhaling the bracing aroma of ozone. Naturally Trixie came with us, braving the pebbles while waiting for the tide to recede revealing the wet sand which presented itself for but a short while each day.

One day after a good lunch Father, Tony and I, with of course Trixie trotting along in company, turned right out of "Crows Nest" heading in the direction of the Lagoon. Somewhere we had seen only from a distance – or on a postcard. It was a lovely afternoon, a gentle breeze keeping the air cool but pleasant. Time was not important so, as we were all enjoying the peramble, we continued walking. From time to time we came across a wooden groyne over which we clambered while Trixie, usually a few yards in front, nimbly jumped or climbed. We had been going for nearly an hour when suddenly we froze, our hearts standing still. A short distance ahead stood an extra large groyne towards which Trixie had happily trotted and which she was now about to scale but on the other side was deep, fast running water. The harbour entrance leading inland to the Lagoon! Panic stricken, Tony called out "Trix. No. Stay". A combination of the urgency in Tony's voice and her unequivocal obedience brought Trix to a halt, literally in mid-air, dropping her straight down on the top of the groyne. The front half of her body and two front legs precariously dangling over the wooden structure and perched above a ten foot vertical descent into the sea. The weight of her tummy and back end prevented her from falling while we sped across the intervening few yards and grabbed her, pulling her back down onto the safety of the beach. Fear, relief, shock, all emotions which jostled for dominance while, trembling, we hugged our girl. Her obedience had saved her life.

Still shaking, we decided that was enough for one afternoon and turned back towards home, Mother and tea.

Next door but one to "Crows Nest" lived a charming lady named Cathy with whom we became good friends partly on account of a mutually shared obsessive love of the sea, partly as fellow animal lovers and dog owners. Cathy was proud "mum" to two small, unclipped poodles. One black called Nicky, the other his son Pepe, a light coloured little chap with a huge sexual appetite for his own kind. A problem indeed for his father as well as other little boy dogs in the area!

Both dogs adored their mistress, spending their days roaming on the beach while Cathy swam, or lazing in the enclosed glass porch room, sitting on her clothes on the sofa or jumping up at her as she moved around the home. Where-ever Cathy was Nicky and Pepe were not far away.

On one occasion, Cathy recounted how she gave them their annual bath. They were unceremoniously picked up one at a time then "dumped" in the sea. As they were not accustomed to sea water exposure, this must have been quite a shock to their systems – as well as their pride.

"Blue Dolphin", the bungalow between ours and Cathy's "Windy Ridge" also became available for holiday rental. Being not only nearer to Cathy with whom I swam four – five times a day, but also at that time superior domestically to "Crows Nest", we decided in future to holiday next door. So for the next eight years "Blue Dolphin" became our home for two weeks each September.

While in the area it was customary for us to visit the Spiritualist Church in Sudley Road, Bognor, where the folk always offered a warm welcome and were only too pleased for Trixie to accompany us. Used to coming to our Spiritualist and Congregational Churches back home, Trix was always as good as gold. She sat in front of us quietly taking an interest in all that was said and done while obviously seeing, naturally, all those who were present from both worlds.

Like all animals she was very sensitive to the life forms of "dead" creatures both human and animal.

Trixie had no difficulty seeing our dear little Billy. On one occasion shortly after her arrival Trix had looked keenly ahead of her putting up a paw to whack Billy, where-upon she was gently rebuked being informed Billy was part of our family also. Henceforth they lived harmoniously together.

Chapter XIII

Whether Billy accompanied us on our trips to Sussex is open to specu-lation. However, as long as we were all together as a family whether on the beach, in St Davids or in our own home, Trixie was contented. At St Davids she would sit on the doorstep watching us working in the garden, having tea or just chatting. It was home from home for her as was proved one year on the last day of our holiday at "Blue Dolphin".

Gertie had been replaced by Sally, a 1948 Austin 10, slightly larger than the 8. Father and Tony had loaded the car in readiness for the return journey then driven round to St Davids ahead of Mother and myself who stayed to finish clearing and locking up prior to walking across the rear of the beach, over the grassy scrublands to say our goodbyes to Aunty Winnie. Being at best a 3–4 hour journey home, Trixie was to stay with us to enjoy a last run across the grass before setting off.

After locking up we looked round for Trixie calling her name. No response. With mounting anxiety we searched the area surrounding the bungalow without trace. By now we were becoming panic stricken, calling her name, asking the neighbours or anyone in sight if they had seen a black and tan Manchester Terrier with a curly tail. Where could she be? In desperation we almost ran round to St Davids to enrol the help of Father and Tony. We had to find her, there was no way we would go home without her.

As we drew near to the bungalow relief flooded over us as Trixie came bounding across the verge, nose wrinkling, tail wagging in cir-cles, body wriggling in sheer delight at the sight of us. The front door being closed neither Father nor Tony had any idea Trix was there. She must have seen the car go or discovered it gone and in thinking she had been left behind, run across to St Davids where, the rest of the family, assuming she was with us as planned, were totally unaware of her presence. Oh, how she was hugged – whatever would we have done if we had lost our dear Trixie? It does not bear thinking about.

Much as we loved Trixie she was not always an angel. How well we all remember the hot summer day we were travelling home from Sussex when we stopped at the Arundel roundabout on the A29 for a cup of tea from the thermos. Having pulled right off the road Trixie, who never strayed far from us, wandered around the immediate vicinity enjoying a good sniff followed by a lovely long roll in the grass – oh, sheer heaven. Wait a moment, what was that dreadful smell? Oh no Trixie, what have you done? She had rolled in human excrement, on one of the hottest days of the year with a long, tiring journey ahead! We washed her down with water from the container we always carried for the radiator, smothered her in talcum powder, opened the roof, the windscreen, the windows and still we could not rid the car of the awful stench. As soon as we arrived home it was straight into the back garden for a bath. We still loved her dearly though!

Chapter XIV

In addition to our two weeks in September each year on the beach, we also enjoyed a fortnight away elsewhere in May or June. Among other lovely counties our parents had toured North Devon extensively in the early and mid 1920's with the result we enjoyed several holidays in Coombe Martin and Woolacombe Bay exploring the surrounding areas which, in the 1960's were still comparatively undiscovered by the majority. Preferring the freedom of self-catering, we rented either a cottage or house for the duration thus eliminating unnecessary restrictions on Trix whose behaviour was perpetually exemplary.

The summer of 1969 we booked, by way of a change, a flat in Southern Court, Woolacombe Bay. The main property, a charming house in it's own grounds, stands high on a hill overlooking the Bay and commanding a magnificent view from all sides. The surrounding hand cut slate wall, built before the war at a cost of £5,000, is a splendid piece of workmanship, an excellent example of the high standard of the craftsmen of the era. Shortly prior to our visit a two storey house comprising an upstairs flat to sleep six people with a smaller downstairs apartment, had been erected in front of the wall. Tony's fiancée Jean, together with Margaret Gardiner a friend of mine with whom I worked in Kodak House, Kingsway, were travelling down by train to join us for the second week, hence the need for larger accommodation.

Happy, as always, to be with us Trix was excited to explore the temporary home, soon finding her way round, establishing where everyone was busy unpacking and settling in. The owners stipulated in their brochure though animals were very welcome, a small charge of £2.00 a week had to be made to cover any damage caused. This seemed fair enough, after all perhaps not all dog owners kept their pets under proper control all of the time, so a nominal charge was quite understandable.

Naturally a deposit had been made at the time of booking, the balance due on arrival. While Father made a cup of tea Mother walked up to the House, Trixie trotting along beside her, to settle our account. The main entrance door being open Mother rang the bell then waited. Within a few moments the owner, a Mr Russell, appeared smiling a greeting. "Do come in". Mother entered the main hall while Trixie, naturally assuming the invitation included her, trotted along behind. Suddenly realising she was being followed, Mother turned saying "Oh no Trixie. The gentleman did not mean you dear. Go back and stay. Theres a good girl". Bless her heart, Trix retraced the few steps to the front door, sat down and looked up as if saying "Sorry. My mistake, I am back where I should be". Mr Russell couldn't believe his eyes, he was so impressed by Trixies obedience he insisted on waiving the extra charge. He claimed he had never come across such a well behaved dog. Trixie had saved us £4 – a not inconsiderable sum in the late 1960s.

Occupying the flat beneath us were two delightful young ladies on holiday from the Selkirk region of Scotland. Nettie, a dark haired, round faced, jolly girl, was Personnel Manager on a Scottish newspaper while Jeanette, fair haired, taller and with a happy smile, managed her Father's fish retail outlet in their small country town. The girls, who were already ensconced when we arrived, being themselves animal lovers, quickly made friends with Trixie who responded with her usual warmth and affection. So, yet another life long friendship was about to be formed.

Nettie was, at the time, obliged to keep to a strict diet which entailed the buying of fresh chicken each day. As her daily purchase frequently exceeded her appetite, Trix became the eager recipient of the residue meat which Nettie presented to her on a plate each morning.

The holiday passed quickly. Never-the-less we made the most of every day either sunbathing on Woolacombe beach or visiting nearby Croyde or Saunton Sands already well known to our parents from former years before we were born. Trixie revelled in long walks across the hills or the sands, nimbly making her way over rocks and through pools, always close by us, always taking a keen interest in all things new.

Much as we enjoy getting away for a while and experiencing the joys of other folks country or seaside, home is always wonderful to return to. A sentiment shared by us all. Before the cases were even unloaded

Trix would be up in her chair or on the sofa happily content to be at home again.

Chapter XV

Basically a very healthy dog there were the odd occasions when Trix needed to visit the Wood Street Practice where she become extremely fond of Mr John Graham who had joined the group in the late 1960's on the retirement of Mr Pickup. Though a visit to the vet was not an event to be relished, Trixie understood the hands that held her and "did things" to her, were only trying to help therefore she was indelibly grateful. Should we meet Mr Graham while shopping in Barnet High Street, Trix would go straight over to him wagging her tail, looking up at him with genuine affection in her eyes.

On the other hand, should any of the family be unwell or confined to bed, Trix would loyally stay with them constantly until they were fully recovered.

In the summer of 1967 Trix became unwell herself. Initially she went off her food, became extremely listless, looked very poorly indeed and developed a high temperature. We rang Wood Street requesting a home visit so, after morning surgery Mr Harris, another young member of the team, arrived to examine her, establishing she had contracted a serious virus infection. Despite the various medications tried, Trixie's condition deteriorated until Mr Harris warned us there was little hope of her recovery. Reluctantly, he gave her no more than three days to live. Little did he know our Trixie! Almost as though she understood what he had said, she fought her way back from the prophesied passing. Day by day showing a slight degree of improvement until the danger passed, when she began gradually gaining in strength. Mother slept downstairs on the sofa with her for three weeks until Trixie was once again able to cope. During this time we had asked for help for Trixie from those we know who have passed over ahead of us, who are always willing to do all they can to help, and administer the natural rays necessary for healing to be accomplished.

One evening a week a healing sanctuary was held in the front half of our through living room. Those in need would come seeking relief from what-ever ailments afflicted them. The session would commence at 7.30pm continuing through sometimes until 10 o'clock. Trixie always sat patiently beside those receiving healing, watching all that was taking place. Not only humans visited our sanctuary, animals including dogs would come in the pursuit of the alleviation of suffering. All were greeted and welcomed by Trixie. When the last patient had departed she would jump up onto the stool and sit there looking up, waiting for her healing which she absorbed gratefully.

Her psychic abilities, like many animals, were by nature strong and evident. Monday to Saturday inclusive Trixie was taken for a walk three times a day – morning, lunchtime and evening. However, Sunday was usually a day for being at home all together so walks were often reduced to once round the block during the afternoon. Occasionally one of us would take Trix out in the morning but this was not guaranteed.

One bright sunny Sunday I was eating a late breakfast while Trixie adorned the end of the sofa as usual. Busily concentrating on the fried bread and baked beans on my plate I pierced a piece of bread with my fork and, while lifting it to my mouth thought "It is a nice day, think I will take Trixie for a walk this morning". Like a shot Trix was off the sofa, over to my side sitting there wagging her tail like mad and looking up with joy and expectation written all over her face. My mouth closed on the bread as a smile of wonder followed in the wake of it's consumption. She had read my thoughts as they were transmitted!

However, not every experience gave Trixie such delight. Mother often visited an elderly lady who lived with her husband in a small bungalow situated at the other end of our road. A good few years older than her partner she made the most of her aged frailty while he waited devoted on her day and night. Their main living room was small, dark and stuffy, not at all conducive to the well-being of spirit or body. Trix would at times accompany Mother on her visits but after only a short while, anxious to be out in the fresh air, she would pick up her lead, walk over to the door then look back as if to say "Come on. I've had enough of this, let's be going". As the lady in question was a compulsive chatterbox making escape difficult, Trixie was occasionally taken along for the express purpose of effecting an early retreat!

Like all life forms, Trixie's sensitivity could cause her distress as well as pleasure as was demonstrated painfully clearly when one night, exhausted at the end of the week dealing with the general public in a vastly overheated Electricity Showroom, my brother did not take kindly to being woken up at 2am to let Trixie into the garden for a second time. Though in reality he was devoted to her, his nocturnal debilitation temporarily over-rode his devotion compelling him to rebuke her with threats of what would happen if she woke him again. Instantly regretting his remarks he attempted to say sorry and fuss her. Too late. Though she must have known Tony spoke in haste and would never be unkind to her, Trixie was hurt and determined to let him know. She refused to have anything to do with him. Spent her penny then marched straight back into the house, up into the armchair. Now fully awake and feeling absolutely weighed down with remorse, Tony was finally forced by Trixies steadfast disregard for his attentions, to abandon all attempts of reconciliation that night.

Next morning he was up bright and early downstairs to make his peace with Trix only to find her in the same fixed state of mind as on the previous night. Towards the rest of us she was her usual warm, loving self. Eventually time forced Tony to once again abandon his efforts and head for the Showroom in Palmers Green, some six miles away. Unable to console himself he rode all the way home lunchtime with a bar of chocolate for her and a packet of her favourite polo mints. Mother, who was just about to take Trix for her midday walk, had reached the front gate when Tony arrived. He jumped off his scooter, calling Trixies name and rushed over to her. She totally ignored him and began trotting off on her walk as though he didn't exist. Poor Tony – he certainly didn't deserve this – Trix was adamant she was not going to forgive him lightly. It eventually took three days for the breach to be healed – true to her sex she had administered just punishment for what she considered unforgivable behaviour.

Chapter XVI

Where we all went, there went Trixie. I well remember one bitterly cold winter night, the snow had been falling all evening while Mother and I were visiting Stanley Poulton a dear, close friend and brilliant medium who would only accept self-perfection in his work but loved to relax with his friends when the opportunity arose. By the time we left Stans bungalow in Barnet it was almost midnight, with the snow already several inches deep. "Sally" started after one or two pulls, however having slithered gingerly to the bottom of the hill, her engine cut out. Several times I pulled the starter to no avail. What could we do? The snow was still falling heavily, it was late, there was no one around. Fortunately a telephone box stood a little way down the road so, leaving Mother in the car, I reluctantly rang Dad. No answer. I rang again. Still no answer – he must have gone to bed! Despairing I telephoned Mr Ryder our neighbour who, being still up, kindly doned his overcoat and went across the road to knock on our door, waking Dad and Tony to relay our plight.

Back in Barnet some four miles from home we waited in "Sally" absolutely frozen, not knowing what was happening. A little under half-an-hour went by when suddenly into sight came "Topsy", Tony's Austin, bowling along Mays Lane towards us through the snow with Dad, Tony and Trixie on board – the whole family had clambered out of bed to come to our rescue. Being young I had erroneously flooded the engine, thus by the time help arrived with the petrol now cleared, "Sally" purred into life at the first pull. Bless their hearts, we received not a single word of anger or criticism from either Dad or Tony, just lots of wags from Trixie who was delighted to see us.

Though always overjoyed to see any member of the family, there was one occasion when Trixie was anything but pleased to be confronted by what I brought in with me. Each year during the third week of March Kodak Limited paid all employees a percentage of their last five years earnings. After buying presents for the family I would purchase something for myself with the result one year I bought home a 28 inch high white fluffy teddy bear nightdress case. Trixie took one glance then backed away looking up as if to say "what on earth is that? It is nearly as tall as me, I don't like it!" Even when Teddy was placed high up on the sideboard he was given the wary eye and ever-after kept at a distance.

Unlike large manmade creatures, Trixie loved animals so when she found a hedgehog in the back garden in distress she rushed indoors to fetch who-ever she could find to help her.

The poor little chap, having been made comfortable on soft bedding in a cardboard box placed by the fire, still looked sadly so, Trixie with her caring nature stayed by him all afternoon and evening. Unhappily the hedgehog was dying and during the course of the night passed over into the next world.

Next day Trix began nibbling and scratching – the fleas from the hedgehog had taken up residence in her fur. During the period we were endeavouring to eradicate her unwanted visitors, Trixie learnt when asked "Trixie – fleas?" to come running over, roll on her back exposing tummy and legs ready to be examined for the irritating insects. Examination completed she received a pat, told she was a "good girl" and given a Find – a special treat of some kind, usually polo mints.

As she advanced in years, in common with all life forms, Trixie slept a lot during the day. When setting off for work in the morning Father would stroke her head gently, saying "Theres' a good girl Trixie. Have a good days sleep ready for a good nights sleep tonight". Something she would certainly do – though when Father was on late nights, arriving home around 11pm, as soon as she heard his key in the door Trix would be there to greet him. They developed a game between them. Our stairs opened at the top onto a wide landing to the left of which was the upper section of the stairs wall behind where Trixie would hide while Father slowly crept up the stairs calling out in a playful voice "I'm coming after you Trixie – I'm coming". On reaching the top he would pop his head round the corner calling "Boo", while putting out a hand to tickle her. Whereupon Trixie, ecstatic with excitement and laughter would wrinkle her nose imitating a sneeze, wriggle her body and wag her tail simultaneously.

One night Trixie decided to play a joke on Father. He crept up the stairs as usual but when he popped his head round the corner Trixie was not there! She was hiding behind the bedroom door laughing all over her face as if to say "I've caught you this time – I'm not there, I'm hiding here!" Oh how we all laughed with her. Father made such a fuss of her, saying "you monkey – you made a fool of me that time didn't you young Trixie?" Can anyone doubt the intelligence of our canine companions?

In June 1969 Tony married, moving into a flat some four miles away. Naturally, though he visited us often, Trixie pined for him. She knew we all adored her but at the same time she knew it had been Tony who brought her home to us from Battersea. Sitting in the living room one night Father said "Listen. Trixie is crying!" We listened. Incredible as it seems Trix was sitting on the door mat literally sobbing. Something I had never heard before nor since. It was heartbreaking. We rushed over to cuddle and comfort her – our dear, dear Trixie. We must all give her the extra love and attention she needed.

Chapter XVII

In the spring of 1970 I went with friends from Kodak to see the musical film "Oliver" in Leicester Square. Having enjoyed it tremendously I purchased tickets for Mother and Father to see the Matinee on Saturday the 4 April. Father's birthday being April 29th, this was to be an early birthday present.

Cockfosters Station being the terminus, only one train in four completes the full journey so on the appointed day I drove our parents to Arnos Grove Station, four stops down the line, to minimise their wait. Trixie sat on the back seat of the car until Father had vacated the front passenger seat. Wishing them a pleasant afternoon, we watched them enter the station, eventually disappearing from sight.

I turned to Trixie saying "Come on Trix over onto the front seat". Ever obedient, she attempted to jump over beside me only to collapse back onto the rear seat again. Panic stricken I tried to soothe her, telling her to stay there, not to move. I would get her home as quickly as possible. I drove home in a state of numbness until, having parked in the drive, I opened the house, rushed into the sitting room to ensure her bed on the sofa was straight then hurried back to the car to carefully pick her up, carry her indoors and place her on her own bed. What to do next? Tony being at work was not contactable, no one answered the 'phone when they were busy and Saturday was the busiest day of the week. I could have a message flashed on the screen in Leicester Square, however Father had a heart condition. What affect would such action have on him? No. There was no way of contacting any member of the family. Best to keep Trixie quiet and telephone Wood Street. Mr Stockman who was on duty, was busy in the operating theatre. He would come as soon as he was free.

Meanwhile Trixie lay very still on the sofa. While pleading for spirit help I spoke quietly to her, stroking her head tenderly. At one point she roused herself, obviously wishing to do wow-woz she made her way slowly to the garden door, down the lawn to the dell at the bottom. Having spent her penny she was unable to manage the return walk to the house so I gently picked her up, carrying her back onto her rug. Again I rang Wood Street only to discover Mr Stockman was still in the theatre. The nurse was very understanding, promising he would come as soon as possible.

Soon after this Trixie slipped into a coma. I felt so helpless, so alone. The afternoon dragged as I watched the clock. Having arranged to collect our parents from Arnos Grove Station when they rang, it was necessary to order a hire car to meet them.

Eventually the telephone rang – not wishing to cause Mother and Father distress sooner than necessary I hastily explained it was not possible to come out however a car was on its way to pick them up.

They arrived home about 5.30–6pm worried and anxious to know what had happened. They were devastated to hear the news of Trix, to realise they had been enjoying "Oliver" totally unaware of her plight. Tony and Jean were not on the telephone so Father immediately drove over to fetch them. This was very much a family crisis, we should all be there for Trixie.

Just before 7pm Trixie passed peacefully into spirit, the family who loved her so much round her bed emitting a combination of deep genuine love and heartbreaking sorrow. Within a few minutes the doorbell rang. Mr Stockman came in and sat sympathetically on the sofa next to Trixie while I lifted my head from hers, tears pouring down my face.

Confirming her death he said "a dogs life is so very short compared to ours and when you are young their life has spanned so much of your own. It is very hard to cope with". What a kind considerate man.

After a few words with Father, Mr Stockman gently lifted Trixie off the sofa carrying her out to his car, ultimately to a humane disposal. As he drove away we turned to each other in benumbed disbelief at the events which had so suddenly and swiftly overtaken our family.

Eventually Tony and Jean returned to their flat leaving Mother sitting in the armchair by the fire, Dad making a cup of tea while I sat on the hearth rug staring blindly into the fire. Trixie would be back with us we knew, as soon as her spirit had recovered from the trauma inflicted on her physical body during it's last few hours. Dear Trixie – at least we would have her spirit with us.

About ten minutes to nine we were still sitting by the fire when a movement behind us attracted my attention. Turning I was amazed to see the door open and Trixie come dancing into the room, straight over to us where she sat down wagging her tail, smiling her doggie smile. I looked at her thinking "No, it can't be. Not yet, it is too soon surely" Not at all – it really was Trixie, rested, refreshed after her transition she was back with those she loved so dearly.

Though of course she no longer needed feeding, grooming or any of the other material attentions necessary when in the physical, Trixie stayed close to us riding in the car with us, walking, sitting in the garden, she was never far away. I remember one summers afternoon being fast asleep in a deckchair in the garden when awoken unexpectedly by a nose nudging me and someone dancing about beside me. There looking up laughing, was Trixie. What a wonderful experience. How lucky we were to still be able to see and sense Trixie. What a tremendous comfort it was – in fact it still is.

Regrettably not everyone is so aware of those who have passed on ahead of us. Father had a dear friend who visited him every few weeks. Basically a good, kind man but possessing a closed mind, steeped in dogma. The first time he came to see us after Trixie passed, he sat down in the armchair by the fire as usual. Trixie, delighted to see her friend, ran over to him wagging her tail, looking up at him expecting her usual greeting. Alas Bert was completely unaware of her presence, he would not have been unkind to her for the world, he simply could not see her – was not aware of her, as far as he was concerned she no longer existed. Seeing what was happening I mentally called her over to me, explaining to her, her friend didn't know she was there. Instantly a sense of understanding flowed from her and she sat down beside me taking, as usual, a keen interest in all that was going on, content just to be there with us.

Strange, all the years we had Trixie, no one ever saw her bury a bone she had been given. Yet, on many occasions after her passing, while working in the garden one or other of us would turn up bones she had obviously buried.

Chapter XVIII

As Father was nearing retiring age the three of us spent that summer, with the exception of a week holidaying in Kessingland, Norfolk and visiting relatives in Belton, touring the South Coast looking for a suitable town in which to settle. First consideration was Father's heart condition. The location chosen must be reasonably flat, at the same time be within commuting distance of London for me.

As is so often the case, we eventually came full circle deciding upon Aldwick just outside Bognor Regis, only a short distance from Aunty Winnie. The terrain was perfect, the 7am train would get me to work on time, and in addition the area was already our second home where we knew and were known by many good folk. We settled on a lovely house in Aldwick Gardens and quickly found a buyer for our home in Cockfosters.

Father had an appointment with our solicitor to sign the contract at 10am on Monday the 21 September. Ten minutes passed nine he had just finished washing the breakfast things and was in the dinning room putting them away. Mother was upstairs busy making the beds. Suddenly hearing a heavy thud she called out to ask if everything was alright. Not receiving a reply she went down to find Father dead on the floor – he had experienced a major coronary and died instantly.

Although I was able to see and converse with Father his sudden, unexpected passing from this life was a terrible shock to us all. However, the thought of Trixie's joy at welcoming him was a great comfort. The two would be together, able to enjoy each other's close company again. Trix had someone she knew and loved with her now – they could go for walks together, she would love that, so would Father.

Having left his body for medical research there were no funeral arrangements to occupy our minds. A memorial service was held in our Congregational Church in Cockfosters, led by the Rev. Keith Trice with our dear friend Stanley Poulton giving a heart rendering address and Ena Berril, another friend, appropriately singing "If I can help somebody".

Chapter XIX

The house seemed empty, large, very quiet. Within just over a year we had diminished from a family of four people with a dog to just Mother and myself. All thoughts of moving were set aside, this was our home. The home we shared with those we loved.

That autumn saw the three day working week which brought with it the additional problem of out of sequence timing of street lighting. During daylight hours the lamps were burning uselessly only to switch off once darkness fell. Twice in one week an attempt was made in the early hours of the morning to break into our house. Still shocked by Fathers passing, alone in a detached house with the telephone downstairs and no dog, Mother and I were scared to say the least. To lie in bed listening to someone trying to force open first a window then the back door is not a pleasant experience. Eventually we agreed, for safety as well as companionship, we must have another dog.

For a number of years we had supported Wood Green Animal Shelter so it was natural when seeking another dog, to turn in the first instance to their Country Home near Royston in Hertfordshire. One afternoon Mother, Tony and I eagerly drove the 30 or so miles, full of hope and anticipation.

On arrival we parked beside the cottage and went in to see Miss Girling, the kindly lady in charge of the Shelter. We would prefer a bitch however we would be more than happy to offer a loving home to any dog of a size we could handle.

Regrettably, having visited the animals currently awaiting adoption we had to agree they were either too large or bearing in mind the guard dog aspect, very small.

Seeing our disappointment Miss Girling offered to telephone a lady she knew "just down the road" who ran kennels, sometimes taking in strays giving them shelter for a day or two to see if anyone claimed them. Our luck was in. The police had taken in a dog who had been found straying in local woods. They believed he may have been dumped from a car by cruel, heartless people. He had already been there several days with the result he was due to be put to sleep the next day. That was it. Whatever size, shape, colour or breed we would have him. There was no way we could let him die knowing we could have saved him.

Having told her colleague we were on the way, Miss Girling gave us directions, assuring us it was only a couple of miles down the road. So off we set anxious to collect our boy. Where was that turning on the left we were looking for? Surely it must be round the next bend – we must have come five miles already. Eventually we found it – ah now the kennels could not be much further, they are just down this turning. Well, they should be. These country miles – we'd been driving nearly half an hour already. At last the dwellings came in view – we had been on the right road after all.

As we drove up to the house a lady came out to greet us. Taking us round to the back of the property she led the way to an enclosed run where we were instantly greeted by a large sandy coloured dog, very thin but with an extremely energetic tail. Bless his heart, he was lovely. The lady repeated the story Miss Girling had told us, seeming only too pleased for us to take him.

He came eagerly with us, jumping onto the back seat of the car, settling himself in. Off we set once more, this time in the direction of home.

The journey through the open country passed quite quickly. Our boy was as good as gold. Strange though, as the fields gave way to more residential scenery our boy seemed to grow larger. By the time we reached home it was obvious he was really quite a big dog.

First thing to do was give him a drink and a good meal then telephone to make an appointment at Wood Street for him to have a thorough check-up.

Gosh, he was hungry. Hoping to find a new companion we had, in readiness, bought several tins of dog food together with a packet of Winalot biscuits. He ate the lot. We wondered if bearing in mind his height and shape, his rib cage was pronounced, he may be a greyhound – it seemed a strong possibility. Mr Harris would be able to tell us tomorrow.

Young Johnny from across the road had been excitedly watching for our return. We were therefore no sooner indoors than he was knocking on the door to meet the new arrival. He made such a fuss of our boy. What were we going to call him? It was agreed, to his great delight, Johnny should help choose a name so it was his suggestion we finally accepted. Kim was with us.

The next day, which happened to be a Monday, as arranged we took Kim up to see Chris Harris at Wood Street. Yes, Mr Harris agreed, he certainly was a lovely dog, rather on the thin side however that could soon be put right with good feeding. We were told he was definitely part alsatian, though there was no greyhound in him. His ribs were showing through as the consequence of starvation. He was still young and would be a very large dog when fully grown. In fact, much as I may wish to keep him, he was really not the right dog for us. He needed at least an hours exercise night and morning. Would I, travelling to London to work each day, be able to give him that? Would I be capable of managing him when he became an adult? Heartbroken I had to admit Mr Harris was right – Kim required a different type of home to the one Mother and I could offer. Love was not enough in this case – a strong hand, plenty of daily exercise, ideally open space to roam in, all essentials we were not in a position to provide. Reluctantly I agreed, for Kim's sake, to get him into good physical shape then find the best possible home for him. Mr Harris' actual words were "feed him up, stuff all you can into him". With an aching heart I took Kim out to the car and we drove home.

Naturally the people at work heard all about Kim. What a lovely natured boy he was; what Mr Harris had said; how anxious I was to find a good, kind home for him where he would receive all he needed.

A young girl had recently joined both the Company and our Medical Sales Department, in the General Office. On the Wednesday she came to me enquiring whether we had found a home for Kim, if not she would like to have him. She lived with her parents in Kings Langley where they had quite a lot of land attached to their property. She promised he would be very well looked after and loved dearly.

With mixed feelings I agreed to her bringing her parents over on Friday evening to meet Kim. It had to be clearly understood no matter how much they wanted him, he must take to them also.

That week I followed Mr Harris's instructions to the letter. Kim ate 39 tins of meat, 5 lbs of dog biscuits and drank seven pints of milk. By Friday evening he looked a different dog, his ribs had disappeared under firm flesh, his coat was gleaming, he eyes were bright. The change that had taken place in bearly a week was remarkable.

Not realising they were a prospective new family, Kim welcomed the girl and her parents warmly which helped to immediately endear him to them. With a lump in the throat, choking back tears I agreed to let Kim go with them straight away. The quicker the break the better for all concerned and the quicker Kim could settle down in a permanent home.

After a cup of tea Mother and I took Kim out to the waiting car where he had to be persuaded to climb in – if the police had been right and he had been dumped from a car it would explain his reluctance. Re-assuring him we stepped back onto the pavement as the car pulled away with Kim looking back at us, puzzlement written all over his face.

Mother and I literally ran back into the house, straight into the lounge where we burst into tears. We knew we had made the right decision for Kim, He would soon settle down and have a wonderful life – he was obviously loved already by his new family but oh, how we would miss him.

Kim did settle down in his new surroundings where he lived a full and happy life. His name was changed to Cuss, something he accepted easily. I was shown photographs of him from time to time so I was able to see for myself how well adapted and contented he looked. Our initial sorrow at parting from him was softened by the knowledge all was now well with him.

Chapter XX

Two weeks after Kim left us I decided to make another trip to Highway Cottage. This time young Johnny came along with me together with my friend and next door neighbour, Helene. Johnny, who had never visited an animal shelter before was full of excitement at the prospect, bombarding us with questions throughout the entire journey.

Eventually we arrived, explained to Miss Girling what had happened to Kim and with her blessing went in search of "our" dog. We quickly found an adorable little golden tan mongrel with one ear standing to attention while the other bent over cutely at the tip. She was still young though would not grow much larger than a whippet. She had been born in the Shelter so was not house-trained. No problem. I didn't mind that, we would soon help her to learn. All was settled – Kim as we called her, was coming home with us.

Helene sat in the front of the car next to me while Johnny sat happily in the back looking after Kim. We had only driven a few miles when Johnny called us to stop. Kim had been dreadfully sick. Poor little mite she did look poorly. Having cleaned her up we set off again with Johnny lovingly nursing her in the back. This young man was a natural with animals. Kim was terribly ill four or five times on the way home and no one could have nursed her better than Johnny, he was patience and understanding personified.

On reaching home Johnny carried her indoors where we laid her on the end of the sofa to rest. Mother was delighted to see her though distressed at her ordeal.

Gradually Kim began to look a little brighter, then to take an interest in her surroundings. Where was this? Funny, there were no other dogs around, however these people were making a great fuss of her so never mind about doggy pals for now, just enjoy all this attention!

Having explored the house, the garden came next. Emm, not bad. Quite a lot of interesting ground to cover out here. A more detailed inspection could wait for now though – how about something to eat?

The remainder of the day was spent happily becoming acquainted. Kim would have to have a special bed, however in the meantime a pile of warm rugs and blankets on the landing behind the wall where Trixie used to hide from Father, made a snug boudoir.

An appointment must be made with Mr Harris for Kim to be checked over and have her inoculations. I would attend to this first thing in the morning.

Early next day Mother and I made a trip to the pet shop to purchase a harness and lead small enough to fit Kim. Born in the Shelter this was a new experience, something it would take time to get used to.

The shop did not currently have a suitable sized bed however further stocks would be in shortly. Meanwhile we purchased a green squeaky mouse which Kim took to immediately. She loved it, playing happily by herself on the hearth rug pawing it, jumping on it, biting it – the squeak was such fun!

Having telephoned Wood Street at 8.30 that morning, I took Kim up to see Mr Harris that afternoon. This time size was no problem. Yes, Little Kim was a lovely girl. Of course having been born in the Shelter she would require complete training, that should not be a problem. So Kim had the first of her two injections. Everything was fine – what a relief.

That evening we decided to take Kim over to see Tony and Jean. It was time they met the newest member of our family.

Before we reached the top of our road Kim was sick, the four mile journey was a nightmare for her. Obviously the problems of the homeward journey were not the result of nerves at leaving the Shelter or simply a stomach upset. Our little Kim could not travel by car. Although we sub-consciously knew the truth, we tried to tell ourselves her repeated sickness was co-incidence. Surely next time she came in the car, she would be fine. It was just a matter of getting used to it.

Sadly this was not the case. Poor Kim could literally not travel more than half a mile in the car without being appallingly sick. This presented a serious problem for us. Aunty Winnie, for whom we now had Power of Attorney, was in a Home in Sussex necessitating our making the 98 mile trip every few weeks. For Kim this would be cruel torture. The choice appeared to be between drugging her everywhere we went or leaving her behind. Neither solution was satisfactory or appealed to us. Slowly, reluctantly, the awful truth began to present itself. For her own sake, much as we had already learned to love her, Kim must go back to Highway Cottage where Miss Girling must be told of her travel sickness. She would be kept there until a home was found with people who did not have a car.

I could not believe it. Once again we thought we had found our dog and once again, having formed a strong attachment, we were having to be parted. I discussed the matter with Mr Harris who agreed it was the only kind thing to do.

Sunday morning arrived in company with the pouring rain. With Little Kim tearing at our hearts strings we wrapped her up and put her on Mother's lap in the car. The nearer we came to Highway Cottage the worse we both felt. The tears were unashamedly pouring down my face as I drove through the driving rain. A journey wet both inside and outside of the car.

Miss Girling took one look at Kim and said "Oh, poor little thing" then took her from our arms carrying her straight into the hospital wing of the Shelter.

On her return, we explained both Kim's sickness and our necessity to travel regularly. To our relief Miss Girling instantly agreed with our course of action promising to keep Kim at the Shelter until the right people, without a car, came along. No matter how long it took they would keep her. We handed her Kim's vaccination card together with a donation covering the cost of the final injection then with mixed feelings of sadness coupled with relieved gratitude for her well-being we took our leave of Highway Cottage heading for home.

We kept in touch with Miss Girling enquiring after Little Kim and were delighted to learn she quickly recovered, settling in again with her friends at the Shelter. It was almost two months before Kim was homed, however the wait proved well worth while. A charming middle-aged couple living not far from Highway Cottage, who never had nor wanted to have a car, gave her a loving home where she quickly became the most cherished member of the household, living a long, happy life.

Chapter XXI

After our two failed attempts at adopting another dog we decided to wait a little while before trying again.

One day in early December while Mother was out on her own, the telephone rang. A gentleman, having established Mother was not at home, began speaking of a little dog for whom he was trying to find new owners. Being at a loss to understand who he was, he explained Mother had answered his advertisement in the Barnet Press. An animal lover he was in the fortunate position of being a gentleman of leisure able to devote his time to rescuing animals as a prelude to finding good homes for them. He was currently seeking such a home for a little Sheltie, would we be interested in accepting her? This being the first I had heard of the matter I would obviously wish to discuss it with Mother. However, yes we were anxious to find another dog. A Sheltie was a little on the small side as our new companion was to double as a means of protection. Could I ring him back later that day?

The beans had obviously been spilt, so on her return Mother was forced to admit she had been trying to find a dog to give me in time for the Christmas break.

My desire to have another animal being so strong, it was very tempting to accept the little Sheltie in desperation. Eventually however, it was agreed if the gentleman could find a good home for her we would wait a little longer – a slightly larger dog would really be more suitable for us.

A few days before Christmas the gentleman telephoned us again. He was trying to find a home for a young collie cross bitch, approximately 18 months to two years of age. The people she was with had a young child and the wife complained she could not cope with a dog as well. The dog, who was named Candy was always getting out and wandering off. If a home was not found for her by Christmas she would be put to sleep. She sounded perfect, just what we were looking for. The right age, size and sex. Also Candy had apparently been spayed while in a previous home. Without hesitation we jumped at the chance to adopt her.

The present owners lived in Harrow so we were given their telephone number to ring and make arrangements with them direct. Trembling with anxious excitement I dialled and spoke to a Mr Williams who appeared only too anxious to pass responsibility for Candy to someone else. It was agreed Mother and I should drive over the next morning, which was Sunday, to collect Candy – he would not change his mind would he? No, definitely not. Candy must go.

After a hurried lunch we set off for the pet shop in New Barnet with a view to purchasing a new bed, blanket, food and water bowls, biscuits, Brush and comb, tinned meat plus anything else that happened to catch our eye.

All were procured except the bed which, as only very small sizes were in stock, had to be ordered. The Goddards bed was far superior to any other make, comprising a strong steel folding frame with surrounding linen draft proof curtain, and a sturdy suspended canvas base raised four and a half inches from the ground. At £4.10s, a not inconsiderable amount in 1970, we felt it to be a good investment. How right we were to be proved!

The morning could not come quickly enough. It all seemed too good to be true. Despite his assurance to the contrary, I was pessimistically on tenterhooks dreading Mr Williams telephoning to say he had decided to keep Candy after all.

We had arranged to call to collect Candy about 10 o'clock so we were up early, ready to leave by 9.15am. Once Trudy, (the little dark blue Ford Anglia with the inverted rear window which we were, by this time running) was out of the garage I again gave Mr Williams a quick ring to let him know we were on the way, confirming also his resolve to stand by his decision.

Although travelling at the permitted 30 mph, Trudy seemed to be crawling, the journey taking for ever, although in fact we achieved a pretty good time of 35 minutes from door to door. Fortunately Mother, who was an excellent navigator, knew the area well so we were not forced to suffer the additional stress of taking the wrong direction.

Having parked outside the little semi-detached house we walked up the front path, knocked on the door and were instantly greeted by loud barks from within.

The door opened to reveal a man and women in their early to mid thirties. Behind them, sitting on the stairs halfway up the run was one of the prettiest dogs I had ever seen. Her long, gold, pointed nose gracefully projecting from her golden face framed by two tall black silky ears standing proud. Her black coat blazened with white and gold chest, long rich golden legs and tri-coloured plumed tail.

Mr Williams warned us we would not be able to "get near her" straight away, it would take a while. It had taken him a good half-hour before he could approach close enough to stroke her when he had collected her from her previous owners. In those days she had been named Mandy but as their little girl was called Mandy, they had renamed her Candy. I did not think much of either name but kept my own counsel. We could sort that matter out when we got home again.

In preparation for this moment I had taken a pocket full of doggie chocs. with me. These I now produced in the palm of my left hand, crouched down to Candy's eye level and approached her gently talking softly to her. Within two to three minutes, to the utter disbelief of Mr & Mrs Williams, she was eating out of my hand, wagging her tail and making friends. She was adorable, it was love at first sight for both of us.

The Williams seemed genuinely pleased to see how well Candy and I were getting along. They produced a chain lead from the kitchen which immediately sent Candy into realms of delighted scampering. Having clipped on the lead, we thanked the Williams, said goodbye and took Candy out to the waiting car.

Without hesitation Candy jumped onto Trudy's back seat next to Mother, full of anticipation of whatever was in store. As we pulled away from the house Candy stood up looking around her. What was this? What was happening? Why was she being taken away by these, albeit nice, strangers? She thought this had just been a bit of a lark but she was being taken away from where she lived. All the way home Candy stood up in the back of the car, paws resting on the rear of the front seats, staring straight ahead out of the windscreen while Mother held tightly onto her lead.

Once indoors Candy sniffed all around then proceeded to inspect every room in the house until a knock brought her running, barking to the front door. It was Johnny. Could he please come in to see our new little dog? Would this one be staying? What was her name? We assured him this little dog was here for keeps, she was the right size, a good traveller and no way would we part with her under any circumstances.

Like us, Johnny was not impressed with the name Candy. It took only a few seconds to decide on her new name – Kim.

After lunch, having taken her on a conducted tour of the garden, I clipped on Kim's lead and took her for a 15 minute walk round the block. Though delighted to be out, Kim was obviously feeling very unsure of herself. She walk steadily without stopping, sniffing or even turning her head to look in a different direction.

That evening she ate a good meal before settling down on the blankets we had arranged for her on the landing behind the wall where Trixie had waited for Father and the two previous Kims had slept. The Williams had warned us that she would jump on the bed during the night and sleep there but we had been adamant this would not be allowed.

Next morning I woke after a good nights sleep to find Kim asleep on the bed beside me. I had not felt her jump up or even been aware of her during the night. How could anyone be cross with her? I just laughed, giving her a big hug in exchange for a lick on the face.

As was Kodak policy in 1970, the London offices closed for ten days over the Christmas period thus allowing me time to get to know Kim better before having to return to work and leaving her with Mother during the day.

Next on the agenda was the visit to Stockman and Partners for a thorough check up. We were delighted to be told Kim appeared to be in good health – she was a lovely young dog. Mr Harris was very pleased for us – third time lucky he said as he wished us a long and happy life together. Having been given her vaccination jab we set off for home feeling on top of the world.

Chapter XXII

We soon realised Trixie must be helping Kim, or Kimmy as she was frequently called, to settle in as she often stared hard and long watching a life-form at her own eye level, often unseen but felt by us. Never was there any hostility on her part, almost as though she accepted this was also Trixie's home too.

Kim must have found Trixie's presence a source of great comfort as her past experiences were obviously causing her an element of subconscious distress.

One evening she was fast asleep on the hearth rug. Suddenly a blood curdling shriek echoed in the room. I shot out of the armchair – whatever could it be? Perhaps a fox in the garden? No, it sounded nearer than that. It was Kim! She was still fast asleep but the cry had come from her direction. Yet she looked alright. Maybe she had been having a bad dream – a nightmare. It was all quiet again now though and she looked peaceful enough.

This proved to be the first of quite a few nightmares Kim experienced during her early months with us. Her awful cry never failed to send a shiver down the spine of anyone who heard it. Yet once she was awoken, soothed and returned to sleep, tranquillity overcame her once more.

Gradually the nightmares faded away.

During those early days Kim stayed very close to me while out on walks especially when a man passed by, she would shy away from him clinging close to my legs. Obviously at some stage she had suffered at the hands of a man which now manifested itself in the form of a cringe when outside the house coupled with warning barks when indoors. At some time she must also have been kicked by a child riding on a bicycle as, if ever one passed her on the pavement she would ran at it barking and snapping. A reaction foreign to her normal good natured, loving temperament.

Christmas time there were gifts for her on the tree and like Trixie, she loved being given presents, looking at them down her elegant long golden nose, going mad with excitement as they were unwrapped, then pouncing on the contents eagerly either playing with or eating them, tail wagging furiously the whole time. All except one were gleefully appreciated. The offending present proved to be a squeaky rubber toy mouse, similar to the one Little Kim had loved so much. On hearing the first squeak Kim shot into fast reverse with a look of astonishment on her face, head on one side staring at the offering which made such a hideous noise. No way could she be persuaded to make friends with a mouse, or any other creature, who insisted on emitting a disgusting, high pitched sound like that! There were plenty of silent creatures who would not answer back and who could be played tug-of-war with or shaken all over the floor without raising any objection – best concentrate on them and ignore that other thing.

As Kim settled down it became obvious she had no road sense at all so it was necessary, when out-of-doors and off our property, to keep her constantly on the lead. It seemed a shame, but better safe than sorry. Kim did not appear to mind – she would dance up and down playing with the lead as we walked along, thoroughly enjoying herself. When tired of this game she would suddenly take great interest in what was behind the walls or hedges we were passing. Each gateway or entrance in the sidewalk her nose, followed by her whole head containing a pair of curious eyes would turn, extend into the opening allowing a thorough examination of the interior to be made. As she continued walking during this operation it invariably happened that she was still busy looking when the gap came to an end and the wall or boundary recommenced. Consequently, many is the time she just touched her face on a wall coming very close to a hard knock. However these near misses left her quite unperturbed as her curiosity had to be satisfied, a want which remained unchanged throughout her life.

In the joy of Kim's company the Christmas leave soon came to an end and it was back to work once more. This was to be Kim's first day at home alone with Mother so lunchtime I telephoned to see how the two were fairing.

Poor Kim, she could not make out where I was. She had spent the entire morning going from room to room and back again crying, trying to find me. Mother had done her best to comfort her and tried to tell her I would be home soon.

Needless to say, when I eventually arrived home about 5.45pm Kim could not contain her relieved excitement. What a re-union! Lots of hugs and fuss, licks, wriggles and wags, her mind must have been so confused and worried all day.

By the end of the week Kim had become accustomed to the daily routine, she knew I disappeared after her morning walk and she spent the day with Mother who took her for a short walk lunchtime. She could not understand where I went but was sure I would re-appear at the end of the day when she would have another walk followed by a good dinner. To make life even more bewildering, having become used to this routine, suddenly there were two days when we were all at home together. These were wonderful times, longer walks, frolics in the garden, trips to the park, visits to strange places, even new people coming to the house to make a fuss of Kim!

During the early part of the following week, while at work, I received a panic stricken telephone call from Mother. Kim had disappeared. There was no sign of her anywhere. Mother had searched every part of the house and garden, even been out in the street but Kim had gone. The police had been notified and issued with a full description of her.

Worried to death I arrived home to find Kim was still missing. How could she possible have got out? There was a five foot fence down either side of the garden with a brand new seven foot fence across the bottom. There was no way round the sides of the house she could have got out as these too were securely fenced. I would have to take the car and drive round the streets looking for her while Mother waited indoors in case she returned home.

I spent best part of an hour driving around looking for her, becoming more and more concerned for her safety. Eventually the sensible course of action seemed to be to return home in case there was any news of her. As I drove round the bend in our road there she was, trotting along the righthand pavement, full of beans and large as life. As the relief flooded over me anger followed in its wake. I pulled over to her, stopped the car, opened the door and said "Kimmy – where have you been? You naughty girl! Get in at once. We have been worried to death about you". Quite unconcerned she hopped in, jumping up on the rear seat. Within less than a minute we were home.

Mother came rushing out and when she saw Kimmy in the car hurriedly warned me not to be cross with her. She had been on the telephone to Wood Street to ask their advice. If, on Kim's return she received lots of fuss coupled with a good meal, she would always come back but if we scolded her and were cross, should she ever get away again she would remember the telling off and not want to return home. We had to remember also that she had been used to straying while living with her previous owners. She was not being naughty just, to her mind, behaving naturally, "popping out for a while".

The following week I received another desperate telephone call from Mother – Kim had vanished again. After searching the house, garden and surrounding roads, Mother had spent best part of an hour in Hadley Woods – which was only five minutes walk away – calling Kim and asking everyone she met if they had seen her. All to no avail. It was beginning to get dark now – where could she be? While we were discussing the problem Mother broke off our conversation to answer a knock on the front door. Over the telephone I heard a relieved exclamation followed by the chatter of voices. Suddenly Mother remembered I was on the other end of the line so came to explain. Johnny, from across the road, had been walking through Oak Hill Park about two miles away when he spotted Kim playing with other dogs. As soon as he called her she came running over to him wagging her tail with delight. Realising we must be going frantic with worry Johnny had brought her safely home. How grateful we were to him – he was certainly growing into a responsible young man.

On one other occasion Kim went off on her adventures this time coming home of her own accord. How she was getting out still remained a mystery for which no one could offer an explanation. Then one Saturday afternoon while working in the back garden I suddenly spotted Kim up on top of the compost heap by the bottom fence. The light dawned as I rushed down the winding steps into the Dell calling to her to stop. I grabbed hold of her, pulling her back into the garden. So that was how she was making her get away! An initial jump of some four and a half feet to the top of the compost then a final spring of two and a half feet over the fence and she was away across the open woodland behind us and the world was her oyster – or to be more accurate, her playground.

Now we knew Kim's secret the solution was simple. I reduced the height of the compost by a good two feet making the more difficult leap up over the fence impossible – Kim was safe in the confines of our garden at last.

Though her excursions out alone were over, Kim's life was not dull by any means. Being young she loved to play with everything soft she could find including our slippers. Consequently, in an attempt to regain control of our own footwear, Kim had a pair of cheap soft slippers bought for her. These she could and did play with to her hearts content, they were shaken, bitten, tossed, pounced on and generally enjoyed to the full.

When summer came she was tethered and played happily in the front garden while I cleaned the car. The rag mats made by Wyn, a friend of ours, were given the same treatment as the slippers. Being tough, even though held firmly between strong young teeth and shaken all over the lawn, they did not tear. Chasing and catching a ball in mid air – at which she was very clever – was terrific fun but did not present the challenge offered by a wriggling mass of rug!

Another great sport in which to revel was called "see them off" which entailed, on the word of command, dashing out into the garden barking like mad to chase away the pigeons who were helping themselves to the bread put out for the little birds. The fact we actually wanted her to bark a lot coupled with the success of her efforts, made this game particularly satisfying.

It was while playing outside we noticed Kim digging up something and eating it. Whatever it was it was undoubtedly delicious. Closer inspection revealed more old, mouldy bones, obviously buried many moons ago by Trixie because we had never given Kim bones. Wood Street advised against it these days and with doggie chews beginning to appear in the pet shops, bones were not really necessary for dental or other canine toiletries! To wash down these disgusting snacks Kim discovered a marvellous source of drinking water in the garden which eliminated the need to trot indoors when thirsty. The watering can was left full, ready for use and being on a level with Kim's nose a long pink tongue quickly found it's way into the cool refreshing liquid. When this was removed another supply was located close at hand in the birds drinking bowl on the corner of the lawn!

Like Trixie, Kim quickly learnt the meaning of the word wow-woz, also that obeying the instruction meant either about to go out in the car or time for bed. One morning Helene called us over to the fence smiling broadly, she had something to tell us. She had recently married a charming young Hungarian boy who spoke very little English. Henry and Helene slept in their back bedroom, retiring the previous evening about 10 o'clock. They had been in bed 15 minutes or so when I let Kimmy into the garden to do wow-woz. She had been reluctant to comply with my request, preferring to wander round the lawn sniffing, hence my repeated "Kimmy, *do wow-woz*". Henry, anxious to increase his knowledge and understanding of the English language, turned to Helene with a puzzled expression on his face and asked "Please, what is wow-woz?". Whereupon Helene burst into fits of uncontrolled laughter only increasing poor Henry's bewilderment!

Chapter XXIII

Prior to his passing, Father had shown an interest in purchasing an Austin Cambridge A55, Mark 1 so it was natural when deciding to change Trudy for a larger, more comfortable motor, to begin with Father's choice. Having viewed a couple of Austins, the salesman at Stewart and Arden persuaded me the Wolseley 16/16, though similar in shape to the A55, was a superior vehicle. However, as owners were and still are disinclined to part with them it could take some time to obtain one. Not to be deterred, I eventually located one through Finchley Motors, a small one man concern in Finchley Central who, even though she was less than a year old, persuaded her owner to trade her in for a brand new sports car thus releasing the Wolseley for me.

The first glimpse of her brought an involuntary gasp of awe, respect and admiration. Could she really be mine? This vision of elegant quality. Being parked behind the small showroom in an even smaller yard, which she filled, the effect was breathtaking. Her stainless steel and chrome trimmings gleaming among the chocolate brown bodywork. Her name was to be "Rebecca", after my Paternal Grandmother. Great Grandfather had entered into a "mixed faith marriage" at the end of the nineteenth century, hence the name "Rebecca". Grandmother had died in 1945 but I had been privileged to enjoy her helpful, loving companionship ever since.

Arriving home with Rebecca, Kim jumped in as soon as the door was open. Yes, she liked this – the front seat was of course hers as always. Much more room, greater comfort, far easier to see out of the numerous, large windows. She sat there looking as proud as punch.

To confirm her sovereignty I brought out Trixie's tartan travelling rug which Kim had inherited, then persuaded her to jump down onto the driveway for a moment while I placed the rug on her seat. In an instant she was back in the car on the rug, head held high, quite at home. During her young days though not sick, Kim was at times restless in the car with the result, when undertaking a journey of any length, Mr Graham prescribed travel pills for her. These were very affective helping to calm her down. Only when she wanted to do wow-woz did she fidget, barking her urgent need until the car stopped allowing her out to relieve herself.

Chapter XXIV

Living in Cockfosters we were surrounded, in addition to natural parks and woods, by wide open spaces where it was always necessary to watch Kim carefully because of her intense love of water – particularly if it was stagnant, dirty or smelly! I am sure she could sense water half a mile away as she would suddenly be off like a shot. By the time I caught up with her she would be having a wonderful time splashing about in pond, river, stream or ditch. Even green slime was no deterrent to this water crazed animal! Many is the time she has had to be taken straight home for a good bath leaving, unfortunately and despite open windows, a strong reminder of her exploits behind in Rebecca.

One regular outing which concluded with a romp in a slime covered pond was our attendance at the Potters Bar Dog Training Society. Each Sunday morning approximately 70–80 dogs of every size, shape, colour, breed and cross-breed imaginable congregate in a large field the other side of town on the edge of the country, accompanied by their Mum or Dad, to learn the correct way to sit, stand, stay, walk to heel, walk on the lead and generally become the personification of canine obedience.

I am proud to say Kim was a very good pupil, receiving high praise from the class instructor for her efforts. The only exercise which gave problems was the "Kim sit – Kim flat" command. To sit was no trouble it was only when I had to gently pull her front legs forward to teach her "flat" that at each attempt she yelped and cried. This dilemma must be sorted out – a visit to Wood Street needed to be arranged. Otherwise, these mornings were a great success. It is true to say as an owner I learnt as much about the right way to give a command as Kim learnt about obeying my instructions.

The subsequent visit to Mr Stockman revealed that at some time Kim had been spayed but whoever had undertaken the operation had, for cheapness used stitches that would not dissolve. Therefore when trying to teach her "flat", the stitches had pulled causing her discomfort.

Unfortunately there was now nothing, short of a really unnecessary operation, that could be done. Therefore this particular lesson was henceforth abandoned.

Once the Sunday morning training session was over for the day it was time for a free run in the open country beyond the tutorial field. Off the lead and Kim was away. Running all over the place darting here, there and everywhere, playing with other dogs, thoroughly enjoying herself. All this running and playing makes a girl warm though – time for a dip in the pond. Never mind the slime on top, the water underneath is lovely! Despite the bother of getting her home to be cleaned up I really did not mind Kim's frolics in the pond – she enjoyed herself so much it was a pleasure to watch her.

Living only a few minutes walk from Hadley Woods and Jacks Lake I would often take her over there for a run through the undergrowth followed by a dip in the lake which, though deep in the middle, is comparatively shallow round the edge, at one point along the bank tapering to a few inches.

Towards the beginning of March I began reacting to Father's sudden passing and was consequently off work for six weeks with delayed shock. Not understanding the reason, Kim was delighted to have me home all day especially as most mornings it meant a walk through the woods to the lake with Helene, her baby daughter Mary and their rather over-weight Beagle, George.

Though she dashed on ahead Kim always returned to us periodically to make sure we were following. Poor George could not keep up with her so resigned himself to trotting along behind with us. As Mary was in a pushchair our pace was naturally much slower, therefore more in keeping with George's age and figure. He was not however deterred from taking the dip once the lake was reached. He waded gently out until the water lapped around his tummy then, to Helene's disgust, would proceed to enjoy a long drink. No amount of scolding from Helene ever made the slightest scrap of difference to him. Fortunately Kim never acquired this rather dubious habit.

One afternoon, for a change, we walked down through the village to Oak Hill Park where Mary was able to indulge in numerous activities in the children's play area. Afterwards we walked along the path which ran beside a shallow stream flowing between two four foot steep embankments.

Kim thought this wonderful! She ran down into the stream, splashing along to her hearts content. George decided he too wanted to join in so half fell, half ran down into the cool water. All was well until Kim ran nimbly up the opposite bank out onto the grass again, when George resolved to follow suite. The only problem was, try as he might, he couldn't climb out of the stream. In desperation and laughing till the tears ran down our cheeks Helene and I slid down into the water, got behind George and the two of us pushed with all our might in an endeavour to heave him up the slope. Poor George lost all his dignity that afternoon but eventually, after nearly 20 minutes hard, hilarious pushing we succeeded in heaving him back onto the pathway.

Chapter XXV

Kim really was settling down extremely well now her unplanned trips over the top of the compost heap were curtailed. We quickly became great pals, together at every possible opportunity. If I were sick she would stay by my side constantly and if confined to bed, she would either curl up on the bottom of the eiderdown or stretch out alongside me as she did during the night.

Her own collapsible bed had arrived within ten days of our placing the order however, apart from trying it out for size, Kim had not used it, continuing to sleep with me.

She became protective of anything of mine including my bed, consequently Mother – who insisted on making the beds herself after they had aired for a couple of hours – had either to turn her off or wait her chance until Kim was in the garden.

When out in the park or open space Kim retained her allegiance to me. Not that she didn't get along with other dogs, she loved to play with them and was off like a shot out of a gun to join in the fun as soon as her lead was unclipped, tail held high wagging nineteen to the dozen. If however I stopped to make a fuss of another dog she would deliberately turn her back, ignoring the intruder!

Although Kim was by no means a fighter I became concerned one day to discover the presence of an extra piece of ear. Disturbed she may have sustained an injury at sometime, along we went to Mr Stockman for further investigation.

She stood on the table as good as gold while he examined her. Gradually a broad grin spread across his face. "Look", he said holding out the obscure object, "there is nothing to worry about, it is just a piece of matted fur, have that off in a trice". With a quick couple of snips the "extra ear" was no more. Feelings of relief mingled with embarrassment – what a twit I was! More careful grooming was the order of the day from now on. The trouble was Kim did not like being brushed and combed, taking the first opportunity to wriggle free and escape out of sight. A firmer hand was needed, especially as she was developing her adult coat long, soft and silky with golden feathers down her legs and a most beautiful long golden feathered tail.

Chapter XXVI

Come summer Mother and I decided a couple of weeks holiday were needed. Being of Norfolk origin we made Southwold our choice and subsequently booked a self-contained ground floor flat facing the land based lighthouse, for a fortnight.

This was to be Kim's first holiday with us. When the cases came out of the cupboard together with all the clothes and holiday paraphernalia Kim was not sure what to make of it all. Obviously this was a new experience for her. In an attempt to reassure her I repeatedly told her she was coming with us and packed a large basket with many of her personal things including toys, brush and comb, towels, shampoo (better safe than sorry!), raincoat, bowls, biscuits, tins, tin opener, water bottle, fork, blankets and bed. While in someone else's property Kim must sleep in her own bed. Hopefully she would be so tired after a day of new adventures she would sleep soundly where-ever she was.

Sitting on Rebecca's front passenger seat, Kim enjoyed every mile of the journey, taking a healthy interest in everything passing the window while making the most of refreshment stops to explore the fascinating new smells exuding from the surrounding countryside.

Arriving at the flat we unloaded Rebecca, let ourselves in through the front door into the main living-come-dining room and straight through into the kitchen to put the kettle on prior to unpacking and making up the beds. Meanwhile Kim, having taken herself on a tour of inspection, returned to the kitchen in search of food.

After a good meal, followed by half-an-hours relaxation, it was time to take a stroll down to the beach then back round the town, home. This would double as Kim's evening walk. She must be tired after the excitement of the day so a short perambulation would suffice. Tomorrow afternoon we would take Kim for a lovely long run on the beach, along to the River Blyth just this side of Walberswick. She would love that.

Next day, as planned, we set off down to the beach turning right in the direction of Walberswick, Kim running along in front of us investigating this exciting new terrain.

Partly from what knowledge we possessed of her background, partly from her excited reaction to everything, it was obviously Kim's first visit to the seaside. Despite her love of water she made no attempt to venture out into the sea, contenting herself with splashing along from time to time in the shallows along the edge of the shore. It was a beautiful day, neither too cold nor too hot – just right for a good long walk, breathing in the clean fresh air. This would give us all an appetite. We should certainly all sleep well tonight.

After we had been walking for some time Kim began to slow down, preferring to trot along at a more leisurely pace. Eventually we turned for home feeling we were really giving Kim a treat – what a lovely long walk. Trixie would have loved to come – maybe she was with us. She had certainly stayed close to us since her passing and knowing her excitement at the sight of suitcases, it was more than feasible she would not miss a chance like this to enjoy once again the delights of a holiday by the sea.

Perhaps we had walked Kim too far – she seemed very tired. We were both still quite fresh, however it was obviously too much for Kim – maybe she was still recovering from the previous day's journey?

When we got home Kim had a long drink then just flaked out in her bed, exhausted. By now we were becoming concerned – we had been walking for about an hour and a half but surely Kim should not be as tired as this? Maybe the sea air had been too strong for her? Best to see how she was in the morning. Meanwhile a light supper followed by a quiet evening seemed the best policy.

Next morning Kim still appeared very fatigued so we decided to cover the settee with a travelling rug and lay her on there to rest.

The whole day she spent sleeping peacefully, waking only occasionally, looking up to ensure we were still there then returning to a tranquil slumber. Mother and I passed the day reading, at the same time keeping an ever watchful eye on our Kimmy. We must be very careful not to take her so far again – she was obviously not strong enough to cope with long walks.

The following day, much to our relief, Kim was her bright, perky self again anxious to be off out. Most of the holiday we spent quietly sitting on the beach, wandering around the town or enjoying short walks through the surrounding country.

Not far from Southwold, in the little village of Belton we have relatives whose farm has been in the family since 1896, when purchased by their Great grandfather, an old trawler skipper and publican. Ever since our Great-grandfather moved down to London at the turn of the century we have maintained a link, albeit loosely, with this branch of our Norfolk kinsfolk always visiting them when in the county. This trip was no exception so, having telephoned first, we set off one afternoon to take tea with them. Cousin Chris now ran the farm with his Father Jimmy, wives Lillian and Edith working alongside them while Cousin John ran his own business on the outskirts of Great Yarmouth and his wife Diane looked after their baby twin daughters. Laurie, now in her 80's, rather deaf otherwise as alert and quick as any 20 year old, was the matriarch of the family. Her mother had been sister to my Great, Grandmother, she was therefore old enough to well remember three generations of our line. When we arrived she took us into her own room where the tears unashamedly ran down her cheeks as she recalled my Father, saying in her broad accent "He were a good man. He were too young to die. Too young".

Among the animals living in the farmhouse were Sally, the 14 year old sheepdog, Micky the white West Highland Terrier and Sydney a large white walled-eye (one blue, one green eye) cat who predominantly ruled all. As official farm cat he had, to date, killed a total of four dogs who at different times had been unwise enough to venture onto the property. Because, of course, straying dogs are a dangerous menace to the farm animals.

Kim, who normally considered all cats were put on this earth for her to chase, took one look at Sydney instantly concurring to his supremacy. While he sat by the fireplace nonchalantly washing his paws, Kim sat opposite him looking as though butter would not melt in her mouth. Throughout the afternoon she maintained a safe distance from Sydney who continually displayed cool indifference towards this visitor to his domain. He left no-one in doubt he was Cat-of-the-Farm.

Chapter XXVII

All too soon the holiday was over so it was home once more, back to the old routine. Despite her little upset at the beginning of the holiday Kim appeared to have enjoyed herself. Never-the-less she was also pleased to be on her own home ground again, free to come, go and do as she wished.

Our next trip, very soon, must be down to West Sussex. Aunty Winnie now residing in a local Home, St Davids had been sold and the proceeds invested to maintain her.

No longer having anywhere to stay during our regular visits it was necessary to locate accommodation in the town. Bognor being a small, friendly locality we asked the sales assistant in the local drapers, while making a few purchases for Aunty, if she could recommend somewhere we could stay where Kim would be welcome. Without hesitation she directed us to Mr Reg. Wheeldon at Northolme Hotel on the edge of town. Thanking her, we made Mr Wheeldon our next port of call.

Northolme proved to be a large corner establishment only a few minutes walk from the seafront. Marvellous for Kim's early morning walks – she could have a run on the beach which, when the tide was out, was golden sand.

We were in luck. Mr Wheeldon would be only too delighted to put us up, Kim as well. He loved dogs, in fact all animals. He owned a dog once, a faithful friend named Toger who had been his constant companion for many years.

He proudly led us to his "special accommodation for guests with babies or dogs" – a self contained downstairs flatlet comprising twin bedroom, large kitchen/diner, bathroom, separate toilet and a back door leading straight into the garden. Absolutely perfect for our needs. Should Kim wish to go out during the night – not that she ever did – I could take her without disturbing the rest of the house.

Mr Wheeldon left us to unpack and settle in, informing us dinner would be at 6.30pm. What a charming man, what an extremely good friend he was to become to us over the many years ahead. An upright, alert man of good physic, having retired from the Army Catering Corp he now ran Northolme with two of his sisters Elsie and Ethel. Much to his delight Kim took to him straight away, sensing his affinity with animals.

Once we were installed, Kim soon settled down to inspecting every corner of the flatlet, taking a particular fancy to the backdoor mat from where she could lie watching everything we did.

Unfortunately Kim had to stay in the flatlet while Mother and I went in to dinner – a new experience for her. However she had eaten a good supper and must be tired after a long day so hopefully she would sleep. Wanting her to learn the phrase "we are just going to dinner Kim – we will not be long", I repeated it several times adding "stay, there's a good girl".

On return to our room after a delicious meal, I made a tremendous fuss of her simultaneously presenting her with a small titbit saved from my plate. The experts tell us a dog never knows if its owner will come back when it is left alone. However, Kim quickly came to understand that morning and evening we disappeared for a short while, knowing we would return bringing a scap of something tasty. She was always good while we were out, usually curling up in her bed – since our trip to Southwold she knew she had to sleep in her own bed when away from home.

Aunty Winnie had loved Trixie. She often chatted to her as though she were conversing with a human being. Now she was introduced to our Kimmy – another instant success. Kim's unusually attractive colouring combined with her natural warm affection and appealing face cast a spell over all who came in contact with her. The only occasions she showed reserve was when a strange man came up to her – or to the front door at home. Never-the-less she would accept any male we spoke to first, or obviously trusted, without reticence – demonstrating complete confidence in us.

I was anxious to introduce Kim to all our friends in the area, knowing they could not fail to be enchanted by her. When we visited Aunty Winnie's closest friend Ruth, who lived in a bungalow – aptly named "Ruthena" – just down the road from St Davids, she was made such a fuss of. Ruth insisted on clearing the sofa for her to sit on while we all enjoyed a cup of tea. Not to be left out, Kim was served a dish of tea with two chocolate biscuits. Such spoiling – no wonder she always became excited when we drew up outside "Ruthena", she was sure of a marvellous reception coupled with very special treats.

Ruth and George once owned two King Charles Spaniels whom they worshipped and whose portraits were proudly displayed above the piano in the front room for all to admire. Feeling they were now too advanced in years to be able to exercise a dog sufficiently, they lavished all their affection on animals of their acquaintance, being more than aptly rewarded by the love they received in return.

Visiting Cathy on the beach was, as always, a pleasure. Sharing with her a wonderful dip in "our" sea, followed by a hot cup of tea sitting in her living room looking out across the water. Kim was once again introduced, this time making friends also with Nicky and Pepe who showed absolutely no resentment to this newcomer, simply taking our visit as a matter of course.

Though Kim would not venture in, she braved the hard pebbles coming down to the edge of the water guarding my beachrobe, watching patiently while Cathy and I splashed about joyously, chattering nineteen to the dozen. There was always so much news to catch up with, gossip to exchange. This time Cathy wanted to know all about Kim. A subject I never tired of talking about.

On our next visit Cathy's daughter Rosie was at "Windy Ridge", another friend for Kim. So many new people to meet – what a super holiday this was turning out to be.

Over the next few years the three of us made the trip to Sussex at least once a month. Visiting Aunty Winnie, taking her out, generally coping with her affairs. A task which in itself would fill the pages of a book. Yet so fantastic were our experiences of the various Homes she was in, our encounters with the often corrupt, cruel or downright wicked – even involvement with Interpol – that no one would believe a word. Without the constant helpful support of Mr Ashdown, the

Senior Welfare Officer at that time, our task would have been impossible. It is said that truth is often stranger than fiction, this was certainly the case in the situation which existed then.

During this period Reg Wheeldon also proved a true friend, standing by us on many occasions. He even opened Northolme to us several times during the winter months, sharing his private accommodation with us. Always making us welcome, feeling at home. Always Kimmy was with us.

A favourite outing for Aunty Winnie was the short drive out to Bosham where, when the tide is out, it is possible to drive right round the water's edge. Unable to leave the car, this enabled Aunty to enjoy the sea at close quarters. Also for Kimmy this was a treat as, having driven round to the far side of the little harbour, leaving Mother and Aunty Winnie in the car, I would take her for a walk along the grassy shore path.

Like Trixie, Kimmy also became a regular visitor to Sudley Road Spiritualist Church in Bognor where, having been introduced as the latest addition to our family, she was made equally welcome. She sat quietly by my chair watching, listening to all that took place. After the service receiving as always high praise for her good behaviour.

Chapter XXVIII

At home too Kimmy would accompany me to the various local churches, in particular Potters Bar Spiritualist Church where as a family we had attended services and meetings for many years. I always sat at the back of the little church so there was more room for Kimmy to sit comfortably in front or beside me. Where also, in summer, she could benefit from the cool breeze coming in through the open door. Indeed, again like Trixie, she became a regular member of the congregation. If for any reason I went along without her, I was immediately accosted with anxious enquiries concerning her whereabouts.

One evening, to the great amusement of everyone present, including the speaker across whose face a very broad grin spread, Kim could suddenly be clearly heard, loudly snoring contentedly!

On another occasion I brought the service to an abrupt halt when a huge spider ran out from under my chair. Having watched it for several minutes in increasing panic I let out an involuntary yell as it turned, running back in my direction. Amazingly we were still made warmly welcome whenever we went along!

Mother being a regular member also of Cockfosters URC Church, Kim was often present there during morning service. These visits were also a real pleasure for her as she became known to a great many people demonstrating on each occasion sheer delight at seeing her old friends, receiving in return a warm greeting coupled with loving strokes and pats.

When the URC was not in use for an actual service, Kim would thoroughly enjoy herself trotting up and down the long aisle between the rows of hard back chairs. A harmless activity she was allowed to indulge in as no one objected.

Chapter XXIX

During Kim's daily walks I noticed once or twice she pulled up suddenly, stopping to rest as though walking had, without warning, become an effort. At first I tried to tell myself it was nothing, she was just tired. However, close contact with heart conditions in humans, coupled with the memory of her experience in Southwold, made me certain there was something very wrong with her.

Despite the family's conviction it was pure imagination – and indeed indoors she was full of life especially when a visitor rang the bell – I knew I was right.

A telephone call to Wood Street brought Mr Stockman to the house next day. As always he was very kind, listening intently to what I had to say. When I finished he said "Right, let's have her up on the table and see what we can find out". Gently he picked Kim up placing her on the dinning room table where the French window shed it's light. He examined her thoroughly. Her temperature was normal, her heart beat fine, nothing appeared to be broken or misshapen. In every respect she passed with flying colours.

No. I insisted there was something wrong. Not simply what I con-strude as evidence but a deep inner knowledge. Mr Stockman sat in the carver by the window for a few moments just looking at me. Then he said "Right. I cannot find anything but it is obvious you are con-vinced something is wrong. I'll tell you what we will do. Bring her up to the surgery and I will run a blood test, urine test and an ECG. If that does not show up anything then I will come out on exercise with you."

A wave of relief flooded over me. Mr Stockman may not be able to discover the problem now but at least he was taking me seriously. He was willing to do all he could to try to solve the problem and help Kimmy.

The day after next Mother accompanied me to Wood Street with our Kim who was as good as gold, making no attempt to pull away or struggle. The necessary tests were run. Eventually we were given the results. Kim's heart was enlarged and the right auricle of the heart diseased. She also had a kidney infection.

We were devastated. Surely we were not going to loose our Kimmy now – after all we had been through to find her. We had already lost the physical company of Dad, Trixie and to an extent through marriage, Tony. Not our dear Kimmy as well.

We had to make another Wood Street visit to see Mr Stockman to establish the best course of action to help Kim. We waited apprehensively in the reception area – old stables converted – for Mr Stockman to appear. When he did it was to greet us kindly bringing with him a tall, slim young man with shoulder-length fair hair and a pleasant face, whom he introduced as Mr Winwood. A young vet who had recently joined the practice and to whom Mr Stockman was handing over our case.

He looked so young. For a split second I worried that he may be too young – too inexperienced. As quickly as the doubt arose, it was banished. Young he may be but he must be extremely capable and proficient for Mr Stockman to have taken him into the practice. Only the highest standards were acceptably to Mr Stockman.

From that moment on I had complete confidence in Mr Winwood. A trust which was never to be broken over the many years ahead.

Mr Winwood was replacing Chris Harris who had left the practice to specialise in veterinary work with farm animals, a preference he had increasingly held. Strange really as Mr Harris had once admitted his favourite hobby was eating, he thoroughly enjoyed a good steak. I have never quite been able to reconcile the two conflicting interests!

Kim was given an initial injection to be followed by a course of tablets for her kidney trouble coupled with more tablets for her heart. With a lot of TLC (tender loving care) and the correct medication hopefully things would turn out well. TLC was the one ingredient Kim would never be short of!

During the evening Kim began to wear a pained expression, periodically emitting a pathetic little whimper. That night she slept on my bed as usual, however neither of us had very much sleep. She was restlessly fitful while I snatched cap naps between anxiously watching over her.

Next morning Kim appeared brighter in herself, however we both realised she was far from well thus her usual walks were out of the question at present.

Within a few days, in an endeavour to both encourage her and make her temporary lifestyle more tolerable, I clipped on her lead gently coaxing her out of the front door. Gradually, purposefully with Kim taking slow steps, we walked halfway up the front path to the garden gate. Not very far but an achievement in itself. The following day we attempted another "walk", this time Kim made it all the way to the gate where she received much praise from her overjoyed Mum. It was going to be a long slow job, that was obvious, but Kim was making headway and together, with Mr Winwood's help coupled with regular healing, we would eventually ensure she was as well as it was possible for her to be.

Over the next few days Kim's "walks" gradually extended past four houses to the corner of the road. This was wonderful, she showed no ill effects. Come Saturday afternoon I put her in the car, drove up to Cockfosters – a distance of approximately one mile – and parked in a short narrow turning which leads into the far end of Hadley Woods. She may only be able to make a very short walk at present however there was no reason why it should not be an interesting one. Kim had always loved her runs in the woods from the very first days when I took her there each morning with Helene while home on sick leave.

Mother had come with us today, waiting patiently in the car while Kim and I investigated the grassy undergrowth on the edge of the trees. She loved this, it was certainly better than walking along the pavement! However, fifty yards or so was enough for the first trip. We would come again next week.

Mr Winwood was pleased with Kim's progress, willingly approving her daily exercise, genuinely interested in her case. Like Mr Graham and Mr Stockman he was proving to be a kind, dedicated, caring vet. How lucky we all are to have such a veterinary practice on our doorstep.

Over the next couple of weeks our daily walks slowly increased while our Saturday visits to Hadley Woods lengthened by about 20 yards or so each trip. Come the following Saturday I acquired a clothes line on which to tie Kim enabling her to roam more freely without losing sight of her. My fear being she would wander off into the undergrowth, have a heart attack and I would have difficulty finding her. This way, she was safe. The washing line worked well, Kim enjoyed her freedom knowing as she must, she was held securely.

During the following week I visited a pet shop in Oakwood to purchase at a cost of £3 – an not inconsiderable sum in 1971 – a one inch wide, thirty foot long, black nylon lead to replace the washing line. So much more dignified for a girl!

What a wonderful investment this was. Having a proper clip at one end, it was extremely durable, light in weight and easily washable – a necessity when it had been trailed over muddy ground!

It was in these early days of Kim's heart problems she learnt how to let me know, when on exercise, if she felt unwell. Walking along she would come to a halt and look up wearing an expression which plainly said "Oh Mum, I cannot carry on. Please help me".

In the event she merely needed a rest I stooped down, stroking her head, gently soothing her while she recovered. After a few minutes she would look up with an "I'm alright to continue now thank you Mum" look. On the other hand should more than a rest be necessary she would stop, turning her whole body across my path, lift a paw looking up with appealing eyes which cried out "Please Mum help me. I can't go any further. Please carry me". So, gathering up her lead I careful put my right arm round under her back legs, left arm across her front legs and lifted her into a comfortable position for carrying. Should she feel better after a short distance she struggled, as a prelude to jumping down. Otherwise we made our way slowly home, resting from time to time on a convenient wall until, home once more, Kim rested on the sofa or in her armchair.

Eventually Kim was able to lead a near normal life though, as with all heart patients, it was a matter of being sensible. Not over-exercising, taking the tablets and ensuring plenty of rest. Her wardrobe also became important and like Trixie's, varied to match the elements. In the winter she proudly wore a warm, smart khaki raincoat boasting a wide red strip around the middle while in wet, milder weather she stepped out in a chic black sheen-affect raincoat with a small turn-up collar.

In her own inevitable way she showed her appreciation for all the loving care she received, returning that love many fold. She became an even more devotedly loyal companion, always with me, always taking an interest in whatever was happening. If I mislaid something I only had to say "Kim, where is so and so?" for her to join in the hunt, searching, sniffing in every conceivable place even though she obviously had no idea what we were looking for!

Chapter XXX

As Kim grew into an adult dog so the long silky "feathers" on her golden legs appeared. At the same time her tail developed into one of graceful beauty which flowed in long shades of golden tan intermingled with white and black resembling a silken fan gleaming in the sunlight. The golden fur on her undercarriage likewise grew long and silky while the black on her tall shaped ears lengthened in keeping with her overall appearance of elegance.

Not quite so elegant however, was her habit of eating anything and everything she could scavenge. According to Mr Winwood this is a natural trait for a cross-breed of Kims origins. One of her greatest treats appeared to be enjoying a good chew on a nice woody stick. This I could tolerate. However come autumn she demonstrated her love of another delicacy which was, even if natural – horrific and which I eventually managed (I think!) to persuade her to relinquish. Sitting in the lounge one evening my attention was drawn to a movement around Kim's mouth.

Looking over I was horrified to see slim struggling legs protruding from the side of her mouth. She was eating a Daddy-longlegs and apparently thoroughly enjoying it. Oh, what a repulsive, grisly sight. An involuntary cry followed immediately by a firm rebuke brought only a nonchalant look from Kim while she finished off her tasty snack. What was the matter? Perhaps Mum wanted to share this delicious morsel?

This performance was repeated on several occasions with both Daddy-longlegs and Harvestmen on the menu before the fact we did not appreciate her actions, finally, bewilderedly penetrated Kims mind.

Her regular diet also demonstrated one or two little idiosyncrasies. She had a passion for spaghetti, kippers and brussel sprouts. The latter she not only enjoyed mashed with her meat and gravy but when offered one whole as a treat consumed it with relish, looking up for more.

By way of a change, Mother brought me home a toffee apple one day on her return from a shopping expedition. Naturally Kim must share this. Would she care for a piece of toffee? No need to answer – the speed with which it disappeared coupled with the delightedly expectant facial expression, said it all! By the time only the stick remained, Kim had consumed 90% of the toffee while I munched resignedly on the apple. Highly amused by all this Mother ensured our sharing of a toffee-apple became a weekly occurrence which lasted for many years.

A treat of Kim's I in no way wished to share was her nightly beef hide chew stick. One of the many new products to appear on the ever increasing pet supplies market about that time. Each evening, as we sat for a while after dinner, Kim would jump up, bark, wag her tail excitedly and look straight at each of us in turn to see how long it would take for the penny to drop, her request being understood and granted.

Thankfully Kim always declined any tit-bits offered to her by well meaning friends outside the house. Had she ever accepted I should have become concerned for her safety. With so much dog stealing occurring an easy method of enticing an animal would be offering savoury delights.

Regrettably, particularly during the summer months at holiday resorts, many dogs are stolen from cars when left on their own. For this reason Kim was never left, one of us always with her. The heartbreaking agony of having a pet stolen must be devastating, an experience from which it must be impossible to ever completely recover and one I hope and pray I will never have to endure.

I never took Kim for a walk. We always went for a walk together. She loved to run – how she could run – and play when off the lead, on exercise but always she stayed near enough for me to see her. We enjoyed our walks, whether she understood or not remains to be seen, but I talked to her about the different things, people or animals we passed or who passed us. Consequently walks were an adventure.

London Underground also provided a adventure to be undertaken. An afternoon trip to Oakwood, one station down the line, filled Kim with puzzled intrepidation. She trotted happily along the Cockfosters platform, looked up enquiringly as we entered the waiting carriage, peering up and down, round and about. What was this strange place? What an uncomfortable floor, all hard ridges – oh gosh what can be happening a hissing noise, the door we entered closing and oh … the floor – no the whole room is moving! What a dreadful noise! Oh dear, we are being shaken to pieces. That is better at least we are only rocking from side to side now, though that is bad enough. Oh, thank heavens, we are slowing down, stopping. That funny sound again – the doors are opening but on the other side of the moving room – oh good we are going out. That is better, fresh air! Ah, we are going upstairs now – here we are by the pet shop – what a funny way to come! Her face said it all.

An antic of hers which also brought a smile to the face on any onlooker was the habit she had of standing on three legs while frantically scratching her undercarriage with the her fourth, back leg!

Chapter XXXI

About this time Helene brought news which saddened us greatly. Her Grandmother lived at Wool in Dorset and together with her parents, Henry and the children (in March Helene had given birth to a baby boy named Anthony) she was selling the house next door and moving down to Winfrith Newburg to be near Grandmother.

Since Father's sudden death Helene had come in every day without fail, if only for a few minutes, to make sure Mother was alright while I was at work. On occasions she had taken Mother out with her for a drive or a trip to the shops. A kind, thoughtful gesture which was deeply appreciated.

We were all three loosing dear friends and promised to visit them once they were settled. They had purchased a large rambling cottage with an acre or two of land attached. Ideal surroundings for young Mary and Anthony to grow up in.

Rather a long journey for a weekend trip so Helene promised to try to locate accommodation for us to rent for a weeks holiday the following summer. Something to look forward to.

Prior to their move Helene and family visited Wool one long weekend leaving George with us. He duly arrived complete with a huge basin of cooked meat, one food bowl, one water bowl and bedding. Being friends and neighbours Kim showed him no resentment what-so-ever, accepting his presence in her home with graceful patience. It seemed strange at first walking out with two dogs but Kim slowed her pace to match George's amble consequently the weekend passed pleasantly without disruption.

The day arrived for our dear friends and neighbours to depart, a chapter of our lives seemed to be ending. We had all lived so happily side by side for many years. Life must go on. Thanks to Alexandra Graham Bell we would still be able to chatter and after all next summer would be here before we knew it.

Chapter XXXII

The year wore on. I have always felt strongly the lack of animal representation at the Remembrance Day Service in the Royal Albert Hall. During both wars, particularly the 1939–45 war, animals worked and died side by side with human beings* in the fight for freedom. From the pigeons who flew with the aircrews; to the sniffer dogs; the donkeys and mules who carried arms and supplies up precarious mountain trails; – the camels carrying men and provisions across the desert and the horses who served so faithfully, to the civilian animal casualties all should be remembered with as much love and gratitude as their human counterparts. With this in mind Kim wore a red poppy in her collar as a mark of respect for those animals whose lives were taken in the service of their country.

Kim also attend the Christmas Bazaar held in the Church Hall – known as Freston Hall – at the end of November each year. She loved to greet all her friends, lapping up the fuss and attention of which there was always plenty. Mother served on a stall selling either plants or tinned goods depending on the volunteers available. No longer running the

*Animals At War by Carolyn Barber.

young Pilot Group or being part of the Sunday School I was usually roped in to help her. Kim sat beside us with her lead trapped under the table leg taking a keen interest in all that was going on – greeting each potential customer by standing up, and wagging her tail. Tea time she enjoyed her own dish of tea together with any tit-bits that came her way. By the end of the day she was tired with all the hubbub and excitement but from her laughing eyes, wrinkling nose, happy panting and tail wagging it was obvious she had thoroughly enjoyed herself. All that remained was to have a short walk, followed by a good supper and a sound sleep!.

Chapter XXXIII

By now Tony and Jean had become parents to a bouncing baby boy named Phillip. When a child appears on the scene so often a dog is pushed into the background, building up resentment in the animal towards this interloper now taking all the attention he/she has previously received. I was determined there was no way Kim was going to be neglected in the presence of Phillip or any future children Tony and Jean may have. We loved Phillip, we loved Kimmy. The two were introduced to each other and whenever I spoke to or gave something to one of them, the other received exactly the same treatment. So nephew and dog became the best of friends knowing neither would ever have cause to be jealous or resentful of the other.

Chapter XXXIV

The following summer Helene found a cliff-top house for us to rent, located only a mile or two down the road from their new home. We invited an acquaintance to join us as she had not had a holiday for several years and was in need of both a break and someone to go with.

As the holiday drew near and the packing cases appeared so Kim became excited – like Trixie she knew only too well the meaning of suitcases coupled with increased activity. Mother and I repeatedly re-assured her she was coming too, placing a large basket in the hallway putting one or two of her belonging inside. Interested as ever, a long elegant nose found it's way into the basket to inspect the contents – erm – dog towels, long lead, dog biscuits, brush and comb (yuk not so good), ah – beef chews. No more re-assuring was necessary.

The journey was hot as before long the sun beat down on the car – oh for the old Austins with roof and windscreen to open! Kim was wearing a wet handtowel tied round her shoulders and tummy by means of four tapes sewn onto each corner. This was periodically re-moistened to keep her cool. We also had plenty of water on board to drink.

We were making good time as a friend had sent us easy directions to the M3. Mother had drawn her own map from there, following the roads to Popham, Sutton Scotney, Stockbridge so on to Romsey.

Our smug satisfaction at our progress was about to be dealt a resounding blow. Coming up to a line of traffic on the outskirts of Romsey we were forced to slow down to a crawl then stop. Oh well, no matter we had enjoyed a good run so far, we mustn't grumble at one small hold-up. Soon be on our way again. We all had a quick sip of water then settled down ready to proceed. Instead we sat, and sat and crawled and sat for over two hours. Fortunately we had stopped for a wow-woz break at Popham or the situation could have proved embarrassing. Eventually we moved along sufficiently to be able to see the cause of our delay. At a narrow section of road there stood one man resting on his spade from the exertion of digging one small hole in the road!

It was unbelievable we had been held up over two hours by just this one – rather laid back – workman.

At last we arrived at a sign proclaiming Winfrith Newburg. Not being too sure which way to go we turned left at the Red Lion, drove along beside a small stream into the village consisting of a handful of cottages, one shop and a telephone kiosk from where we were able to call Helene. Apparently we should have turned right down the lane facing the Red Lion and "Gatemore" was to be found a quarter of a mile up on the lefthand side.

How delighted we were to see our friends again. How the children had grown. There was no doubt Kimmy remembered them all. Despite the tiredness she must have felt after the journey she danced, wriggled and wrinkled her nose with excitement at the sight of them. Dear old George was equally pleased to see his friend Kim again after so long and came waddling over to see her, tail wagging in greeting.

Helene's mother produced a much appreciated cup of tea after which Helene, Henry and the children showed us around the property. The house, full of character, had at various times been extended resulting in a wonderful rambling building mainly on one floor with just three small bedrooms on the first floor. Helenes parents sleeping in the downstairs bedroom.

The two large fields surrounding their home also belonged to Helene's parents and here the dogs were able to run – or in George's case amble – freely.

Time at last for Helene to show us the way to our holiday home. She drove ahead of us through the country roads until we wondered where on earth she was taking us. Then away across the fields we saw the house – that was the best way to see it – across the fields!.

Having driven up to the front door Helene used the key she had been given by the owner to let us all in.

Oh, the frowsty smell, the dust covered interior which greeted our hitherto eager eyes. Could this really be the place? Did the owner honestly expect us to pay for this? While there we had a look upstairs only to find the airing cupboard, windowsills, even the beds full of dead flies. Being termed "furnished accommodation", what was presumably meant to represent furniture consisted of two or three broken, dirty items of cheap pre-war construction.

No way were we even going to unload the car let alone move in. What to do? Helene had a brainwave. A Mrs Porter lived on the outskirts of Winfrith in the hamlet of East Knighton, she had often remarked she would like to take in bed and breakfast guests but had never actually begun the exercise being a little nervous at the prospect of taking strangers into her home. Perhaps if Helene were to take us along and introduce us? Mrs Porter knew Helene would vouch for us. Could she be persuaded to help out in this emergency? Anyway, it was worth a try.

Following Helene back again through the lanes we finally drew up outside a beautiful thatched cottage boasting a large, truly colourful English country garden. We waited hopefully while Helene rang the bell then spoke to the lady who answered the door. A lady of perhaps 60 years of age with a thick mop of curly grey hair and wearing glasses – a kind, homely looking lady. Having listened to Helene she looked over to where we were waiting, hesitated then to our joyful relief, nodded her head.

We would have to book into the Red Lion for the night while Mrs Porter prepared our rooms but we could move in with her tomorrow and she would be only to happy to accept our Kimmy.

So began the first of many happy holidays spent with Eileen Porter, a true London lady with a heart of gold and a pot of tea always on the brew. She loved Kimmy and Kimmy loved her. During evenings spent sitting around Eileens magnificent stone fireplace Kim would stretch out in tired contentment after a day spent either on the beach at Lulworth or Weymouth or perhaps visiting Dorchester with it's busy market place; strolling along the river bank at Wareham or Moreton; exploring the various strips of heathland or perhaps visiting friends in Poole or Parkstone.

We frequently visited Helene and family at Gatemore often taking George and Kimmy across the heathland backing onto their property. After an initial trek across the heath with Henry, I realised Kim's capacity for exercise was even less than I had anticipated. Consequently her walks must be strictly monitored again. We had walked her too far, she was exhausted. I thought I had been careful in judging the distance we had taken her but obviously walks required greater restriction. Perhaps another check up with Mr Winwood on our return would be advisable.

All the years I had Kimmy with me in the physical sense she only once asked to be taken out during the night and that occurred while staying with Eileen one summer. Kim always did wow-woz last thing before retiring whether at home or away. This particular night she kept pawing the bedclothes until I stirred when she began running in an agitated fashion between the bed and the door, crying as she went until I hurriedly threw on a robe and took her downstairs, out through the front door into the garden.

Never at any time either before or after this incident did she ask to be taken out once we had all gone to bed but slept or dozed peacefully all night until we enjoyed our morning cuppa when Kim also eagerly lapped up her first-dish-of-tea-of-the-day.

Kim did not always pass through the front door of Eileen's cottage so easily. Hanging either side of her porch Eileen had two beautiful baskets of flowers, of which she was justly proud. Each day they were faithfully watered. A procedure which presented no real difficulty as they hung roughly head high to Eileen who merely reached up to empty her water container over the top of the arrangements. Returning home one afternoon, as we walked up the pathway Eileen opened the cottage door. Busy greeting us, enquiring if we had spent a pleasant day and whether we would care for a cup of tea she didn't notice Kim, who had run on ahead, standing immediately under the right hand basket. As the water flooded the plants, cascading over the edge of the receptacle it absolutely drenched our poor Kimmy who looked up with what can only be described as an expression of astonishment on her face as the water poured off her from every quarter. Always a good sport, she shook herself heartily then, with nose wrinkling, joined in the ensuing merriment.

In the field opposite Eileen's cottage were two charming best friends. Princess a graceful, elegant mare light gingery brown of body with white blazoned down her chest and nose and Lollipop, an adorable, gentle donkey. The two were always to be found together, happy in each other's company they could munch away to their hearts content while watching all the comings and goings through the hamlet of East Knighton. Their field was raised slightly above the road which carried the heavy rush hour traffic to and from the local towns, the Atomic Energy Establishment or Bovington Army Camp.

Each morning as Kim took me for her early morning walk she pulled on the lead down the cottage path, across the road then up the grassy embankment to greet her two holiday pals with whom she was fascinated. She would watch their every movement coming as close to the netting as she possibly could in an attempt to rub noses with them. Despite the promise of a "nice walk", she was always reluctant to leave them, repeatedly turning back to look at them as we took the path up over the hill for our morning constitutional before breakfast.

It was while in Dorset, on the beach at Lulworth Cove with Helene and the children, we discovered Kim's love of ice-cream. One hot, sunny day we were all enjoying a lazy afternoon on the beach when Helene jumped up, grabbed her purse and telling the children to stay with us and be good, set off down the shingle in the direction of the little shop-cum-cafe. Five minutes later she returned precariously carrying six cornets, one for each of us including Kimmy. "Oh", she exclaimed with a laugh, "it is so hot I thought Kimmy would like one too". Holding her own cone in one hand she held the other out towards Kim who looked, took a hesitant lick then having decided this was definitely good to eat, elegantly extended a long, pink tongue down and up the ice-cream savouring the taste with a look of complete ecstasy on her face.

Unfortunately one local beauty spot held nothing but fear for Kimmy. Kimmerage Bay where blasting was frequently taking place. A lovely drive along narrow hill lanes was completely spoilt for her as she sat trembling from head to tail, then climbed down onto the floor in an attempt to hide under the dashboard. Regrettably, we were unable to visit Kimmerage again. It would have been an act of gross cruelty to subject Kim to such conditions knowing how frightened she was.

The gunfire generated by the Army on the heathland around Bovington Camp also brought terror to our Kim – as I am sure it must to many other dogs visiting the area, and was a great inconvenience. I can never understand why greater restrictions are not placed on gun practice during the holiday season in an area so dependent on tourism.

We also spent a couple of weeks one year with Eileen at the beginning of November. A glorious bonfire and firework party was held on the beach at Weymouth. The noise must have been deafening so we stayed in the cottage with Eileen, chatting and joining in the fun of a Party Time tape of London's East End. Apart from thoroughly enjoying ourselves – we laughed till the tears rolled down our faces – Kim could not hear even the distance bang of fireworks so was unaware of anything unusual happening.

Weymouth was only "just down the road" from East Knighton so at least one trip into town was always on the cards. Driving down the hill to the sea then turning left, away from the town up a steep incline to the top, gave vent to a wonderful view across the bay to the docks at the far end of Weymouth. It was an ideal place for Kimmy to have a run on the grass or a scamper on the little beach below where she could run or sniff around in safety, enjoying a paddle along the water's edge. She loved it here.

The beach further along the coast towards Weymouth usually provided plenty of space to stretch out undisturbed but bathing could be rather dangerous as the wash from the large Sealink ferries leaving port, would eventually reach this part of the shore catching bathers unaware.

For some inexplicable reason, not all eating establishments are friendly towards dogs. Therefore, we were overjoyed to find the Criterion in Weymouth only too happy to welcome Kim. Situated on the front we were delighted to be shown to a table in the window where we could enjoy not only the excellent cuisine and service but a splendid view of the sea. Kimmy having eaten her own supper and well behaved as always, sat quietly under the table until, well fed and contented, we paid the bill and left, determined to return on many occasions. Which indeed we did.

Sadly Henry and Helene's dear old George was run over outside their home on the UKAEA road. Before long however, Henry had acquired another dog whom he adored just as much, a Hungarian poynter named Csibsz, pronounced "chibbis". A lovely but crazy young dog who accompanied Henry everywhere.

As time passed Mary grew up and with a daughter of her own moved to Bristol while Antony stayed with his parents working alongside them in their exciting new venture. They became the landlord and landlady of The Stokford Inn, situated on the road between Wool and Wareham where, though the hours are long and the work hard, they are happily content; where both regulars and guests alike are sure of a friendly smile, a warm welcome and good company in an invitingly pleasant environment.

Chapter XXXV

After the long walk across the heath which tired Kimmy so, I took her on our return home to see Mr Winwood. Another ECG was run with the result her medication was increased. Mr Winwood was hopeful the extra tablets combined with more careful monitoring of her exercise would resolve her immediate problem. So it proved to be, although I insisted she had a regular ECG to keep a check on the situation.

She was generally very well behaved in the waiting room sitting quietly taking an interest in the other patients, unless a cat came into the room when she would become quite fidgety as though it were an affront to expect her to sit still in the presence of the enemy. On one visit however, we opened the door, walked in and found every chair occupied by an adoring cat owner cradling on their lap either a box or basket from which emitted the strains of an encaged feline. Kim stood stock still for a moment then, as the next owner was called into the surgery, followed me quietly to the vacated chair and sat on the floor in front of me staring straight ahead of her as though butter would not melt in her mouth. She was definitely outnumbered on this occasion and was only too well aware of it. The time to return to the car and home could not come quickly enough this day!

Whether by car or on foot Kim was always eager for an outing recognising instantly the signs of preparation, becoming excited, jumping up and down, turning in circles. She quickly learnt the concluding tune to Crossroads signalled her evening walk. Where-ever she was in the house or garden the instant the programme closed she appeared in front of me as if by magic – head held high, tail wagging in anticipation which could never be ignored or disappointed.

Only when Mother and I went shopping together was Kim left behind. She would be told "stay Kim, theres a good girl. We are only going shopping, will not be long." This also meant she would be given a "find" on our return. I hated leaving her alone but at times there was no alternative as she really did not enjoy being lugged around the inside of busy shops. The close proximity of many human legs, prams, shopping bags and the like coupled with all the noise was too much for her – or presumably most dogs – to cope with.

The noise of thunder also disturbed Kim alarmingly especially after the onset of her heart condition. She would dash for the nearest place of safety, usually the 7 foot long oak sideboard, crawling under it as far back as possible. Many is the time I have stretched out on the floor with her trying to soothe and comfort her during a storm.

Not always in her own home when a storm sprung up, Kim would quickly find the nearest 'safe' place to shelter. Mother's life-long friend whom we called Aunty Ivy had retired to a small bungalow in Widmer End near High Wycombe. While preparing to return home after visiting her one afternoon, a sudden unexpected storm of unusually violent vehemence sprung up. Petrified, Kim dashed into Aunty Ivy's bedroom straight under her bed where she huddled herself together, eyes fixed in a terror sticken stare. Consequently I spent an hour and a half tucked half-way under the bed stroking her head, whispering gently to her while she trembled from head to tail. A spare

Millophyline tablet buried inside a piece of Frys Cream chocolate was always in my handbag or pocket for just such emergencies.

After stress like this Kim would sleep peacefully at night and I would often wake next morning to find her deep in slumber with her head beside mine on the pillow.

One bright summer morning our walk took us down to the allotments then back home along the pavement on our own side of the road. About 8 houses from home I noticed, to my amazement, a police constable strolling towards us – a most unusual sight. We rarely if ever saw a policeman walking the beat around our streets. A well built man he had a gentle, friendly countenance. As he drew near, a smile spread across his face while he greeted me cheerfully and we exchanged the customary remarks concerning the beauty of the morning. He bent down to Kimmy speaking kindly to her whereupon she responded warmly looking up and wagging her tail enthusiastically. It seemed strange, as he was obviously very fond of animals, he should make a point of bending so low to speak to her yet refrain from actually stroking or touching her. Oh well, never mind, he was a very pleasant person so there must be a good reason for his reluctance to come into physical contact with her. We said goodbye and went our separate ways.

A few yards down the road I turned to look back at him only to find the street completely empty. No sign of anyone. He could not possibly have approached a house in that short space of time or he would still be in sight so where … the light dawned. Of course he could not touch Kimmy, he was dead – or to put it more accurately he was existing on a different wavelength. Yet he had been so real. We had stopped and spoken to each other and Kimmy had acknowledged his attentions. A quite natural, most pleasant, if unexpected, phenomena with which to start the day.

Chapter XXXVI

The house was beginning to seem rather large for the three of us and so intricately had our parents designed and built the garden with its numerous rockeries, flower beds and walkways that it's maintenance alone was becoming a major occupation. Mother therefore decided the time had come to sell our family house, moving into a smaller property better suited to our current needs. A semi-detached would be nice as we would not feel quite so cut-off. Much as we loved our detached house and particularly since Helene had moved away, we were beginning to feel very much on our own, especially on long winter evenings.

Eventually Mother purchased a small semi-detached residence just off the Cockfosters Road. Small being the operative word. However, we must become accustomed to this style of living now and a small park facing would be ideal for Kim to run freely in.

A large pond on the opposite corner would hold lots of interest being home to many ducks, swans, moorhens and even a terrapin. A lot of new friends to make – and feed! Kim was always fascinated by other creatures, she would enjoy standing with her nose poking through the strong wire fence surrounding the water, or even looking beneath the bottom bar of the frame. We had seen ducks waddling under the fence, across the pavement and the grass verge out onto the main road holding up all the traffic until finally condescending to return to their own domain the way they had come.

Maybe the move would not be too bad after all.

We only had four weeks in which to clear and pack the contents of the house, garage, workshop, greenhouse and toolshed which had constituted our family home for nearly a quarter of a century. A close friend from Kodak, Dave Harber, gave us a tremendous amount of help. Indeed without all his hard work I dread to think how we would have managed. It is amazing how much a family accumulates over the years!

Kim, though obviously bemused by all the activity, took great interest in everything going on. She "helped" with whatever I was doing, always there, looking, sniffing, trotting around, her long nose investigating the many boxes, bags and bins. In an attempt to re-assure her I reiterated many times, "Yes, Kimmy you are coming too, dear". Constantly chattering away half to myself, half to Kim asking her if we needed this, that or the other. Where should this go, should we take that, what did she think?

December 10 was booked as Moving Day. Aunty Ivy had kindly come to stay for a few days to help us with the actual move and subsequent unpacking. Dave was also staying overnight ready for an early start next morning. Two of Kimmy's favourite people, their presence would undoubtedly increase her sense of confidence and well-being during the upheaval.

The day dawned bright, the wintery sun shedding a gentle warmth. We were lucky, this time of year it could have been cold, wet or even snowing.

Breakfast over, Kim came for her usual morning walk round the corner, down Edgworth Road happily exploring for the umpteenth time the shrubs and bushes she knew so well, planted in attractive beds either side of the pavement, unaware this was her last walk from our present home.

On our return to the house the two removal vans had arrived, their tailboards already lowered in readiness for acceptance of the contents of our home. Kim looked at them, looked at me then trotted indoors to see what was happening. For her physical safety and my peace of mind I put her on the front seat of Rebecca. There she would feel secure knowing where-ever we were going she would be going too. I then parked on our next door neighbour's drive. From here Kim could not only see us but watch everything going on. Molly Edwards, our good friend and neighbour, kept an eye on her while I popped over periodically to make sure all was well. After a while Kim became bored with the seat, preferring to clamber down onto the floorboards where from time to time she turned in circles scratching away at the carpet in an attempt to curl up and settle. Consequently it was not long before the carpet began to tear, breaking away into several small pieces. A shame, however it was more important for Kim to feel and be safe. A carpet could be replaced, our Kim could not.

An hour or two later the vans were packed ready to move off. Mother and I, having popped over to say goodbye to Johnny and Mrs Ryder earlier, took our leave of Molly thanking her for her kindness. We would miss these good folk whom we had seen move into the area as their houses were built but when all was said and done we were only moving about 2 miles away, we would see them again.

One or two special treasures were coming with us in the car which meant, with the boot full and two thirds of the back seat packed high, rather a tight squeeze. Dave sat in the front passenger seat with Kim on his knees while Mother balanced precariously on Aunty Ivy's lap in the rear. What a crazy, comic picture we must have made! Despite the natural sadness we felt at leaving, what had for a quarter of a century been our family home, we could not stop laughing as we waved goodbye to our friends and drove the short distance to Bramley Road and our new home.

On arrival we found the removal men waiting in the vans for us to open the front door so they could begin unloading. I drove up onto the concrete drive, parking the car halfway up to allow the men access through the garage into the back garden.

Extricating ourselves from Rebecca, I took Kim inside the house to let her have a look around. She was greatly interested, running here, there and everywhere looking into this room then the other, up the stairs, round the large square landing, into the bedrooms and down again. "Emm – well I have seen all there is to see – now what? Ah, back into the car. Good, we must be going home – should be nearly lunchtime!" Kim looked slightly bewildered when she was put back on Rebecca's front passenger seat, the window opened and the doors closed behind her. However, I felt she would be safer there than running around the house with the doors open especially as number 58 was situated on a slip road facing a turn-in from the main road to Enfield carrying fast moving traffic.

Dave helped the men unload while we three ladies attended to the most important chore of all – putting the kettle on and making the tea! It is a pity we could not have had androids of Dave who worked with care and precision. The so called "removal men", employed by a well known local firm, confessed to being no more than odd job boys travelling around the country and knowing nothing of the art of removal – as became painfully obvious by the amount of damage they caused to our possessions.

By the end of the day we were all exhausted. Kim had found her bed but chose to settle herself in the armchair where, with a full tummy, she slept peacefully.

Moving home is never easy, there are so many jobs large and small to be completed before the feeling of being "settled" may be enjoyed. A wall to be knocked down, rooms to be decorated, carpet to be bought and laid, sockets to be installed, locks to be fitted, the cage put up behind the front door, these things all take time.

When Kim first came to us she made a habit of tearing up anything which happened to pop through the letter box onto the mat. Although we didn't mind about the telephone, gas or electricity bills the respective authorities all sent duplicates as they still expected to be paid, hence the metal cage! The telephone itself had also attracted our Kim's attention. If it rang while we were out she would stand on the bottom stair from where she could reach the low windowsill then pull the receiver off the hook. We discovered this was how she managed it when one day we came running in from the garden to answer the ring and caught her in the act. In this new house we made sure the phone was on a high hall table, well away from little straying paws!

Chapter XXXVII

We were very lucky with our neighbours in Bramley Road. Adjacent to us lived Peggy and Frank Poole, two of the nicest people you could meet. They both adored animals and took to Kimmy immediately, consequently she responded to them with equal enthusiasm.

Walks took on a new interest now for Kimmy as the surrounding area presented many fresh smells to be sniffed and enjoyed. Between our slip road and the main road was a grass verge approximately 12 – 15 feet wide edged with trees, bushes and hedging. This haven for dogs stretched along Bramley Road from the Cockfosters roundabout, by the duck pond in one direction to the beginning of Oakwood Station in the other, a distance of approximately two thirds of a mile. Kim's early morning preamble usually took us along the verge one way or the other where we frequently made the acquaintance of other dogs undertaking similar exercise. Never one to get into a fight or cause trouble Kim would always greet her fellow canines with a sniff and a wag.

Just across the main road was a small park where Kim could safely run free, something she loved especially if a ball came along with us! The exercise was good for her although, because of her heart condition, I was always a little apprehensive when she tore round the fields, she could run so fast. At one time Mr Winwood had said to me "She could live many years but you must accept she could just as easily collapse suddenly when running in the park. It is better for her to run and enjoy what-ever time she has than to live a longer but restricted life." I never forgot those words, they haunted me, especially when Kim was playing or chasing with other dogs. I had to make a very conscious effort not to be over-protective with her but to let her enjoy herself naturally. By the same measure the memory of Mr Winwood's words ensured I loved and treasured Kim every day of her life as though it were her last. This created an even greater bond between us which still exists today.

At one time, when Kim had been unwell for a few days, I taught her to poke her nose into my bag and "find", an expression which meant there was a treat for her. For months after that whenever I had been out and returned home Kim would immediately become very excited and her beautiful long muzzle would take a nose-dive into my basket or bag to see what I had brought her. A favourite treat was a small bar of chocolate which not many years previously would have been a "penny bar".

This was fine until one day in a local shop the lady in front of us put her shopping bag down on the floor while paying for her goods. "Ah" thought Kim "a find". Down into the lady's bag went Kim's far-reaching nose! In horror, I pulled her away, apologising profoundly to the astonished owner, trying to explain Kim's action was the result of my stupidity in teaching her such a trick. From then on Kim's "find" was presented to her by hand on my entry through the front door.

Having developed a taste for chocolate, other than the Frys Cream in which she took her daily tablets, when we all went out in the car Mother started the habit of buying her a small Milky Bar. Quick to learn, while we sat alone in the car waiting, she would sit quietly looking out of the window at what was happening outside. As soon as

Mother came into view Kim was up on her hind legs, her front paws hanging over the back of the front passenger seat eagerly watching as Mother approached the car, opened the rear door and climbed in. Immediately Kim's tail would wag nineteen to the dozen while her nose searched out the chocolate she knew was about to be unwrapped for her.

Chapter XXXVIII

By Christmas the house was beginning to look more like "our home". Kim had become accustomed to her new environment and life was starting to settle down to a normal routine once more. The weather being bad, Dave was not overkeen to make the journey to his parents in Devon so accepted an invitation to spend the holiday with us.

As usual on Christmas morning we all opened our presents after breakfast. Kim wriggled, danced and wrinkled her nose with excitement as one by one her presents were opened for her. Gleefully she accepted each gift, taking it gently in her mouth then tossing it on the carpet before rolling on it as a prelude to playing with or eating it.

Dinner time came. After giving Kim her own plate of Christmas fayre we sat down with relish to consume our own.

The first course over, I cleared away the dishes in preparation for the Christmas Pudding which, steaming hot, I carried proudly in. The aroma was scintillating!

As I passed through the hall the telephone rang. Holding the Pudding in one hand I lifted the receiver with the other to hear a voice ask for either Mother or me. Having introduce myself, the voice promptly informed me Mrs Winifred Minihane had just died in St Richards Hospital, Chichester. I was dumbfounded. What was Mrs Minihane doing in St Richards? We had spoken to the people at the Home were she lived, only two days ago and were assured Aunty Winnie was fine. Apparently she had been taken ill suddenly and transferred to hospital without anyone seeing fit to inform us. Not only were we next of kin but held Power of Attorney for her. Dazed, I confirmed we would travel down to Sussex the next day to attend to her affairs.

Dave rang his parents to let them know he would be arriving Boxing Day. We hastily finished Christmas Dinner then made preparations for the following day's journey.

We were over a hundred miles, four hours driving time in those days, away from where Aunty Winnie lived. Reynolds, the well known South Coast firm, had all the details of her funeral on file hence all that was required was a telephone call for the wheels to be set in motion. Being

December 25th I assumed an ansaphone would take my message, amazingly however, with Reynolds usual first class efficiency their staff were on duty. The personification of kindness, they quickly located our file assuring us everything would be taken care of exactly as we had arranged a year or two previously.

Reg had sold Northolme Hotel at the end of the summer season purchasing a smart newly built house in Felpham, just outside Bognor. He and his elder sister Ethel, (Elsie having passed over the previous year) had moved in the week before Christmas. He knew most people in Bognor, perhaps he could suggest alternative accommodation where Kim would be welcome?

No way! We must take them as we found them – packing cases and all – but he would not hear of us going anywhere else.

Next day, with Kim on the front passenger seat as usual, we drove down to Sussex this time with heavy hearts. Dad would look after Aunty Winnie until she became settled in her new life and Trixie would be over the moon to see her again but we would miss her presence in the material world, as indeed would Kim. The two of them had been great pals. Aunty Winnie loved dogs consequently both Trixie and Kimmy had thought the world of her.

The weather was bitterly cold. We had made the journey several hundred times in every kind of weather Mother Nature could produce from scorching hot sun to dense fog to thick driving snow. This was to be our final trip on Aunty Winnie's behalf.

We arrived in Chichester early afternoon, already feeling very tired as well as very cold. Kimmy stayed in the car while Mother and I went into the hospital to identify Aunty Winnie only too find the duty doctor had already undertaken this office. After visiting the Chapel of Rest, we returned to Kimmy and drove over to the Registrar's Office. Luckily I was able to park right outside. Whether I was the only person to require his services this day I cannot tell however, despite my efforts to dissuade him, he preferred to chat rather than attend to business with the result it was two whole hours before I managed to get away. Kimmy and Mother were by now, frozen to the core.

It took us about half an hour to drive to Felpham then locate Reg's new house. How glad we all were to be in the warm, in the company of two such good friends.

Two days later Ruth, Aunty Winnie's good friend, accompanied us to the new Chichester Crematorium for the funeral service which was tastefully conducted by the resident minister and ably handled by Reynolds. Kimmy stayed in the car, waiting patiently, though was of course delighted to see us return to her.

A few days after that, with all business matters completed, we thanked Reg and Ethel for their extreme kindness – their true friendship and made the return journey to Bramley Road.

Chapter XXXIX

Our neighbours to the right of us moved up to the Midlands early in the new year. Their house was bought by the Home Office and shortly after, Mr & Mrs Macklyn together with their teenage daughter Linda moved in. Like Peggy and Frank on our left, Mr & Mrs Macklyn proved to be the best neighbours anyone could wish for. They also loved animals with the result Kimmy was constantly in her element – being made a fuss of by kind people from both sides of our home also receiving, from time to time, a plate of tasty morsels from both neighbours. Mr Macklyn proved to be very much like my Father in many ways. Both were very kind, compassionate men who were also extremely sensible and capable. Whether the similarity – Kimmy knew Father well of course because of his frequent presence with us – attracted Kim or whether it was something else, I would not like to say but she became devoted to Mr Macklyn. Whenever she caught sight of him she was immediately overtaken by coyness. Wriggling from side to side she would descend to ground level, her nose wrinkling while she emitted squeals of ecstatic delight. Her devotion was always rewarded with lots of strokes and fuss accompanied by "Hello Kimmy. Hello old girl. How's my girl today?" More often than not Kimmy would promptly roll over to have her tummy tickled and was never disappointed!

Though Mr Macklyn was her idol, being a very affectionate dog, Kimmy loved all her friends dearly, always greeting them with warm sincerity.

Once a month, either we would visit my friend Alice (another Koda-friend)* or she would spend the evening with us. Either way it was another occasion for Kimmy to be lovingly spoilt but not spoiled. She sat next to Alice on the sofa licking her face while Alice stroked her head gently, talking to her – holding a conversation with her. When coffee and snacks were served, Kimmy too enjoyed her bowl of tea "with snacks"!

When we moved to Bramley Road I missed the squirrels who used to play in our garden chasing each other up and down the rose trees, all over the lawn, they came fearlessly up to the house. Therefore, Dave bought me a soft toy squirrel sitting in an upright position with its paws

---

* 'Koda' is the 'in-house' term for staff and anything relating to Kodak.

held out together in front of it. It was beautiful, however something was missing. The light dawned. The paws were together but empty – they needed to hold something – of course a nut! One was quickly located.

That looked much better.

A few days later the nut had disappeared. Funny, it must have fallen out or been accidently knocked onto the floor. Yet there was no sign of the nut anywhere. Oh well, never mind, I'll put another one there. This happened several times. Then I found pieces of broken nutshell in the corner of the lounge and again in the dining room. How on earth did they get there?

It was only a matter of time until I caught the culprit. Coming quietly upstairs one day I found Kimmy standing by the squirrel – which was sitting on a miniature chair on the landing – gently removing the nut with her teeth! She was helping herself to something highly desirable she had found placed at her own level. Carrying it downstairs she cracked open the shell to savour the contents at her leisure. Naturally we saw the funny side of the whole incident. If Kimmy liked nuts why should she not have them? So, whenever she removed the squirrels nut it was replaced ready for her next little indulgence.

There were times though when she had to carry her treat a little further than just downstairs before being able to enjoy it. The Oakwood pet shop was now only five to ten minutes walk away from home so if our steps led in that direction it was tempting to call in and buy a long chew stick – something that was becoming increasingly popular with most dogs. The shop also, naturally, held many glorious smells for visiting canines – all those sacks, packs and boxes containing unimaginable delicacies! Our purchase having been made Kim took the chew gently in her mouth as we set off in the direction of home.

She trotted along the pavement beside me proudly holding the chew stick between her teeth. Not until we were home and settled down did Kim attempt to eat her treasure, then she stretched out on the lounge carpet holding the 10" chew between her paws and began gnawing.

Maybe it was this habit which gave her the idea or perhaps she simply took an instant dislike to the gentleman in question. Whichever, walking along the pavement towards the pet shop one day we were overtaken by a middle-aged man minding his own business. Suddenly Kim leapt forward at the man's rear end, snapping shut a set of razor sharp teeth only an inch from his trousers. Fortunately he proceeded on his way totally unaware of the painful experience he had narrowly missed. Never before had she, nor after, did Kim do such a thing again. What could it possibly have been about that particular gentleman's person that made Kim react so? Various suggestions spring to mind – maybe his aura was showing agression within himself; maybe he reminded her of someone at whose hands she had suffered previously; maybe she simply had a mad moment – all conjecture because we shall never know.

Chapter XL

One aspect of Kim's nature we were familiar with was her fascination with other animals. Phillip now had a younger brother Keith and the two boys had an adorable white and grey rabbit named Snowy who lived in a warm, well constructed hutch Tony had built which measured approximately 9/10 feet in length. As soon as we drew up outside Tony's ground floor maisonette Kim became excited and could not wait to rush round the side of the property into the back garden where Snowy lived. The kerfuffle brought Snowy to the wire mesh to see what was happening. The expression on her face clearly said "Oh, it's you again, might have known. Nice to see you, what's going on out there today?" Kim stood rigidly facing Snowy, her alert ears cocked, her bright eyes gleaming above her long pointing nose and her luxurious tail alternating between standing straight up and waving vigorously. The two would stand interminably just looking at each other. Everytime Snowy moved from one end of her run to the other Kim always followed.

When holiday time came round. Tony asked if we would look after Snowy and her new house-mate, a lovely little gingery guinea-pig, for two weeks while they were all away. He had a friend with a small van and the hutch would just fit inside. Yes, of course, we would love to!

Friday evening prior to the family's departure Snowy and Pig, complete with their home, arrived. Kim was beside herself with excitement, running backwards and forwards watching the hutch brought through the garage into the back garden and laid gently down on the lawn. Immediately Kim was round the front to see her two friends, who must have been totally bewildered by all this movement and upheaval. How re-assuring for them to see Kim's familiar face and realise that even after their experience of being taken away from their own garden, transported then carried into a strange place that they were still with friends they knew and trusted.

Never having looked after a rabbit before I was determined to take the greatest care of Snowy and Pig. Each day they had clean newspaper and hay in the hutch, fresh lettuce, carrots and meal together with fresh milk.

First thing in the morning Kim was out in the garden and up to see the two friends. She spent hours sitting or standing in front of their hutch watching them, taking great interest when they were cleaned out or taken onto the lawn for a scamper. Snowy had a small harness she wore for her own safety but I preferred to let her run freely and keep a close eye on her until discovering she could move faster than I could catch her. Then the harness came into its own.

On the second Saturday afternoon I went out to see Snowy and Pig and was horrified to discover a large tear in their wire. How on earth could that have happened? Had a fox tried to get at them? Surely not in broad daylight. Could it possibly be Kim? I rang Wood Street to ask their advice. Fortunately there is someone on duty 24 hours a day and they are always willing to help or advise. Apparently Kim was the most likely cause of the damage, a dog's paw/claws are, pro-rota to their size of course, equal to a bear's paw in strength. This was a relief as no way would Kim harm either Snowy or Pig. There was obviously no ill-intent behind the action and the wire was soon repaired.

The two weeks passed quickly and before we knew it Tony and his friend were loading the hutch back into the van to take Snowy and Pig home. We were all three sad to see them go. We had really enjoyed having them with us.

Five days later, Tony telephoned to inform us that no way would we be looking after Snowy again. Why? I had tried to look after her properly. They had both received lots of love and attention together with good food and drink. "Precisely" came the reply "You looked after them so well Snowy has been pining for four days and not eaten a thing. We have only just succeeded in getting her to take a little food."

Another visitor to our garden came in the shape of a very large tortoise I found in the middle of the road. He stayed with us for several days until, unable to trace his owner, he was found a good, caring home. What a wonderful fellow he proved to be. He happily munched away on the luscious greenery provided for him and popped his little head out to rub noses with me, listening to all I was telling him. Kim, fascinated by this stranger, followed him all over the garden sniffing at him, obviously not quite sure what to make of him. She had never seen a lifeform moving around in such a large shell-house before. Again, we were sad to see our guest leave but he went to a home were he could roam freely unpestered by a nosey dog or other creature forcing unwanted attentions on him and well away from a busy main road.

Chapter XLI

Attention to the cooking pot is an area in which I tend to be rather lax at times. Although Kim's favourite dinner was liver, at least once a week she enjoyed fresh steak and kidney, a special treat because she was such a good girl. To bring out the best flavour it needed to be cooked slowly under a low gas. On the evening in question Kim's meal was prepared with seasoning and gravy powder then put on the stove to gently simmer. An early evening Sherlock Holmes film was on the television, an entertainment not to be missed. Kim followed Mother and I into the lounge so we closed the door and settled down to enjoy a nostalgic trip down Baker Street in the company of the great detective.

Nearly an hour and a half later, the film concluded, I opened the lounge door onto thick, dense smoke! Oh my hat! Kim's meat! Mother rushed into the kitchen to find the meat totally disintegrated and the saucepan burnt as black as pitch while I ran to open the front door to release some of the smoke. The whole house was full of it. Although we managed to clear the smoke from our home that evening, the aroma hung around for a further two or three weeks.

Like Trixie, Kim had been taught, by means of warning her when a meal was too warm to eat comfortably, the word "Hot" meant it would hurt or was dangerous. On this occasion the word proved a gross understatement!

Because I adored Kimmy and made a fuss of her, friends and family tended to think that she was an old softy. How wrong they were! Kim proved herself as capable and ferocious as any guard dog when the need arose. We were woken about 2am one morning by the sound of Kim racing downstairs barking vociferously. Springing out of bed I chased down after her to find her jumping up at the front door, snarling, growling and barking like an animal demented. Through the small window in the door, clearly discernible was the outline of a man in the porch. Telling Kim she was a good girl and warning Mother to stay where she was, I ran back upstairs and dialled 999. Within a few minutes the police arrived, gave chase to the now absconding intruder eventually catching up with and arresting him.

Well done Kimmy, what a good girl! How she was praised and fussed not only by Mother and I but over the next few days by neighbours, family and friends alike. A special treat in the form of a chicken dinner and bar of Frys Chocolate cream – minus tablets – was her extra reward. Never again would anyone call her "soft". A dog who has known cruelty or suffering will always defend the person or persons who subsequently gives them lots of love and a good, caring home. Nothing can compare to the devotion between a "rescued" dog and its adopted owner.

Chapter XLII

Kimmy soon discovered another treat which gave her infinite pleasure. Ted and Pete were two mechanics attached to Finchley Motors where I had purchased Rebecca. As the land on which the garage was situated was due for redevelopment they were forced to find alternative accommodation. Eventually their search led them to a lock-up at the rear of "The Albion" public house in Union Street, Barnet. Should it prove necessary to leave the car there overnight, the journey home by public transport could not be simpler. A 107 bus from the end of Union Street ran right passed our front door, in theory every twenty minutes. However, a wait of nearly an hour was never unusual on this particular route in the 1970's.

On the first occasion Pete's father, affectionately known as "Pop", kindly gave me a lift home. Two days later when I went to collect Rebecca, Kimmy naturally came with me. We waited patiently at the bus stop for about 15–20 minutes, Kimmy presumably wondering why on earth we were standing on the same spot for so long. There was the park only a few yards away – a run in there would be much more fun than standing still doing nothing!

At last the 107 came into view rambling round the bend in the road, between the cottages on one side and the tree covered verge on the other, swaying unsteadily as it progressed towards us. Eventually reaching the regulation stop it pulled up, the doors opened and we all clambered aboard.

Dogs are required to travel on the top deck so up we scrambled, Kimmy being goaded up the stairs in front of me. Ah, the front seats were empty, good we could enjoy to the full the view as the bus trundled down into the village then up the hill to Barnet.

To enable Kimmy to see out of the windows I lifted her up onto my lap. She loved this – so many interesting things to look at from this exalted position. Then suddenly she spotted the wide-angle security mirror affixed to the righthand corner of the ceiling just above our heads. She sat perfectly still for a moment staring at her reflection. Suddenly up went her ears, over to one side went her head, then to the other side. She looked at me as if to say "What on earth? There is a small dog up there in the corner.. ??" Then back to the mirror again, head thrust forward. Next she tried to get up to inspect the mirror closer – no go, two hands held her tightly.

By this time, the scattering of other passengers near the front of the bus had noticed her fascination with the mirror and were beginning to smile and chuckle at her antics. Unperturbed by their attentions Kimmy remained steadfastly engrossed by the reflective movements of this miniature canine apparition up there in the ceiling. Lost was her interest in anything passing outside the windows, this new weird and wonderful phenomena was all absorbing and, to the amusement of our fellow travellers, continued to be so throughout the entire journey.

All too soon our stop came into view. Gathering up my gloves, handbag and Kimmy we prepared to make our way back along the bus to the stairs. At least I did. Kimmy did not want to leave her new found friend in the mirror. She repeatedly stopped, pulling on her lead, turning her head round in an attempt to look once more up into the corner until, in desperate fear of missing our stop, I picked her up and carried her to the top of the stairs.

Now she knew what the big red monsters were, Kimmy developed a passion for them. From the day of that first ride Kim never passed a stationary bus without pulling towards the door which, if open, was a terrible source of temptation to her and on more than one occasion I had to pull her back to prevent her trying to board. She would even pull towards a bus that was slowing down as it approached a stop. They attracted her like a magnet.

Kimmy and I were destined to take several bus rides to and from Barnet over the next few years and she never lost her love of the experience. Should "her seat" in the front of the top deck be occupied she would sit on my lap staring doggedly in that direction. The instant the offending passenger stood up to get off, Kimmy would begin to fidget until we moved into the vacated seat where she could once again delight our fellow voyagers with her enthralment of the strange little dog up there in the corner of the roof.

Chapter XLIII

After Dad passed over I had to undertake more jobs of a heavier nature with the result my previously beautifully cared for nails began to look very sorry for themselves. Try as I may nothing seemed to help them so, in desperation, I asked our mobile hairdresser Sheila, who lived just around the corner from our house in Cockfosters, if she could recommend anyone. Why yes, her good friend Beryl was a qualified beautician, she was a part-time college tutor and national examiner who, in addition, had recently begun her own mobile beauty business. Sheila put us in touch.

So began Beryl's fortnightly visits, which were to continue for nearly thirty years, to restore and maintain my nails and constantly attempt the preservation of my face!

Kim immediately took to Beryl who, being an ardent animal lover, made a tremendous fuss of her. On her second visit Beryl arrived armed with several dog chews as a treat for Kim; this endeared her all the more to Kimmy who henceforth went crazy when, from her seat on the blanket box in Mother's room, she espied Beryl's car pull up outside the house. After rushing downstairs to greet her and nosing around in one of Beryl's many bags for her "find", Kimmy would follow us upstairs then stretch out on the bed beside me while Beryl worked.

During our many chats covering every conceivable subject from make-up, to in-depth philosophy, I discovered Beryl and her husband Arthur were also proud "parents" to a dog named Kimmy. A black collie cross breed with a lovely nature, only Beryl and Arthur's Kimmy was a little boy dog. In addition, their family included two female cats (who had produced ten kittens between them) and two teenage daughters Sharon and Debbie.

When we moved to Bramley Road my Kim, having been told Aunty Beryl was coming, would sit on the lower bend of the stairs with her eyes glued to the casement window watching, waiting, full of anticipation until Beryl's arrival.

No matter how much Kim loved someone though, she would not allow them into the house without our approval or presence as she fervently demonstrated one December evening.

My eldest nephew Phillip attended a local church school where, every Christmas for a whole week, the pupils gave a most impressive evenings entertainment based on a seasonal theme. Naturally as proud Grandmother and Aunty we went along to add our support both to the school and young Phillip.

Kimmy of course was not allowed in the hall so reluctantly we had to leave her at home. However, Peggy was kind enough to come into our house and sit with her while we were out, relieving us of the worry of leaving Kim alone after dark. Two years running this arrangement worked extremely well. The third year however, when we gave Peggy the date of the performance she was terribly upset as she would be in London that evening with friends at a concert. Oh dear – what were we going to do? There was no way we would even consider leaving Kimmy alone at night.

As soon as Frank heard of the predicament our worries were over. Bless him – he readily offered to look after Kim. "No problem" he said "Kimmy knows me, we are good friends. You leave me the key and when you have gone out I will come in and bring Kimmy indoors with me. She will be fine. You go and enjoy the evening".

With our minds settled we gave Kimmy a lot of fuss, told her Frank would be in to see her very soon, then got Rebecca out of the garage and drove to Winchmore Hill where we spent a thoroughly pleasant evening watching a first class show. Once the production was over and we had duly praised Phillip for his polished performance, we were anxious to get home to Kimmy as quickly as possible.

As I pulled into the drive so Frank, who must have been watching for us, opened his front door and came over to meet us. Immediately my heart stopped. What was wrong? Had something happened to Kimmy? Was she alright?

Apparently Kimmy had never been better! It was poor Frank who was distressed. Shortly after we had driven off, he had opened our front door calling to Kimmy as he did so. He could advance no further. Kimmy came tearing down the stairs growling, snarling and ferociously baring her teeth. No amount of coaxing or comfort talking by Frank would calm her. Mother and I were out of the house therefore **no one**, not even someone she knew and loved well, was coming in while she was on guard duty. Frank was not allowed to put a foot over the doorstep. As soon as he tried Kim went crazy growling, snarling and snapping even louder than before leaving him in no doubt about the reception he would receive should he be foolish enough to attempt crossing the threshold. Those razor shape fangs were waiting. In desperate surrender Frank closed our door again, reluctantly returning alone to the house next door, leaving Kimmy in total charge of our home.

Amazed at his account of the evening's events, Mother and I apologised profusely for the unnerving experience to which Frank had been subjected. It hardly seemed credible. However true it must be as there stood Frank alone and inside our house Kimmy was barking wildly with excitement at our return. We knew now that no unwelcome intruder would ever enter our property while Kim was there, or if they did it would be to their peril.

A few months later I was at home on leave for a few days when a knock sounded on the front door. Kim came running into the hall with me, barking loudly as usual. Before the door was fully open a short, busy little man muttered "Electricity" and began to push his way in. Immediately Kim flung herself forward, hackles up, nostrils flared, snarling through bared teeth. The offensive little man stopped dead in his tracks, looked at Kim then reversed into the porch informing me he was coming in to read the metre. Whereupon I assured him he was *not* coming in until he had produced, and I had inspected to my satisfaction, his identity card, especially as he was not dressed in EEB uniform. After fumbling unsuccessfully in various pockets, he announced he could not find his pass but was coming in anyway. Not only did I verbally assure him he was not entering our property but Kim, who seemed to sense his determination intensified her warnings. Eventually the objectionable man admitting defeat, retreated down the driveway muttering angrily to himself.

Needless to say I promptly followed this distasteful incident with a telephone call to the Electricity Board offices and, having been informed their men were in our area that afternoon reading metres, lodged a complaint. The young man to whom I spoke was most apologetic assuring me the man would be dealt with in no uncertain terms for his officious behaviour and failure to carry identity.

Once again, when the need had arisen, Kim proved herself anything but an "old softy".

Chapter XLIV

As time went by Kimmy required stronger tablets for her heart condition. Though she was always game for a walk her daily exercise varied in length according to how she was feeling.

At home she sat in the easychair with her head and chin resting on the upholstered arm while her tail hung down through the open side of the chair, in a resplendent, flowing cascade of golden fur. Another favourite place for repose was underneath the capacious oak sideboard (which Uncle Fred, being an acknowledged and talented cabinet maker had made as part of his and Aunty Winnie's first home in the 1930's) where, stretching out full length on her side or curling into a ball she was able to doze undisturbed. Often while deep in sleep her legs twitched, her tail wagged furiously or on occasions she issued forth a joyful bark. At least the nightmares had long since ceased and been replaced by dreams of a happier nature.

The older she became the longer the fur on her feet grew until, at times, she accidently stood on it thus necessitating a quick trim. The effect of the lengthened fur was quite becoming, giving her legs and feet the appearance of a miniature carthorse which, with affection, I often referred to her as.

Despite her now advancing years Kim always took an early morning stroll round the garden while I prepared the birds' breakfast. She inspected the plants, examined the vegetable garden in detail and, if she could get away with it, took a quick sip from one of the birds drinking dishes. Come the winter snows she suddenly forgot her age becoming once more a young, playful over-grown puppy. As soon as the back door was opened she was out like a streak of lightening. Down the garden, burying her nose as she went in the soft white snow which covered the lawns, then lifting her head high, front legs splayed, laughing and sneezing with excitement. Turning in joyful circles, running this way and that, biting into the snow recovering with relish a mouth of the frozen liquid. Tail wagging nineteen to the dozen.

Like most collie crossbreeds, Kim's love of a good game coupled with her sense of fun was eternal. One of her greatest loves was a 12" high orange teddy bear with a white tummy and white nose which I bought her one Christmas from Woolworth in Palmers Green. Teddy

Paddy in 1927
Our parents much loved Airedale/Wolfhound

Late 1930's
A very young Tony cuddles Tiger his cat and best friend

Patch on the verge outside Aunty Winnie's bungalow
at Aldwick Bay, West Sussex

Billy in the garden at Hamilton Road, Cockfosters

Trixie with her puppies in the box Dad made for her

Mother with Trixie and her puppies

Trixie takes 'Cheeky' out for his first walk on the lead

Lulworth Cove Beach

Watched by Mary,
Helene offers Kimmy
an ice-cream . . .

. . . and she throughly
enjoys it!

Back home in her armchair

Wood Street Veterinary Hospital Barnet

The main entrance of the Hospital as it is today, 124 years after
the first veterinary surgery opened on the site in 1880

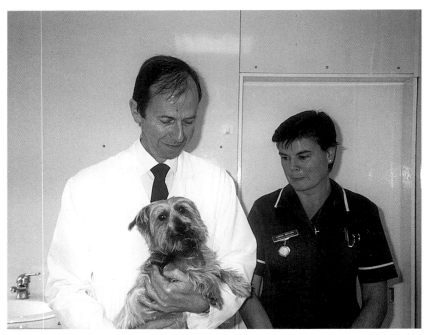

Vet. Mark Winwood and Practice Manager Carol Brown
examine Miffy in the main consulting room at the hospital

Madelaine, the Receptionist, on duty at the front desk

Both Blackie and Tessa love to sit looking out of the
bedroom windows

74 Wood Street
Barnet
Herts.
EN5 4BN
Telephone: 0181-449 0074
Fax: 0181-447 1950

Consultations by Appointment:
Monday to Saturday-Morning
Monday to Friday-Afternoon & Evening
All Other times-Emergencies only

29.12.99

Dear Blackie & Miffy,

I am sure that your 'mother' will read to you my thanks for the excellent Clotted Cream that arrived at the practice for me. The cold weather meant that it arrived in absolutely perfect condition and was attested truly delicious by all who tried it.

I hope that you all had a happy Christmas and managed to avoid the many & varied viruses doing the rounds. May I take the opportunity of wishing you all a happy & healthy year to come in 2000.

My thanks once more

Kindest regards

Mark

Example of the letter Mark Winwood always wrote to thank my
dog or dogs who sent him Cream from Devon at Christmas and
from holiday, whenever/wherever they went

went everywhere with her. Practically every day he was shaken wildly then licked with loving affection. Also to receive many a wash from Kimmy's endearing tongue was "Felix" a white fur fabric cat who sat on a Victorian lady's chair I had purchased at auction in Wareham.

However, one furry animal who attracted Kimmy in a different way was an elegant Afghan Hound bitch, a lovely dog with a pleasant nature who lived, with half a dozen cats, in an upstairs flat a little way down the road. For some inexplicable reason the Afghan and Kim went crazy whenever they met. As soon as they espied each other the provocative barking began in earnest. Both dogs strained on their leads pulling towards each other. Though what exactly would have happened should they have been released from their restraint will never be known. Quite probably they would simply have stood facing each other at a loss to know what to do – having cried wolf once too often.

I sometimes wonder whether the Afghan's bright blue track-suite mackintosh had an affect on Kim – maybe she wanted one to add to her already ample wardrobe! The first time I saw the Afghan wearing this incredible garment, it was difficult to control the laughter. Her entire body from her neck to the base of her tail and all four legs were hidden under bright blue nylon. In later years I not only realised how sensible the suit was but purchased similar wear for my own dogs – though in a more subdued colour.

Chapter XLV

In November 1976 I took voluntary severance from Kodak. After the new building at Hemel Hempstead was completed and occupied in 1971 only a comparative handful of us were left in London, housed in the office block that had been built on the site of the old Holborn Empire destroyed by enemy bombs during the Second World War. Syd Marshall, the Principal of the School of Medical Radiographic Photography, and myself, the administrator, were the London based members of the new Marketing Education Centre at Gadebridge on the edge of Hemel. Eventually it was decided to relocate the Medical unit out of London; as I did not want to move house I decided the time had come to investigate the outside world. Life in Kodak had been wonderful in those days despite its enormity it was very much a "family" firm, offering a secure and happy environment in which to spend ones working day. However, sad though the physical parting maybe, life must move on.

Having worked like a beaver to leave everything in apple-pie order ready for the hand-over to Gadebridge, there had not been time to think of looking for a new post. Consequently I was destined to spend a while at home before attending two Management courses prior to accepting the next assignment. Kimmy was over-joyed to have her "Mum" at home. She was able to make longer walks, became more playful and – to quote Mr Winwood – "her life is more interesting so she feels better in herself".

Christmas drew near and we invited a lady in her mid-sixties, who would otherwise be on her own, to stay with us over the holiday. Not having seen Mildred for some years we were unaware, until she informed us, her constant companion was a little dog named Sweetie-pie. Of course the little dog could come – Kimmy was very good about allowing other dogs in her home. She knew she was very much loved and always came first. Our guests accepted the invitation to stay for the four or five days of the Holiday.

The guest room was made ready in good time for the visitors' arrival a few days prior to Christmas. Answering a knock at the door we caught our first glimpse of Sweetie-pie tucked under Mildred's arm. A little chihuahua with an insolent stare and arrogant manner. As they crossed the threshold and stood in the hall Kim looked up at Sweetie-pie then at me with a look which clearly said "what on earth is she doing up there – why isn't she on the floor like me"? Sweetie-pie looked down at my Kim with what can only be described as a look of supercilious disdain. Oh dear, what had we done? What were we in for in the days ahead?

It soon became obvious Sweetie-pie was Mildred's "familiar". When not tucked into her Mum's arms, she followed her everywhere with an air of haughty contempt for Mother, Kim, myself or anyone who dared enter our home. Bless her heart, Kimmy was so patient though utterly bewildered by this contemptuous little creature which frequently yapped – as opposed to barked – for no obvious reason. So obstreperous was her yap even Peggy and Frank next door commented on it's stentorian volume. The thickness of the walls prevented them ever hearing Kimmy barking when indoors, thus they found it unbelievable when Sweetie-pie's voluminous tones penetrated the dividing brick structure.

Come mealtime Sweetie-pie was picked up by her adoring Mum who held her up to her neck or over her shoulder. Our objections to Sweetie-pies close proximity to the table fell on deaf ears. The little dog herself looked at us with an expression which loudly declared "hard luck I am up here and staying whether you like it or not – I reign supreme where-ever I go". Kimmy looked at the dog and it's owner in disgust before taking herself over to her armchair where she sat watching the proceedings with nonchalant interest.

Upon being informed Sweetie-pie slept *in* her Mum's bed, Mother expressly requested she refrain from doing so while with us. There was no objection to her sleeping on top of the bed – indeed Kim always slept on mine – but not inside the bed please.

Next morning when Mother took a cup of tea in to Mildred's room, Sweetie-pie was nowhere to be seen. "Where" Mother inquired, "is Sweetie-pie, is she all right?" "Oh yes" answered Mildred lifting the bedclothes, "she is fine. She is in here with me". No amount of remonstrating made the slightest difference to Mildred or her precious Sweetie-pie. Each morning the dog was to be found cosily tucked right down inside the bedclothes with her Mum.

Mildred and her canine companion settled themselves into our home with the air of a deigning monarch.

Outwardly unperturbed by this intrusion into her home and life, Kimmy behaved like the well-mannered lady she was. Despite Sweetie-pie's constant insufferable presence Kim went about her daily life as though nothing untoward were happening. When Sweetie-pie pushed her way in front of Kim to steal some of her food – not that she really wanted it having just consumed a saucer of her own victuals – Kim merely waited patiently while the irritant was removed. Every time Kim settled down in her armchair Sweetie-pie tottered over, stood immediately in front of her deliberately taunting her host. The fact her pathetic antics were ignored seemed to make no difference to Sweetie-pie and she was obviously too full of her own importance to realise how ridiculous she looked. The only outward sign Kim made of even acknowledging her existence was to look up at me with a look of patient forbearance.

Christmas over, Mildred and Sweetie-pie were due to return home to Kent when the weather took a turn for the worst. The snow began to fall heavily stopping only when the ground was covered to a depth of almost a foot. Not to worry, Mildred announced, she would stay a little longer – there was no need for her to rush away.

A week later, the snow still on the ground and showing no signs of thawing, Mildred decided she would have a hire-car to take her all the way home. Mother and I agreed it was the best plan – there was no way of telling how long it would be before there was an improvement in conditions. The forecast was bad.

The car was duly booked to collect Mildred and Sweetie-pie at 10am on Friday morning. Excitedly, I gave Kimmy a hug telling her our visitors were departing – our home would be our own again.

Just before 10 o'clock Mildred, having left me to bring her luggage down into the hall, descended the stairs like an aging Prima Donna Sweetie-pie having, preceded her mistress, scuttled into the lounge to have one last taunt at Kimmy. What a surprise she was in for!

Kimmy having seen the luggage in the hall realised our visitors were leaving us. She had been tolerance and patience personified for the last ten days or so, now it was her turn to repay this obnoxious little fiend for all her contemptuous behaviour.

She chased Sweetie-pie all over the lounge snapping at her bottom. In and out of the chairs, round the table, along the sideboard, back again through the table legs, this way and that. There was no escape.

Having seen what was happening, I closed the door to prevent Sweetie-pie absconding. I knew Kim would not hurt or even touch her but she was entitled to give this self-opinionated little creature who had done her best to make Kim's life a misery, a dose of her own medicine. I was certainly not going to intervene. Sweetie-pie's tail was tucked between her legs as she darted this way and that yelping like the coward she was.

"What is going on?" called Mildred from the hallway. "It is alright Mildred" I replied. "Kimmy is just saying goodbye to Sweetie-pie". "Oh, good, that is nice" came the response.

The car arrived sharp to time and it was with a sigh of relief we waved Mildred and Sweetie-pie goodbye – forever!

Chapter XLVI

November the 12th, 1977 was our parents' Golden Wedding Anniversary. Very special flowers for Dad in front of his portrait and something nice for Mother. What she would really like, she told me, was a good pair of gloves. Certainly. We would go along to Bradfords in Southgate on Saturday afternoon and she could choose what-ever she liked – no expense spared.

Naturally Kimmy came too. It was a pleasant dry afternoon so we left Rebbecca in the car park next to the field at the top end of the high street and walked its length to the ladies outfitters the far side of the shopping centre.

Twenty minutes later, having discovered and purchased a pair of gloves which, though by virtue of the origin of their material were repugnant to me, delighted Mother. The afternoon's shopping over, the three of us made our way back up the high street. As we reached the gap in the two bar fence which served as the car park entrance Mother suddenly gasped as she fell over an uneven paving stone, crashing to the ground, her right hand under her. A very agitated Kim immediately pulled over to her wanting to see what had happened. Mother said very little as I helped her up – only that her hand was hurting but she was alright. No, she did not want to go to Casualty, she would be fine, she just wanted to get home and have a cup of tea.

Next morning the hand was still giving trouble so, turning a deaf ear to Mother's protestations, I took her to Casualty at the local hospital a couple of miles down the road. This time Kim had to stay behind, it was not advisable to leave her in the car alone for heaven knew how long. Also the hospital was surrounded by open country, consequently the car parking area was quiet and virtually unoverlooked.

After the usual three hour wait, Mother was seen by the duty doctor then sent along to Radiography to have the hand and fingers radiographed. Back again to Casualty for another lengthy wait. Eventually her name was called. We went into the tiny consulting room where the young doctor, holding the radiographs up to the coldlight illuminator, marvelled at Mother's courage. Apparently she had broken the back of her hand, thumb and finger! The appropriate dressing was applied and she was instructed to report the following Tuesday for treatment.

For the next few months I drove Mother to hospital accompanied of course by Kimmy, first three times a week, then twice and latterly once a week until the hand was finally declared better.

We drove into the small car park bringing Rebecca round to face the nearest building – the maternity block – for protection from the wind while Mother made her way across to the main hospital. All during the long winter months Kimmy and I wrapped up in our thick coats, huddled together under a pure wool tartan travelling rug to keep warm. The weather conditions were truly arctic with Kimmy and I often sharing a hot water bottle and a thermos flask of hot tea in an endeavour to beat the cold. The ground frequently covered with several inches of frozen snow while flakes continued falling unrelentingly from above.

She was wonderful company those afternoons when time passed slowly. Always responding to my chatter in one way or another. Taking a shared interest in any welcome diversion going on around us. An ambulance arriving across the way; the occasional car driving in or departing from the car park; a train in the distance making it's rhythmic passage through the countryside; a hospital float slowly progressing along the Authority's pathways to deliver or collect laundry or other supplies.

One of the most rewarding pastimes proved to be watching the birds and squirrels scavenging amongst the undergrowth only yards away from the car, quite unperturbed by our presence or that of other intruders into their world of grubs and shrubs.

By the time Mother's visits were no longer required, the warmer days were creeping in, with the blessing we did not have to continue our waiting sessions in the heat of the summer.

Chapter XLVII

As Kimmy grew older she lost her slim youthful figure though I failed to completely recognise the fact. I loved her so much I only saw her endearing personality so consequently became annoyed when folk declared she was "putting on weight". However, it did become necessary to add another couple of inches to the pale blue and grey coat I had knitted for her a year or two previously. In an attempt to reduce her body fluid she was given at least one bowl of fennel tea a day to drink. Amazingly, despite it's strong flavour, Kimmy loved it drinking the entire contents of her dish non-stop. The tea achieved a moderation of success as Kimmy lost 3 or 4 lbs as a result.

She obviously felt the cold more, as during the winter months, she snuggled right down each night under the sleeping bag on top of my bed. Her presence discernable only by the curiously shaped lump moving gently up and down to the rhythm of her breathing. Mr Winwood assured me she was perfectly safe, apparently dogs are quite capable of surviving under a pile of blankets, or similar, for many hours.

Her own Goddards bed was placed in the lounge for her each day, just in case she wanted it. Having recently changed my own bedding from the conventional sheets and blankets to a continental quilt, it seemed a shame no one had as yet produced something similar for pets. Suddenly an idea came – a baby's cot eiderdown! The very thing.

The following Saturday I took a trip into Enfield Town to scour Pearsons (the one and only department store) and as many baby shops as it took to procure what was needed.

To my delight a little shop in the main street produced the very thing. I purchased two, one pale blue and green depicting little boys in baggy trousers and a similar one coloured blue with pink. The two lady assistants thought it a wonderful idea to utilise them as a pet bed, indeed one of them had bought something similar for her cat.

I carried them home on the bus filled with anticipation at Kim's reaction to her present. Always coming up to expectation she sniffed them, danced in circles of delight then, as the blue and green quilt was spread out on the lounge carpet, promptly lay down in the middle of it. Her tail wagging joyfully, her face upturned towards Mother and I, eyes sparkling with pride and pleasure in her latest acquisition. So pleased was Kim with her eiderdowns that she began curling up in her bed during the daytime instead of sitting in the armchair.

With the success of the first two quilts I later purchased a third in pale yellow. Now there would always be two in use and one in the wash.

Come summer Kim began to scratch. Only occasionally at first then the scratching increased and was accompanied by frenzied sessions of biting and nibbling the skin. Close examination revealed little red patches where she had attempted to relieve herself of the irritation. Otherwise her skin was as clean as a whistle. No sign of the expected fleas. Along we went to Mr Winwood.

By process of elimination we realised Kimmy was only affected thus after being in the long grass. She had the canine version of hayfever! Fortunately one quick injection solved the immediate problem though the allergy was to return each year with the onset of summer.

Occasional she also needed ointment to clear her ears. This presented no problem as, having complete trust, she stood perfectly still while the drops slid slowly into place. What-ever needed to be done to her she never made a fuss, always accepting it was for her own good.

Not that she was perfect by any means and in later years developed the habit of poking her nose into the wastepaper basket in my bedroom, retrieving any soft contents such as tissues or cotton wool, then tearing it to shreds all over the floor. Time after time she entertained herself this way. It was impossible to be cross with her because she was by now getting on in years.

Chapter XLVIII

We had never really been happy in the little house in Bramley Road, despite our marvellous neighbours. The house was so small in comparison to previous homes, our furniture took most of the available space. We were plagued by giant spiders and were constantly being rescued by both Peggy and Mr Macklyn to whom we shall always be grateful. Worst of all, the house was occupied by unwelcome visitors from long ago.

Often we would be woken during the night by the sound of machinery being used or the bed being shaken violently. On one occasion, when my own bed was being thus shaken, I told the mischievous entity to "shut up and go away". It responded promptly by leaving my bed and going into the next room where it began furiously shaking Mother's bed! Needless to say she did not appreciate the boisterous intrusion.

Our good friend Stanley Poulton visited the house for the express purpose of helping with this matter. The disturbances were reduced slightly but so numerous were the "visitors" that to clear the building completely was a mammoth task requiring ongoing attention.

Surprisingly Kim took absolutely no notice of any of our unwanted guests. She must have been able to see them as, like Trixie, she always responded to the presence of family or friends who had passed on. Up would go her head when a kind person stroked her. She also sat keenly watching, with a wag of her tail, Dad or any amicable soul who visited us. So, once again, the job of house-hunting began.

Chapter XLIX

In June 1980 we received, from a local agent, attractive details of a semi-detached property in Chase Road, only a mile distance from where we were at present. An appointment to view was made for 12 noon the following Saturday. Being so close to hand, we left Kimmy at home and walked down the road and round the corner. Lined either side by 70 ft trees standing on grass verges outside the properties, Chase Road had a lot to commend it. Approaching the front door of number 66 a warm pleasurable feeling swept over us. The door was opened by the husband and as soon as we stepped over the threshold we knew this was the right house. An all embracing sense of well-being, peace, tranquillity and security embraced us, which grew stronger as we viewed each part of the property.

Built just before the last war, the rooms were large and airy with plenty of window space allowing the sunlight to flood the interior. This was to be our home, no doubt about it.

A large patio door opened onto a garden just the right size for us to manage yet big enough for Kimmy to roam round the lawn during her morning preambulation. She would love it, both the house and the garden.

Friday the 26 September dawned misty, however before long the sun was breaking through. Having accepted a twelve month assignment with a statutory body in Paddington in March, I had taken three days leave. We were up and dressed by 6.45am. Breakfast over and Kimmy taken for her morning walk, the days work began.

Hoults, the removal contractors, had been with us the previous day undertaking the bulk of the packing. They arrived at 9.15am this morning ready to load-up the huge Eurovan.

Aunty Ivy was unable to help us on this occasion but Alice called in to see if she could give us a hand. Tony also spent the day with us so we were in no way lacking willing helpers. As on the previous occasion, for safety, Kimmy stayed in Rebecca. Having sat looking out of the open window for a while watching the men go to and fro she decided she had seen all there was to see so curled up on her front seat and drifted into a peaceful slumber.

Around midday, with the house almost empty, tummies began to rumble. Grabbing a purse then jumping in beside Kimmy I drove down to the local fish and chip shop to buy lunch for everyone. Arriving back at the house we realised all the china and cutlery was already on the van. Never mind – Kimmy had her dish of water which could be emptied and utilised for her piece of fish. The rest of us could sit on the floor eating cod and chips with our fingers out of the paper. Not very elegant but good fun!

Peggy and Frank, who came in to see how things were progressing, had a good laugh at our improvised picnic. We were sorry to be leaving all our good neighbours. Kimmy would miss them sorely and they would miss our Kim – she had become such pals with them all but, only being a short distance away, hopefully we would all still meet from time to time.

Lunch over, I began to load Rebecca with those precious items which required special transportation. Her space now being invaded, Kimmy took a keener interest in what was happening. She had seen this kind of activity before but as long as she was in Rebecca all would be well. The back seat was piled high with familiar possessions; ah now here came her bed, it was being put in the boot – good.

By 5.30pm the van was finally closed-up ready to move off. I had already made five trips round to the new house with the car fully loaded – where did it all come from? Had all these things really been in this little house? No wonder we had been so cramped for the past few years. Now it was time to say au-revoir to Peggy, Frank and Mr & Mrs Macklyn from whom Kimmy received many pats, strokes and kind words. Alice had had to leave us mid-afternoon but Mother, Kim and I clambered into Rebecca for the long journey down the road and round the corner! Tony came along behind in his car and Les one of the Hoults men, brought up the rear in his own car with the boot full of the last of my cactus plants which would not fit into the van.

The Eurovan was waiting outside number 66 as we drew up. Although Kimmy had come with me on the previous five trips she had remained safely in Rebecca. Now it was her turn to inspect our new home. She pulled eagerly down the path in through the big front door where she was unleashed to explore by herself. She ran into each downstairs room where she had a good look and a sniff around before making her way upstairs to see what was up there. Then outside in the garden which had not been touched since we viewed and agreed to purchase the house back in June. The grass was so tall we almost lost sight of Kimmy who was having the time of her life investigating every nook and cranny.

At last the unloading was finished. The contractors had left, Tony had gone and we three were on our own. Tired, dirty, surrounded by packing cases, boxes and heaven alone knows what else but in our own home at last. The first job was to feed Kimmy, then have a cup of tea, make the beds and prepare a meal. Here a slight problem arose. Although gas pipes were laid to the house, the gas had not been taken into the kitchen. Consequently dinner comprised two eggs each boiled in the kettle!

We all settled down quickly in our new home. The space coupled with the peaceful atmosphere was sheer heaven after the old house. Kimmy very soon made friends with Kitty and Max, the elderly couple living in the house attached to ours. Max particularly was very fond of dogs having had several of his own throughout his long life.

Both Peggy and Mr Macklyn visited us and, needless to say, were given a tumultuous welcome by Kimmy. As always she offered Mr Macklyn her tummy for tickling and was not disappointed!

Although happy in the house and garden, for some reason Kimmy was extremely reluctant to go for a walk outside the front gate. Concerned about this, I took her up to Mr Winwood who diagnosed deficiency of sight due to cataracts in both eyes. Dear Kimmy, we must take even greater care of her now. Perhaps if I kept her close to me on a short lead she could be persuaded to come for a walk. Regrettably though this was not the case. Try as I may she would not venture beyond our frontage. Indoors she did not have a problem as the furniture was arranged in a similar fashion to that in our previous homes.

In November we decided it was time for a short break by the sea to recoup our energies after the strain of moving and settling in. We began our mini-holiday by driving down to visit Hove en route for Bognor.

Having spent a couple of hours with friends in the town we drove down to the sea to spend a few moments in peaceful solitude with the elements. The wind was howling as we stood on the front watching the boiling sea, Kim's fur being blown straight back along her face and body. Her ears flattened against her head. We could hardly hear ourselves speak above the roar of the waves crashing down on the shingle then being sucked back under the next oncoming wave. Eventually we clambered back into Rebecca and made our way along the coast to Bognor.

Over the next few days Kim made the most of the fuss and attention she received from all our friends, showing her delight at renewing old acquaintances, in particular Cathy on the beach and Reg and Ethel whom we visited in Felpham. It was just like old times.

Come Sunday morning, as pre-arranged, we called to collect Ruth from her bungalow in Nyetimber to bring her back with us for ten days, George having recently passed over. She was delighted to be in a position to visit us at long last and, an ardent animal lover whose own two dogs had passed over, was thrilled at the prospect of living with Kim for a while.

Kimmy was genuinely pleased Ruth was with us as they had always been the best of pals. By keeping her closely between the two of us, Ruth and I managed to persuade her to come for a short walk round the block, a tremendous achievement. One we repeated on two or three occasions during Ruth's visit.

When the day came to drive Ruth to Victoria to catch the mid-day train home, the three of us were very sad to see her go. Would she come back to spend Christmas with us? Yes, she would be delighted to!

Leaving Mother in Rebecca to look after Kimmy who was nervous of all the hustle and bustle of London, I walked to the train with Ruth seeing her safely aboard. As the train snaked it's way along the platform and out of the station I made my way back to Rebecca for the drive home to Chase Road.

Needless to say Kim was greatly relieved to be in the peace and quiet of her own home once more. After consuming a bowl of biscuits and liver – her favourite – she curled up in her bed in the lounge for a good, long sleep.

Before we knew it Christmas was upon us. To Kim's utter joy Ruth arrived on the 23 December in time to help put up the tree and decorations. Though now approximately eleven or eleven and a half years of age and despite the fact she was not only slowing down but experiencing odd bouts of sickness, Kim was still young enough in heart to thoroughly enjoy the festive season. Christmas morning she turned in circles of excitement at the sight of so many presents. Her nose went into each parcel in turn. Her tail wagging crazily as her own packages were opened for her, pouncing on the contents as was her want. What a wonderful Christmas she was having!

Come January she was unwell again necessitating another visit to Wood Street. She experienced a bout of sickness which, thankfully, eventually cleared up but not until we had experienced a great deal of worry and anxiety.

Chapter L

By now young Phillip was nine years of age and old enough to spend the occasional week-end with us. He was very fond of Kimmy and, had it been possible, would dearly have loved a dog of his own. However, it was not really feasible at present. He helped me in the garden then came with me to the Council Tip to take the rubbish – all activities he described as "fun and interesting"! Naturally Kimmy always came too.

A special feature of these week-ends was the Midnight Feast which took place when Grandma was, supposedly, asleep in the next bedroom. Not wishing to sleep alone in the guest room, Phillip always brought his own sleeping bag, unfolding it onto our lounger which was placed at the foot of my bed. Thus Phillip, Kimmy and I shared the same room. Having procured an ample supply of crisps, chocolate and other such goodies during the afternoon, as soon as Grandma's light went out the feasting began. Kimmy happily joined in the excitement. Unperturbed by such extraordinary behaviour, she eagerly consumed her share of crisps and chocolate (a special treat on a special occasion) along with half a dozen dog chews.

Keith, who was still only five years of age, longed for the time he too could stay with Grandma, Aunty and Kimmy. He was promised that when he was a little older, in a year or two, he could come as often as he liked providing of course Mummy agreed. This had to satisfy him for the time being. He was equally as fond of Kimmy as Phillip was and never missed an opportunity of putting his arms around her neck to give her a hug and a big kiss. She was so patiently gentle with him, always standing still to allow him to demonstrate his love for her.

He became aware of the fact the lead belonged to Kimmy and some- how hooked onto her. One afternoon, while the whole family watched fascinated, he explored every part of her anatomy in an attempt to attach the lead to her. Where did it fix on? He dived into her long fur a dozen times trying to discover the answer without success. Eventually as a reward for his efforts, he was allowed to watch the leash being clipped on then to take her for a walk round the lounge. He was so proud, so pleased with himself. He was taking Kimmy for a walk all by himself!

No longer enjoying the walks of her youth Kim's claws grew unchecked by nature, consequently it was upon Mr Winwood and his claw clippers the task of a regular manicure fell. Unfortunately the trimming of each claw – was accompanied by a loud snap which fright- ened Kim so much she struggled frantically to escape. With each ses- sion – which occurred every two to three months – Kim's terror increased. The only answer I could think of was to ask Mr Winwood sif he would be kind enough to visit Kim at home and clip her claws while I put on a record of loud music and turned the volume up. Understandingly kind as ever, he agreed to try my idea.

Two days later, as I opened the front door Kim came to see who was calling. The instant she recognised Mr Winwood she trotted back into the lounge. She knew this man – he belonged to the place where she was taken to have, among other nasty things, needles stuck into her. He was the man in the white coat who "did things" to her. What was he doing here? She was in the protection of her own home. Oh dear, he was following her into the lounge. Quick, dive behind the sofa. Good he was sitting down talking to Mum. Now what is happening? Mum has made the box in the corner make a very loud noise and **he** is opening his bag and looking this way. Help!

It took several minutes to catch Kimmy who suddenly found a serge of youthful energy in her attempts to avoid being caught. Success at last! I was able to grab her as she made a bid for the door and hold on to her while Mr Winwood undertook the work that had to be done. Although she struggled Kim was definitely not as badly affected as on previous occasions. The experiment had proved sufficiently successful to warrant it's use in future.

When Mr Winwood had taken his leave of us, Kim decided it had been a very exhausting morning, she was therefore entitled to lunch followed by a good, long, uninterrupted sleep. Within a few minutes of emptying her bowl, her gentle snoring was echoing from the armchair where she had settled herself comfortably.

In her advancing years she tended to snore more often than not. At nighttime I often lay awake quietly laughing to myself at the sound of Mother, in the next room, and Kimmy on my bed snoring in unison.

Chapter LI

The end of March saw the fulfilment of my London post and once again I was at home with Kimmy who as always, despite her age, was good company and a pleasure to be with.

Come April Kimmy was again unwell and under the care of Mr Winwood for a couple of weeks. She suffered from bouts of biliousness which must have made her feel rotten though she never made a fuss or "complained".

Towards the end of April my third nephew Colin was born at UCH. As always Kimmy was introduced to the new baby and the two were fussed over simultaneously thus ensuring a firm bonding between them.

The beginning of August I decided the small front bedroom could do with redecorating – a nice new wallpaper was what was needed. With the requisite materials purchased and work well under way, it being Saturday afternoon, a short break seemed like a good idea. The Grove Retirement Home, situated a little further down our road, were holding an Open Day so, leaving Kimmy to guard the house, Mother and I went along for an hour. It was a very pleasant interlude. A lot of effort had obviously been put into the event with many tables of goodies on sale which had been made by the occupants. With the sun shining brightly through the windows and everyone happy and cheerful the afternoon was a great success.

We had only been back indoors long enough to make a fuss of Kim when the telephone rang. A call we were never to forget. Keith had been knocked down by a car in the road outside their house and was at that moment being taken by ambulance, with a police escort, to a London hospital. His injuries were extremely serious and he was unconscious.

He lay in a coma for just over a week. Then at 4.19pm on Sunday the 15 August, he passed over to join the Grandfather he had never known during his short six years of life in the physical world.

Keith's death was a dreadful shook to our family and friends alike. He was always as bright as a button, very confident and quick to learn while at the same time he was sensitive and affectionate. He adored Kimmy and she him. Many is the time he put his arms around Kim to give her a cuddle while conversationally chattering to her. I am sure he believed she understand every word he said and who knows – maybe she did.

Being temporarily at home and out of the work-a-day rat race I was more aware of Keith than would otherwise have been the case. He did not realise at first he had passed over, believing instead he was on holiday staying with friends who loved him and were taking care of him.

Chapter LII

Come September the three of us went down to Dorset for a week to stay with Eileen. Kimmy was overjoyed to see her friend again, wriggling from side to side and wrinkling her nose in excitement. However, the journey had been rather long for her, leaving her very, very tired. She was therefore only too ready to curl up on Eileen's rug in front of the electric coal-affect fire, quickly drifting into an exhausted sleep, while we indulged in a cuppa and a long natter with Eileen, catching up with all the local gossip.

Though she enjoyed the holiday Kimmy found it rather tiring, taking every opportunity to doze off. She still enjoyed her morning walk across the road to greet Princess and Lollipop, then up over the hill to inspect the hedgerows before turning for home. During the day though she was reluctant to walk very far preferring to curl up on Rebecca's front seat to sleep. However this did not prevent her from gleefully greeting Helene and family who were equally delighted to see Kim. Csibsz ran round and round in circles loudly emitting his peculiar high pitched squeak in welcome. While we all enjoyed a cup of tea, piece of homemade cake and a natter, Kimmy declining the titbits offered her, stretched out on the carpet in a precious pool of sunlight and was soon fast asleep.

All too soon the holiday was over. Sadly we took leave of our friends once more before setting off on the long journey home during which Kimmy slept most of the way.

When we finally arrived home and unloaded the car Kim's bed, which was always packed first as it lay flat on the floor of the boot with everything else on top, came out last. Waiting in the lounge for it to be erected, Kim was in her bed curled up fast asleep again before Rebecca was put away in the garage. Too tired to eat she slept until it was time to go into the garden for wow-woz prior to retiring for the night.

Meals were now something to be eaten as a necessity rather than consumed with relish. A little gentle encouragement was always required these days. Sometimes Kim could be persuaded by hand-feeding to continue eating of her own accord while other days she would gently take the entire meal from my fingers little by little. I always consider a good meal to be of paramount importance, worrying greatly about any member of the family who is not always ready and eagerly willing to devour a plate of good food. Kim undoubtedly sensed this, if perhaps a little over-active emotion on my part, so did her best to respond positively to my anxiety by swallowing as much as she could, if only to please me.

Winter came early in 1981. On Monday the 7 December, the snow fell heavily, quickly covering the ground with a thick soft white blanket, transforming the landscape into one of exquisite beauty. During the day Kimmy was very sick and rather listless. Praying it was just an upset stomach I watched her carefully, adjusting her diet in an attempt to aid her quick recovery. Hopefully a small dish of lightly boiled chicken would soon have her back to normal. Unhappily this was not the case.

When, after two days, Kimmy showed no sign of improvement Mr Winwood called to see her. Hearing the doorbell ring her ears immediately went up as she wearily made her way into the hall to see who was there and whether it was necessary for her to put on a show of aggressive protection. She took one look at Mr Winwood then turned tail, back into the lounge. She may not be feeling very well but she knew who this was! Her anxiety to put as much distance as possible between herself and this man carrying his big black bag of nasties, gave her an increased speed with which to escape behind the sofa.

We all followed Kim into the lounge and sat down allowing her to remain where she was for the time being. A test I had taken half-an-hour previously, indicated an unusually high protein level. This was not good news – however veterinary science, love and healing were all at Kim's disposal. Her course of injections and tablets began. Mr Winwood would call again in a couple of days – hopefully there would be some improvement by then.

Concerned to supply Mr Winwood with an accurate account of Kim's situation I kept a detailed written record of her hourly condition. At the end of each day typing the notes in readiness for his next visit.

Mr Winwood called in each day to see her. No one could have been kinder or more caring. He assured me she was not in pain, just "not feeling very well". Although I knew Kim was really poorly I constantly willed her to recover, never seriously entertaining the thought she would not.

However, Kim was no better. She was unable to retain little if any sustenance. I brought her Goddards bed into the lounge each day putting it near but not too close to the fire. When on Friday the 18 December Mr Winwood called again, his concern was increased. On his concurrence with my suggestions, I obtained in turn a jar of Brands Essence then tins of Heinz baby food in an attempt to settle her system. By now the snow was too deep to get the car out of the garage let alone up the fairly steep drive onto the road. So, determined to procure any-thing that may help Kimmy I walked into Southgate, a distance of a mile and a half, to raid the shelves of Boots the Chemist.

Next day a bus ride to Barnet and a visit to Mothercare produced a small pillow for Kim's bed where she now spent most of the day cov-ered with a soft shawl crocheted by our Aunt Evelyn. At night she now needed help to climb the stairs before being lifted gently onto my bed where she slept soundly throughout the night, waking only occasion-ally for a drink.

One morning during the second week of her illness, an envelope addressed to her arrived with the early post. She had received letters addressed to her before as each Christmas she sent clotted cream to Mr Winwood and his family from Woolacombe Bay Dairy in North Devon as a small thank you for looking after her during the year. Always he wrote to her personally thanking her, saying how much they all enjoyed her gift. This envelope was different, it gave the impression of containing a card of some kind. Showing it to Kim, who looked, sniffed then looked up at me enquiringly I opened it pulling out a Get Well Card! I must confess my initial reaction was – someone has gone mad – much as I love my Kimmy, you do not send cards to dogs! However, over the next day or two she received several more. Having accompanied me virtually everywhere over the last ten years she had indeed made many good friends who were very fond of her. I was touched that so many of them were thinking of her at this time, wishing her well. Surely so much love from so many people must help her recovery. She was also of course on the Healing List at Potters Bar Church where she had remained a regular visitor until her illness.

Despite the worsening weather making the five mile drive extremely arduous Mr Winwood continued to call on Kimmy regularly. As time went on and in an attempt to draw her from her bed to demonstrate her current walking ability I endeavoured to excite her into action with the words "Look whos here Kimmy. Look who has come to see you!" Initially the rouse worked well and she would totter out into the hall to see for herself who this illustrious visitor was. Later she declined to be roused, so in order to judge her progress, or lack of it, Mr Winwood approached her as if to carry out an examination. This had the immediate effect of making Kim leave her bed and head for the hall with Mr Winwood in hot pursuit. He followed her slowly round and round the floor until he was able to satisfy himself as to her present capabilities.

On the 23 December, with Kimmy now taking fourteen tablets a day with little evidence of improvement and as the test results achieved at home had not been conclusive it was desirable to undertake a more intensive examination. Mr Winwood therefore booked her into the hospital for the day on Christmas Eve to undergo further tests. She would be able to come home about 5pm so we would have her with us over Christmas. Unfortunately Mr Winwood would not be there himself, he was due his first Christmas in many a year off duty. However, Mrs Stockman was scheduled to be in attendance.

Kimmy had to be at the hospital by 8.30am. The snow still lay heavily on the ground but the clouds had cleared away leaving a bright blue sky. The snow had mercifully ceased its unrelenting descent a day or two previously, allowing a run to be cleared up the driveway. Wrapped warmly in her knitted coat against the cold morning air, I lifted Kimmy gently onto her tartan rug on Rebecca's front seat, next to me as usual. Her little orange and white teddy came with her for comfort.

The combined rush-hour and Christmas traffic was quite heavy despite the weather. The hospital, situated on a bus route, allowed easy approach as Barnet Council had kept the road well gritted. Pulling up outside the 6 ft wrought iron gate, sited in the middle of an even taller green hedge, I clambered out of the car, making my way round to open Kimmy's door. She offered no resistance to being picked up though obviously recognised her surroundings. Weighing nearly two stone and with no energy to assist me, we struggled up the pathway to the big green front door as quickly as possible to attain the warmth of the interior.

After booking Kimmy in with the young lady on Reception we sat on one of the half dozen or so chairs to await our turn. Kimmy lay on my lap, her head gently cradled in my arm, I was going to hate leaving her here, if only for a day, even though I knew it was for her own good. These kind, knowledgeable people were going to do all they could to help her. The obscured door in the corner recess at the end of the waiting room opened and approaching footsteps revealed a young lady wearing a dark blue RANA (Registered Animal Nursing Auxiliary) uniform and a kind smile. She leant forward saying hello to Kimmy who looked up at her with big soulful eyes. I cuddled her closer to me as the time came for allowing the RANA to take her gently from me. As she passed into the young lady's caring hands Kimmy turned her head to look at me with a questioning expression. With moist eyes I tried to re-assure her that all would be well, there was nothing to fear and she was coming home very soon.

As the RANA retraced her steps back through the recessed door with Kimmy in her arms I hurriedly turned and half walked, half ran through the front door, down the path back to the security and privacy of Rebecca. The strain and worry of the last week or two was beginning to take its toll. 5pm was an eternity away.

Although Kimmy did not make a lot of noise the house was deadly quiet without her. Recently she had had my full attention all day long, now it was a matter of finding something to do that did not require a great deal of application. I tidied up the lounge which was strewn with Kims bedding and the paraphernalia used in nursing her. Then Mother and I busied ourselves by firstly putting up the Christmas Tree in the extension then dressing it and finally putting one or two decorations around the room to introduce the seasonal atmosphere ready for Kimmy's return.

At 4.30pm I started out once more on the five mile trip to Barnet. This time Mother came with me as she too was anxious to have Kimmy back home with us. She waited in Rebecca while I went into the hospital to collect Kim. Yes, she was ready to come home again. She had not eaten anything but had taken a little water. Mrs Stockman declared Kimmy was overweight and was living on the fat in her body – that was keeping her going at present. I felt indignant that my Kim should be described in such terms – she was not overweight! Never mind, she was coming home with us that was all that mattered for the moment. The RANA with the pleasant smile carried Kim, dressed again in her woolly coat, through into the Reception area as her eyes looked up with a mixture of relief and pleasure at the sight of "her mum". Mr Winwood would be on duty again after Christmas and I was to telephone him on Tuesday the 29th.

Gently the RANA handed Kimmy back to me then opened the front door to allow us to pass through into the cold, dark night. Mother was watching for us, ready to open the car door so I could place Kim straight onto her rug then cover her over with a shawl against the bitter air. We were home indoors within half-an-hour, Kimmy settled once more into her bed by the fire.

Exhausted by the turmoil of the day Kim slept soundly on my bed that night, waking only occasionally to take a sip of glucose water from my fingers.

Next morning being Christmas Day, there were the usual parcels for Kimmy on the tree. This year though instead of dancing excitedly around sniffing her presents, she lay quietly covered up in her bed where her parcels were placed round her. After glancing at each one she returned her head to the pillow to rest. It was heartbreaking to see her so disinterested in an activity she had always enjoyed and loved so much. Next year she would be her old self again – or would she? She did not seem to be getting any better. That she may not recover was unthinkable, she could not have more love or better attention. She would pull through alright. After all she was Kimmy, a strong character and not one to give in easily.

The next few days saw no improvement and on Tuesday the 29th, as requested, I telephoned Mr Winwood with a report. Concerned, he came along to see her straight after morning surgery. This time she did not even attempt to get out of her bed where she had been since I carried her downstairs earlier that morning. Mr Winwood wanted to try something different so, without resistance from Kim, gave her two injections. He would come again tomorrow.

That night as she lay in my arms I began to accept the fact she was physically slipping away from me. So weak was she becoming I could not wish her to continue unless there was a definite improvement very soon. After Mr Winwood's visit next day Kim slept calmly, breathing easily. Maybe the injections were going to work – there certainly appeared to be a slight betterment. Oh – if only …

That evening Mother and I were sitting in the lounge while Kimmy slept peacefully in her bed in front of the fire. Just after 8 o'clock she suddenly sat up vomitting violently. I dashed over to comfort her then rushed into the hall to telephone the hospital emergency service. As luck would have it Mr Winwood was on call. The RANA connected us and I explained what had happened. Kind and gentle as ever Mr Winwood said the description received, coupled with her history meant the time had now come to release Kimmy from her illness. Devastated I begged him to take her into the hospital – she had been much quieter during the day – surely that must be a good sign?

If I could get her up to the hospital they would take her in and see what they could do but he would not allow her to suffer.

Obviously I could not drive and nurse Kimmy at the same time so who would be willing to take us in their car? While Mother hurried upstairs to put on her coat I telephoned Tony. Unfortunately his car was out of commission but if I could get a mini-cab to pick him up he would come with us.

Oakwood Car Hire located in the underground station, just a quarter of a mile down the road, was the nearest source of help. I rang to ask if they carried animals in their cars and explained the situation. They wanted to know if Kimmy was likely to be ill while travelling. Assuring them it was extremely unlikely and in any case I would take every precaution, a young man named Stephen kindly agreed, under the circumstances, to take us. Apparently he is the son of the man who owns the business. Yes, he could drive over to Bush Hill Park to collect Tony before picking us up. He was on his way!

Leaving Mother to watch Kimmy for a few moments I secured the house, adorned a winter coat, at the same time fetching a warm rug to wrap Kim in.

By this time Tony was ringing the front door bell while Stephen waited in the car with the engine running.

Returning to the lounge with the rug I scooped Kimmy and her teddy up in my arms and carried her out to the waiting car while Mother pulled the front door closed behind her.

Tony sat in the front seat next to Stephen. Mother sat with me in the rear. Kimmy lay very still in my arms, just her face showing through the folds of the rug. The night was cold but thankfully the car heater kept us warm during the journey. I constantly soothed Kimmy cuddling her close to me, feeling desperately worried – what would the next few hours reveal?

On arrival at Wood Street we found a RANA waiting for us. A warm bed was ready for Kim in one of the hospital pens. Gently I passed Kimmy into the open arms of the nurse. With a very heavy heart, tears in my eyes and a blanket of total exhaustion enveloping me I tried to reassure Kim that she would be alright, Mr Winwood would take care of her. Assuring me she would be well looked after, the nurse began to walk towards the door leading to the ward. Kim turned her head and looked at me with big accusing eyes which were indicative of betrayal. How could I bring her here then hand her over to someone else? What was I doing? A look I would never forget even though I knew it was only momentary and that Kimmy loved me as much as I loved her and always would. This was the last chance of saving her, it had to be taken.

I should have stayed the night in the waiting room, Mr Winwood would have allowed it but so depleted was I with the strain of weeks of worry, anxiety and emotion, the thought did not enter my head until it was too late.

Stephen, waiting in the car outside the hospital gate, was anxious to hear news of Kimmy. How kind of him to enquire – all we could tell him was she was in good hands. The drive home was agony – we were driving away from Kimmy – if only even now they could make her better.

Tony came indoors with us for a few moments to make sure everything was alright then Stephen drove him home.

It was a long time before either of us managed to sleep that night – our minds were constantly with Kimmy in Barnet. Eventually total fatigue drew up the blessed coverlet of sleep.

Next morning the telephone rang at 7.45am. My heart stood still. Could it be good news? Had Kimmy rallied during the night? Was she now on the long road back to recovery?

The tone of Mr Winwood's voice as he said "hello", spoke a thousand words. No. It could not be true. Yes, it was. He was telling me that Kimmy had rallied a little during the night but then died peacefully about an hour ago.

I hardly heard what he said after that but remember asking him if he would like Kimmy's body – would it be of any use to him for research? Kimmy was with me again now – her spirit would be always close so if her body could be used to help other animals he would be very welcome to have it, she would not mind. He thanked me but declined the offer saying if he could have utilised her physical body he would certainly have asked me.

Putting down the receiver, the tears came suddenly as the cord of self-control snapped. The flood gates opened for a while then subsided as realisation of the pain such sorrow would cause Kimmy. She was with Dad now, he would look after her. Please, please Dad keep her safely with you until I join you both.

During the morning I took her food bowl into the garden filling it with water for the birds. Kim loved to sit watching them promenading around the lawn. This was one way in which she could provide something for her fellow creatures of the feathered kind.

Her bed remained in the lounge though moved to one side, up against Dad's bureau.

Sitting quietly that afternoon a movement suddenly caught my attention. Looking up I saw Dad with Kimmy in his arms gently lowering her into her bed. His thought transference told me she was sleeping now as she needed her rest having been ill prior to her passing.

It was wonderful to see her back in her bed sleeping peacefully – how do people unable to see their pets after death cope?

109

How grateful I am for the ability to do so – an ability increased by the lack of the material hustle and bustle created by going to work each day. A new post within an international computer firm had been offered to me but as yet the premises were not ready for occupation, it would be another 2–3 months.

The weekend passed and Monday morning Mr Winwood telephoned to say he would call in to return Kimmy's teddy and blanket. He arrived after surgery and sat in the lounge taking coffee with us. Such a kind, understanding man. Even though dealing with bereaved owners must, by nature of his profession, be a regular occurrence he offers genuine comfort and sympathy on a personal basis, easing to a degree the deep ache of the physical loss experienced.

He recalled his first encounter with Kimmy when he joined Stockman and Partners back in the early 70's. She had been one of his original patients consequently he retained a special affection for her. Mother and I explained how she had come to us to fill a big gap left, not only by the passing of Trixie and Tony's leaving home to marry, but by Dad's untimely death. Since Mr Winwood had warned me many years previously Kim may live a long and happy life, at the same time her heart, due to it's disease, could give out suddenly, I had loved her every day as though it were her last.

We discussed the possibility of another little dog joining our family at some future stage but it seemed unlikely. Mother was getting on in years and I would have to be out at work all day for the next twenty years. However, what would be, would be.

That evening Mother and I were sitting in the dining room in the front of the house, going through the motions of trying to eat something, when suddenly my attention was drawn to the corner of the room as the door opened. In trotted our Kimmy! Not the elderly, slightly overweight Kimmy who had so recently been with us but the young, slim Kimmy of her former days. When we pass beyond the physical our spirit body returns to the form we held in our middle years as this is our true age.

Delighted to see us Kimmy was laughing in her own inimitable way. She came over to the table and sat down between us, looking up from one to the other, her tail wagging nineteen to the dozen.

Chapter LIII

From then on Kim was with us constantly. At first, as is so often the case, unaware she was no longer in our material world. When realisation came it brought with it the usual initial distress of physical parting.

Something she had not done during her lifetime she jumped up on my lap while I was sitting in the rocking chair, curling up closely as if in dread of being parted from me. I tried to mentally re-assure her, asking Dad once more to help and comfort her; to explain to her what had happened and that we all still loved her and could be together spiritually.

At night Kim came upstairs with us, curling up on my bed as usual. I was very aware of her weight – as Mother had been of Billy's many years before – and spoke to her as I had always done, receiving in return the warmth of her presence. I had placed her little orange and white teddy bear beside my pillow so she could have it with her. There it remains to this day and always will until I join her.

She accompanied us in the car as she had always done, sitting on her front passenger seat taking an interest in everything we passed. She was there when Mother and I took a special flower arrangement to Potters Bar Church in gratitude for her life and all the help she had received. She was there when we took flowers for her to Freston Gardens Church. When visitors came to the house she ran out to greet them, delighted to see them despite their inability to see her.

When Beryl came, she was greatly saddened to hear the news but aware of Kim's closeness, was pleased to know she was with us still. Her own Kim had only recently experienced the same transition and both Beryl and her husband Arthur had, on numerous occasions, heard and sensed their Kim around the home.

The weather remained bitterly cold with fresh snow falls. Friday the 8th was the coldest January day since 1890.

On the Saturday, standing in the kitchen I thought to myself "will walk down the road to pay the papers, it is a nice afternoon. Kimmy, Trixie coming for a walk?" Immediately, the two were there beside me, full of expectancy. Suddenly a little voice by my right elbow piped up "and me". I looked down in astonishment to find Keith standing there looking up with a big grin on his face. "Hello Keith, yes of course you may come too".

So, the four of us set off down the road together, happy in each other's company. To all intense and purposes I was alone but to any-one able to see beyond the physical into the etheric or spiritual world this was far from the case.

When we reached a road junction I automatically transmitted a warning to Keith to wait at the kerb, the road was dangerous. The instant the sentence left my mind and simultaneously with Keith's laughter, I realised of course he was safe. He could no longer be hurt by the traffic.

We made our way across the main road and into the paper shop where Trixie, Kimmy and Keith all waited with me at the counter, looking up expectantly. The light dawned – they all wanted a Milky Bar! I paid the weekly account, purchased three medium sized bars, thanked the proprietor and left the shop. Outside on the pavement the three of them clustered around, turning eager eyes in the direction of the chocolate. I was just on the point of unwrapping it for them when I suddenly realised how insane it would appear to anyone passing by! A lady standing outside a shop, unwrapping chocolate bars and holding them down in mid-air!! With a chuckle I told them they must wait until we arrived home as anyone nearby would think I had gone mad. They accepted this without question, so off we set for home where, having struggled free of outer garments, I removed the wrappings from all three bars placing them where the trio could help themselves.

Note:
Perhaps I should explain here for the benefit of those who may have difficulty following these events, that though the physical body has ceased to exist the etheric and spirit bodies, which are contained within the physical and are governed by the mind, live on within and around our world but at a different rate of vibration. With either the natural or developed ability to penetrate this finer sphere, it is possible to enjoy the fellowship of those who have "gone on ahead". Because all substances are made up of millions of atoms revolving around each other, everything in the material world has it's counterpart thus allowing the use of similar artefacts in the higher realm. Consequently Trix, Kim and Keith were able to take and eat the counterpart of the chocolate bars, after which, the taste of the physical chocolate was greatly reduced.

The sound of Kim's collar jingling, of her shaking herself or running up and downstairs became again familiar noises around the house even, from time to time, the sound of her bark. One evening, whilst sitting on the lounge floor, she came over to sniff the plate of sandwiches which constituted my supper though, as in life, she would not touch.

Chapter LIV

In March that year, now several months after the initial offer, I began employment with the multi-national computer firm in their newly opened branch only three miles from home. Not wishing to use Rebecca each day, mainly because it meant leaving her in the road outside the office block, I had, with the kind assistance of Mr Macklyn, purchased a secondhand blue Morris Marina – named Clara – to travel to and from work.

Though the introduction to computers presented a new interest, the position itself had been grossly over-stated during the interview and in reality held little to commend it except the steady income.

With increased activity in the material world my ability to commune quite so closely with Kimmy decreased a little, being replaced by deep, grieving sorrow for the loss of her physical. I still heard her around the house, felt her on my bed each night and spoke to her as usual but the intrusion of the monetary requirements of life took their toll.

During this period I learnt, for the first time, the true meaning of grief and intense sorrow. At times, while driving home of an evening, the cascading tears brought about by the profound aching pain of unutterable sadness, forced me to pull into the side of the road while the floodgates released their oppressive burden.

Chapter LV

One morning in May, the 5th to be exact, a young woman from my department telephoned to say she would be late in to work as she was going to take her dog to be put to sleep – it had bitten the children. Almost before she finished speaking I interceded with "No, don't do that. I will have her and find her a good home". Well, if I was sure – this was not the first incident, she had bitten the children before. They had taken her from a local shop keeper who, having the Mother, did not want to keep the puppies. They had not managed to find a home for this one it was therefore going to be put to sleep so she rescued her from certain death but now regretted it, she was neither gentle nor good.

It was agreed the woman should leave the dog at home and I would drive her there after work to collect the little one. No dog ever bites without provocation and if children were involved it was pretty certain what had been going on.

5.30 was an eternity away. The hours dragged at the best of times here but this particular day seemed to go on for ever. At last the clock on the wall behind me indicated freedom beckoned once more so, clearing my desk, the young woman and I made our way down to the car. The journey to her house only took about ten minutes and was on my way home. She informed me the little dog was named Tessa and would jump up as soon as the front door opened.

Pulling up outside the little house the young woman led the way up the garden path to the door which she opened with her key.

Immediately we were greeted by a wriggling, squealing, nose-wrinkling bundle of tri-coloured caninimity. Having the appearance of a sheepdog/papillon cross and standing approximately 19"/20" high. She was adorable.

Entering the lounge we were confronted by two little boys with badly running noses, each clutching a slice of bread in grubby little hands. Their mother explained I had come to take Tessa away as they could no longer keep her. These remarks brought forth a hail of protest from the two offspring who, in an attempt to calm them, were promised they should have another doggie later on when they were a little older.

The woman had rushed home lunchtime to wash Tessa's blanket so it would be clean for her to bring with her. Something of her own. In order not to distress Tessa more than necessary, the young woman came home with me to stay for half an hour giving Tessa confidence.

It had been kind of her to wash the blanket but unfortunately it was still soaking wet. Never mind, we took it along with us. Also one or two tins of dog food which would tide us over until I could get to the shops the next day. That was thoughtful of her.

Mother was delighted to see Tessa, what a beautiful little dog. Tessa walked straight in, confident and at home presumably because her mum was with her. We all went through to the lounge where we sat chatting for a while until Mother went out to put the kettle on.

As her former mistress sat drinking tea, Tessa dashed all over the house sniffing into every corner. Obviously she was picking up Kimmy's scent. I mentally explained to Kim that Tessa was not taking her place. She was only coming to stay for a little while until I could find her a good home. She was Kim's guest.

Having completed her exploration of the house it was time for Tessa to venture into the garden. "Oh," exclaimed the young woman, "she will love this. What a lovely garden you have to play in Tessa". Tess obviously agreed as she ran round the garden, in and out of the bushes, up and down the lawn like a dog let loose in paradise. There was plenty of space here to enjoy a good game!

While they were outside, I brought Kim's Goddards bed down into the lounge, placing it in front of the bureau where it had stood for sometime after Kim's transition.

Putting a warm blanket in the bed I called Tessa indoors, picked her up, put her into Kim's bed and told her it was for her. She took to it instantly. Turned round and round then curled up in the middle and sat there looking up at us all as if to say "thank you – it is lovely and it is mine"!

While Tess was happily enjoying her new bed the young woman and I crept out into the hall closing the door quietly behind us and I drove her home. She seemed genuinely pleased Tessa had settled in so quickly.

On my return I found Tessa, very naturally, alarmed by the disappearance of her mum. Agitated she ran hither and thither looking for her. She needed a lot of re-assuring. Maybe a plate of food would help. Rather! Everything else forgotten Tessa cleared the plate almost before I had time to blink. Gosh, she must be hungry – would she like another plateful? The upturned face declared "try me!" A second plate of food vanished equally quickly and a third. No more tonight – I did not want to make her ill but she was obviously starving. Come to think of it the outline of her ribs were showing through her fur. Poor little thing, it was evident she had not been receiving enough food to eat.

The young woman had told me they knew Tessa had been born in February the previous year so she must be only about 15 months old. Still growing.

On close inspection she proved to be even more attractive than I first realised. Long black silky fur ran the length of her back and head to be embraced round her neck by the wide white band of the sheepdog. Down along her sides the black merged with tan then ran into white around her tummy. All four legs, on which the feathers were just beginning to form, were white with occasional small tan spots, rather like the markings of a Dalmatian. The upper front legs suddenly becoming gingery tan as they merged into the black. The effect was to appear as though she were wearing long white evening gloves, while the sparsely spotted white fur spread over her pink tummy. Her head and face, the entire length of which only equalled the length of Kim's nose, was that of Papillon. The soft semi-open butterfly ears showing their lining of black and tan silky hair. The big round dark brown eyes set in the midst of milky tan colouring spilling down either side of her face then to within an inch of the end of her nose which was monopolised by another white band, this time tinged with pink, culminating in a little black tip. Her throat and chest being of purest white into which, at one point, ran the sheepdog collar before flowing down into her tummy. Her long bushy tail, black on top, tan underneath suddenly turned pure white two thirds of the way along, giving the impression of having been dipped into a pot of white paint.

An elegant little creature with a dainty walk which implied she trotted along on tip-top like a dancer. She was certainly very lively and did not hesitate to show a razor sharp set of teeth if approached in her bed.

During the evening Mother picked up the newspaper and before we realised what was happening Tessa was out of her bed, through the open door like a shot out of a gun. She was terrified. Apparently she was painfully well acquainted with a folded newspaper. What had this poor little dog experienced in her former homes? It was not long before we discovered she could not bear her tail touched. Obviously it had been pulled unmercifully, presumably by children as she actively disliked them. Her lead brought to the fore another source of bad memories as, unless I was very careful how I took it out of the cupboard, she would flinch and cower.

The first night she spent with us I carried Tessa's bed upstairs placing it on the floor next to mine. Having followed me into the room, Tess climbed into her bed and sat there for a while watching me move around preparing to retire. When eventually I clambered in, Tessa jumped up beside me. Immediately she spotted Kimmy further down the quilt, stared hard at her then growled.

Horrified by such behaviour, she was instantly reprimanded and told this was Kimmy's home, she was Kimmy's guest. Welcome though she was, she must respect that fact.

Bless her, she immediately jumped down into her own bed and was never to jump up of her own accord again. Try as I may, I could never cox her up though I would dearly have loved to her enjoy the comfort and security of sleeping on my bed with Kim.

It is said a persons bed is the nearest a dog can get to their "mum" or "dad" which is why they will always do their best to curl up there when left alone. It is the closest they are able to get in the absence of the actual physical presence of the owner and generates a feeling of well-being, sheltered safety and comfort.

I noticed, when Tess spent a penny, her urine was thick and sticky like treacle. I remembered reading about a wartime aircrew drifting in their dinghy without rations. Suffering eventually from malnutrition their urine developed a similar, treacle-like texture to that of Tessa's. She was always hungry, this had to be the answer – she too was suffering from malnutrition. So much revealed in so short a time.

Chapter LVI

At 6 o'clock on Friday the 7th May Tessa was introduced to Mr Winwood up in Barnet. He was most interested in our new arrival. She was a lovely little dog. Rather on the thin side. Her ribs were showing through. She would need feeding up. Were we going to keep her?

Much as we would love to I had to work and Mother was getting on in years. Did he know of a good home? Unfortunately he didn't just at the moment. It was a shame as she was a beautiful dog and just right for us. Well, let's see what happens.

Her check-up and vaccinations over we returned home trying hard to convince ourselves it would be best for Tessa to find her a good home where she would be assured indefinitely of company during the day.

A young dog she could easily outlive Mother, now in her 80's, and would have to be left alone all day while I was out earning a crust. How wrong we were to be proved on both counts!

That evening, having given Tessa her supper in the kitchen as usual – her food bowl sat on the raised ledge that formed part of the built-up floor under the side worksurface next to the oven, which had served as Kim's "table", and beside her stoneware drinking bowl – another inheritance from Kimmy – I placed our own meal on the dining room table. Smoked haddock with buttered mashed potatoes.

As Mother was not quite ready I took the opportunity to pop back into the kitchen for a moment. Returning to the dining room, I entered the doorway as Tessa dashed down from the table and scurried away, tail between her legs. My plate was empty – she had eaten the lot! The incredible speed with which she must have consumed my entire meal was amazing. Poor little thing, she must still be starving despite the good food she had received since coming to us.

There was nothing to be gained by scolding her, she was hungry and had naturally enough helped herself to available food. Calling her name gently, I reassured her there was no need to be afraid – she was a good girl and must have been really hungry to have done what she did. If anyone were to blame it was me. I should have realised the effects of her malnutrition were still with her.

In consequence of regular, substantial meals she had put on weight but obviously her hunger remained as yet unsatisfied. Until her appetite waned her daily ration must again be increased and include boiled rice to help sustain her.

Before too long Tessa was no longer attacking her food ravenously, rather eating calmly with enjoyment.

Chapter LVII

The week after Tessa's supper of smoked haddock I decided to buy her a new food bowl so, on the way back to the office in North Finchley, stopped off at a petshop to make the required purchase. While waiting at the counter for the sales assistant to conclude a telephone call, I noticed a little lone creature struggling madly to climb the sides of a dish on the counter. A young terrapin looking sadly in need of love and attention.

My heart immediately went out to him so, having chosen a large round yellow bowl for Tess, I went on to acquire the little fellow – still desperately trying to scale the steep, slippery sides of his prison – together with sufficient food for the next few days.

Terrapins in captivity live mainly on chopped fish, especially herring or sprat which are rich in vitamin A. Raw liver, shrimps, cockles, pondweed, watercress, cabbage, fruit, white bread, hard boiled eggs or tinned dog food etc. Terrapins also require rocks on which to rest while, if they are lucky, soaking up the rays of the sun. The rocks were also available from the said petshop.

We still had two large transparent processing dishes at home which I had bought for Dad just before his death and which he unfortunately had never had a chance to use. One of these would be an ideal tank for "James" during the summer months. Later he would of course require a heated aquarium but for this afternoon his temporary home must be Tessa's new food bowl.

Carrying him very carefully back to the car I placed him securely on the front passenger seat and set off back to the office.

To the amusement of several of the staff, James spent the afternoon clambering around his bowl, which I had partly filled with water, on my desk. He was very cute and extremely responsive to the human voice.

Arriving home with him, Tessa was most anxious to see what I was carrying, jumping up, stretching her neck to peer into the bowl. Of course she could see. The bowl was lowered for her to inspect the contents; for her to become acquainted with James and him with her. They seemed interested in each other, anxious to be friends if at all possible.

Gently James' bowl was placed on the kitchen worksurface while I ferreted around for the processing dish that was to be his home.

Still Tessa's fascination persisted. She stood in the kitchen watching every movement while the dish was filled with water, the rocks arranged neatly and James carefully transferred from his bowl to his new luxury abode.

He remained perfectly still for a while then began swimming around the dish, climbing onto the rocks and generally investigating this wonderful new, spacious accommodation. Sheer heaven after his experiences in the petshop!

Having cleared a space on the kitchen windowsill I cautiously lifted his dish where the sunlight would warm him during the day. At night he would come into the warmth of the kitchen.

Being small I was able to lift Tessa up, holding her over the sink so she could get a closer view of James. They stared entranced by each other until, becoming heavy to hold, I had to put Tessie down on the floor again. Satisfied she had acquainted herself with this latest member of the family and that he was now staying put – for a while at least – she trotted off about her business.

Dinner time came and Tessa was given her big new yellow bowl – yes, it was for *her*. Judging from her initial possessiveness of anything given to and told it was hers, Tessa must have been teased shamefully by – presumably – the children she had previously lived with. I should imagine she had been taunted with things – given toys, treats, whatever then had them snatched away from her again. That would never happen to her again – what was hers was hers and would remain so.

Popping in to look at James once or twice during the evening, he looked very lonely on his own. It would be cruel not to find him a friend – next day I would re-visit the petshop enquiring whether they had received any more little terrapins. Like all lifeforms he needed a companion. I was not really sure how best to look after him so decided to write to the London Zoo for advice and posted the letter on the way to work the following day.

That evening, on the way home, I called into the petshop to find a further supply of terrapins had been delivered. It was heartbreaking to see them all struggling around the bowl on the counter. It would have been wonderful to have been able to take them all home but then the "stock" would only have been replaced again and again. I have an abhorrence of petshops where animals are kept and have in the past complained to the RSPCA when I considered animals had insufficient room. Unfortunately the law only requires an animal, in such conditions, to have enough room to turn around in it's cage. A shameful, cruel and disgraceful law that badly needs changing. In fact, the keeping of animals for sale in shops should, in my opinion, be banned.

However, James had a companion, given the name Joan. Arriving home with her, Tessa immediately wanted to see what I was carrying in the interesting container. Having explained it was a companion for James, we all three went into the kitchen where James came scurrying to the front of his dish to greet me. Placing Joan carefully in the dish beside him I watched while they immediately inspected one another. Emm yes, great joy, a friend! The terrapins seemed delighted to see each other and took to one another immediately.

Leaving them to become better acquainted, I then made a terrific fuss of Tessa. Yes, we had new members of the family but they in no way detracted love and attention from her.

Chapter LVIII

Tessa was obviously still a bag of nerves as she would help herself to any furry toy that happened to be within her reach and shake it vigorously, tearing it to pieces in the process. Given a white chew bone of the largest size available, she would consume the lot in 24 hours!

In fact she would chew anything coming within grasp of her teeth. A favourite object of her attentions was her leather lead. As soon as it was taken down from the cloaks cupboard it became fair game. A good munch while it was being hooked on to her collar was not to be missed, then great sport was to be had jumping up and biting it while walking down the pavement. Much more fun than looking where she was going! When she eventually chewed her way through three leads within a week, the time had come to buy her a chain with a leather handle. This did the trick. A chain was definitely not as tasty as a strap, so time to look elsewhere for a lark.

It did not take long to find a replacement game. Both Trixie and Kimmy had always had a sulphur block put in their bowl of water so naturally Tessa had the same. Needless to say it did not stay there very long! Within no time at all the block had disappeared leaving only broken bits and pieces as evidence of it's former existence. Tessa had found something else to chew!

One afternoon, about two weeks after she arrived, I received a distressed telephone call from Mother. Tessa would have to go. She had caught a bird on the lawn and savagely torn it to pieces.

My stomach heaved at the thought. We loved our garden birds dearly, feeding and watching them all year round. How could Tessa do such a thing? Our other dogs had learnt to live with the birds. To sit and watch them quietly.

Arriving home that night I found it difficult to see Tessa in the same light but tried hard not to let her feel my emotions. The welcome she gave me was as warm as ever, wriggling from head to toe, tail wagging madly. The only possible answer to her actions could be her hunger was still not satisfied, thus she had tried to feed herself naturally. That had to be the answer. We must try to forgive and help her to settle down.

When, after a week of two, her appetite appeared finally satisfied, Tessa continued to chase the birds but more as a sport than a hunt. It took just over a year for her to finally accept our garden birds as her friends to be watched quietly rather than chased. The only exception was the pigeons. Like Trixie and Kimmy she was actively encouraged, when the order "see them off" was given, to chase away these large unwelcome intruders who roughly pushed aside their smaller counterparts. Left alone these bullies would quickly have devoured all the food put out for the little birds. We were happy for them to have their share but not to deprive their smaller brothers of sustenance. However, all three dogs found it impossible to differentiate between pigeons at home and the seagulls they found when on holiday. Consequently many unhappy gulls were chased from their natural habitat whenever our dogs were to be found at the seaside.

Another phrase Tessa had to learn quickly was the meaning of "wow-woz". Being a very bright little creature it was no time at all before she understood what was expected of her when receiving this command. The visit to the garden before going to bed or out in the car usually brought successful accomplishment. Once in the car Tessa was seated on the tartan rug used many years previously by Trixie, then more recently by Kimmy.

Again, like her predecessors, whether in the car or at home, Tessa loved her tummy tickled, rolling on her back in sheer delight while being told "tickle Tessa's tummy" – quite a tongue twister!

Interestingly she chose to frequent some of Kimmy's favourite haunts. In particular she loved to crawl under the sideboard and stretch out or curl up as the mood took her. Considering the distance between the floor and the base of the sideboard measures just 7" this was quite an achievement. Latterly Kimmy had grown too large to enjoy either this hide-away or the area under the spare bed in the guest room. However she had continued to sit happily in the armchair from where she could survey the scene around her. Unlike Kimmy, who had been able to rest her head on the arm of the chair, Tessa could not reach up sufficiently to rest more than the tip of her chin, even then her head was tilted at an uncomfortably acute angle.

Tessa may be small in stature but she was beginning to display a strong character. Consequently I frequently referred to her as "my little girl with a big personality" and what a personality!

I looked after her well, fed her, took her for walks and made a fuss of her yet my sub-conscious still persisted in supposing her Kimmy's guest. Then one night I was in bed looking down at Tessa in her own bed on the floor beside me. She seemed so tiny and alone. "Bless her heart, all she wants is to be loved". The message was received and, overwhelmed by emotion, I picked her up hugged her to me gently but firmly and emitted all the love I could muster. Immediately she responded by turning her face to mine and gratefully accepting all that was given.

From that moment on Tessa became as precious to me as Kimmy and Trixie had been during their lives and indeed still are. Dear Tessa, she was beautiful in every sense of the word, both inside and out. Mr Winwood had described her coat as that of a "tri-colour crossbred", I describe her spirit as "loving, intelligent, gentle yet full of fun".

At that time I had no concept of the full extent of Tessa's true and deep intelligence or development. That was to come later.

Chapter LIX

Our good friend Stan had moved from Barnet several years previously and after a number of various residences was now living in a very nice flat in Hampstead. As was his way, he rang up out of the blue one day inviting Mother and myself over to dinner the next evening. Delighted to learn we had another little dog he didn't hesitate when asked if she may come too. Of course. He was looking forward to meeting her.

This was to be Tessa's first social visit other than, of course, family and friends in our own immediate area.

Travelling against the homeward bound London traffic, the journey was comparatively easy. Tessa, sitting on the front passenger seat as usual, was fascinated by all the new and exciting things to be seen through the window because although she was, as I have already described, nowhere near as tall as Kimmy, she was able to take advantage of Rebecca's high, well-upholstered seat which enabled her to see out of the side window.

Having pulled round onto the drive in front of the block of flats, I first took Tessa to do wow-woz on the grass before entering the building. She would never make a mistake indoors and would ask if she needed to go out but this way she started off the evening feeling comfortable.

Stan as always, welcomed us warmly. He was not only the best friend anyone could be lucky enough to have but an excellent host. "Would Tessa like something to drink or eat". Producing her little orange plastic tea dish I thanked him. She would love a drink of water please but had already eaten her dinner before setting out. James and Joan had also been fed and settled down. He must come over soon and meet them.

During dinner the conversation, naturally enough, turned to Tessa. How I had acquired her and how she was settling in. Stan looked at her for a moment then said, very quietly and profoundly, "That is an extremely intelligent little dog you have got there. She is very highly developed". Words that were to be proved so true time and again especially after her transition, many years later, from the physical world.

Talking to Tessa rather than me, Stan then said he had some lamb casserole left from the previous day, he was sure she would enjoy it. Turning to me, please let her have it, it would not do her any harm. Needless to say Tess required no second bidding. With nose in the dish she quickly cleared the contents, thoroughly enjoying every mouthful. An upward look at Stan and a wag of the tail aptly expressed her appreciation of her second supper. In fact the entire evening was a very happy one.

Chapter LX

By now Tessa had settled down well, acquiring a routine of habits. Each morning as I prepared to leave for work Mother would say to her "Come on Tessa, see Gilly go" and Tess would rush into the dining room, up onto the carver near the window from where she nimbly hopped onto the wide windowsill while the net curtain was pulled aside for her to watch me get into the car and drive off.

When indoors Tessa would spend a lot of her time sitting sideways on the sill, looking out of the window watching the world go about it's business. The vehicles driving past or pulling up outside; people walking up or down the pavement, particularly Mothers with young children who always stopped to look at Tessie and wave to her. Indeed she became quite a feature of the locality! Occasionally when working in the garden I overheard strangers trying to decide whether, as she sat so still, she was real!

The garden itself provided Tess with much entertainment. The comings and goings of the blackbird who nested each year in the conifer hedge which separated our garden from that of our elderly neighbours. The various assortment of birds who, having eaten the contents of the feeding tables on the back lawn, now came to the front for second helpings alongside the birds who lived in the tall trees on our verge. The squirrels who chased up and down these trees swinging through the high branches; the occasional fox trotting by on it's way to or from it's lair in the undergrowth 50 yards down the road or the impertinent intrusion onto our property of a neighbouring cat. The summer bees flitting around the flower beds or the spider sliding down its fine gossamer thread outside the dining room window, all created interest for an alert Tessa to watch.

Quickly Tessa came to know when it was time for me to come home for lunch and again at the end of the day. As I turned into the drive she would be sitting on the windowsill watching, waiting patiently. The instant the car stopped she bounded off the sill, through the chair, out into the hall and up to the door to greet me, tail wagging, nose wrinkling as she turned in circles of delight.

Lunchtime and evening we followed the same routine. Having dumped my bags and belongings on the hall floor, I grabbed Tessa's lead then side by side we dashed out to Clara waiting on the drive. Oakwood Park was less than a minute away, just round the corner. With restricted time it was better to drive there and let Tess have a long free run rather than utilitise the available time walking there and back.

We entered the park via high double iron gates leading along a short road (the property of London Transport) forming a bridge across the train lines. With the exception of week-ends and bank holidays, the gates were kept open to allow the Council Parks Department vehicles to enter and leave without having to stop to unlock and lock the heavy gates a dozen times a day. These vehicles never travelled above about 15 mph, indeed it is unlikely the huge grass cutters could do more than that.

The public were also allowed to drive slowly in and leave their cars along one side of the roadway, which meant dogs and children could scramble out running straight into the park in perfect safety.

Like most of the parks in Enfield, Oakwood is an area of natural grass and woodland boasting, in one small corner, the usual childrens' playground with swings, roundabout, slide etc. and an adjacent pond for sailing toy boats. As a 10 year old I had often cycled over there from Cockfosters where we lived, with friends to enjoy the facilities – gathering a saddlebag full of blackberries along the country roads on the way. Oakwood Park had once – back in the early 1920's – been the grounds of a large house which had long ago been demolished and replaced with public tennis courts.

Visiting the park three times a day it soon became our second home. We went there about 7.45 in the morning before I left for work; again at lunch time and then in the evening throughout the summer until darkness began to draw in early and the gates were closed before we could get there.

The closing time is brought forward by 15 minutes a week from mid-summer to mid-winter when opening hours are once again lengthened by 15 minutes a week till mid-summer.

To prolong our evening walks as much as possible, the lunchtime rush would be repeated at double speed during the autumn until it became a race to vacate the park before we were locked in for the night! Then, throughout the winter, our evening exercise was taken around the local roads.

Always popular with local dog owners, the park proved to be never short of playmates for Tessa who adored the company of her fellow creatures of all shapes and sizes. As the car stopped and I opened the door to let her out she would be off, her little head and body erect with excited anticipation. Her beautiful tail held high, it's white "feathers" falling gracefully down behind her in a waving cascade. Full of energy she loved to flirt, chase and play with anyone who was willing to join in the fun. Should one of the hundreds of resident squirrels be foolish enough to put in an appearance, the sport was increased ten fold. Don't worry about chasing them across the grass or through the woods, jump up the tree trunk after them! They may have disappeared into their drey high up in the branches but no need to give up. Turn, run away from the tree, turn again, run towards the trunk and straight up to a height of 7 or 8 feet before turning in mid-air then running down the trunk again barking with delight.

Mind you, squirrels are for chasing not for catching! On more than one occasion, having spotted a particularly slow squirrel, it would have been easy for Tessa to catch it but each time she visibly held herself back to allow it's escape. Despite the incident of the garden bird when she aptly proved her ability to catch virtually anything that moved, now she was no longer desperate for food, she would not harm but respect all living creatures.

Chapter LXI

Her love of and compatibility with other dogs made her many friends both canine and human. Amongst her special pals was a sweet little sandy/gold coloured mongrel named Jenny, who had come from Wood Green Animal Shelter to live with her new "dad", Paul. About the same size and age as Tessa the two became firm friends. Without any difficulty they were able to spot each other from one side of the park to the other – long before either Paul or I could see them. They would rush towards each other across the open ground like a pair of long lost friends re-united after an enforced parting. Not on the odd occasion was this the case or even once a week but every evening. Paul worked night duty so took Jenny out about 6 o'clock prior to preparing his dinner come breakfast.

Round and round the friends chased, up and down barking and laughing with excitement. Tails spinning in circles as they raced full pelt across the fields and back; then stopping just long enough to face each other with front legs splayed, bottoms in the air before they were off again.

This happy frivolity would last for anything up to three quarters of an hour to an hour with periodic rests to join Paul and myself either sitting on the grass watching the fun or strolling around the park chatting about everything and nothing. Days to be always remembered with pleasure.

Two other very good friends we made were Bill and his retired greyhound Andy. Bill and his wife Rene are lucky enough to live in the house next to the main gate, consequently Andy only had to walk down his front garden path before turning directly into the park.

Andy was professionally trained and raced at Harringay, White City and Walthamstow before Bill, having paid 500gns (£525) for him, collected Andy from Northaw Kennels.

Like all greyhounds Andy was the most gentle, lovable character. While Bill and I walked round the fields chatting, usually about Bill's interesting experiences in the Wartime Royal Navy, Andy – after a brief run round – strolled round with us while Tessa chased about hither and thither.

Despite the enormous difference in size, the two dogs became firm friends. Andy was always the gentle giant with Tess even when she ran between his legs and under his stomach he made no attempt to be cross with her.

I believe Andy was quite attached to me also. I only had to spot him in the park and call his name for him to run over to me and nuzzle his large gentle head in my waist – looking up with big soft brown eyes. Who could not love dear Andy? He had a wonderful home with Bill and Rene who absolutely adored him and, like all animal lovers, were heartbroken when at the age of 15 Andy finally succumbed to old age, passing peacefully from this life into the next but never from our memory or our love.

Not just in the park did Tessa love to play chase. The game frequently extended to our dining room where, holding a rubber toy in her mouth and with sheer delight squeaking it nineteen to the dozen, she would look up at me with big brown eyes full of expectancy, head and tail erect, then run a few paces ahead. Once I had got the message, she'd run and dance round and round the table, doubling back to dart under it and across, trying to avoid being caught – which, of course, she never was. The more I rubbed my hands together calling "I'm coming after you", the more she loved it, the nose wrinkled, the eyes sparkled and the tail whirled.

The squeaky toy she loved most was a 9 inch high white dog of Disney character appearance, with light brown patches, big eyes, black nose and a protruding red tongue curled round it's whiskers. It was never given a name, just referred to as "Squeaky Dog" but she loved it more than anything else. She played with it so much that every three or four weeks after constant shaking, squeaking and chewing it had to be replaced. However as all other similar toys had lost their squeakers within ten minutes of finding themselves in Tessa's mouth, I considered Squeaky Dog to be a good investment for her happiness. Who could begrudge her £1.40 a month when she gave so much love and pleasure in return!

Chapter LXII

Everyone who met Tessa instantly fell in love with her not just for her attractive appearance but her bright, cheeky and intelligent personality. When we took her over to Widmer End to meet Aunty Ivy and bring her home to stay for a while, Tessa thoroughly enjoyed her first ride of any distance. The journey, through Stanmore, Rickmansworth and Amersham, took about an hour. As we pulled into the little cul-de-sac so charmingly named "Harebell Walk", and stopped outside the end bungalow Aunty Ivy opened the door and came out to greet us, calling hello to Tessa as she came. Even though Tess had never seen her before she greeted Aunty Ivy like a long lost friend, thus endearing herself to another new "aunty".

While Aunty Ivy was with us we held one of our regular Coffee Morning events for the local animal shelter. This was to be the first one Tessa had experienced. Kimmy had thoroughly enjoyed these mornings, so many people coming to see her, to talk, stroke and generally make a fuss of her. Now Tessa was to discover the same joy.

She knew something was happening when the furniture was moved around in the lounge; small tables erected and covered; plates of delicious scones, cakes and biscuits appeared from the kitchen, to say nothing of one of Grandma's giant size chocolate sponges which was to be raffled.

Aunty Ivy was in charge of the money – the most important job! Seated in one corner she settled herself in with cashbox and loose change ready to relieve everyone of as much money as possible.

The doorbell rang, Tess ran barking excitedly to see who was there then turned in circles of ecstasy as Alice entered, smiling broadly. Dear Alice, she could always be counted on to help anyone at anytime, anywhere. She loved animals dearly and had made many a donation of both money and goods to the Shelter.

To let her see the Shelter for herself I had driven her there one day for a guided tour conducted by Leslie, who was in charge of the London centre. Alice had been overwhelmed by everything she had seen. The individual houses for each cat, the operating theatre, the waiting area but most of all by the kitchen. Lined up along the top of the work bench, which ran the length of the kitchen, were several rows of gleaming dishes all waiting to be filled with succulent morsels of cat food in readiness for the evening meal.

One look at this array of attendant feline platters and Alice could not contain her delight! Beaming all over her small round face, she enthused rapturously for several minutes, clapping her hands together in wonderment and pleasure. Never did Alice forgot her visit to the Shelter or the sight of those dishes on parade! Often over the ensuing years she referred to them and on each occasion a broad grin would spread across her face as she recalled her first experience of an animal shelter's kitchen.

Now, once again Alice entered into the spirit of helping the Shelter, this time by bringing along numerous cakes, sponges and treats she had baked for the event – and carried most precariously on the bus!

Some twelve to fifteen people, mostly friends from Freston Gardens Church and neighbours like Audrey and Eric Furness who lived facing us, attended this particular Coffee Morning. Most of our guests had, by now, made Tessa's acquaintance through one means or other so were as pleased to see her as she was to greet them. She excitedly nosed her way from stroking hand to ear tickling fingers as she moved around the lounge and garden, occasionally accepting a proffered titbit. What a lovely time she was having!

By 1pm our guests had departed and Tessa had tired herself out, thus as soon as her bed was back in place in front of the bureau she curled herself up in it and drifted into a happy, contented slumber.

During Aunty Ivy's visit we discovered Tessa's strong protective trait. Coming home from work the following Monday afternoon, I put my briefcase and handbag on the floor in the hall while popping into the kitchen to clean car grease from my hands. Hearing me arrive home Aunty Ivy came into the hall to say hello. Suddenly Tessa darted from the kitchen where she had followed me, straight across the hall to my bags where she sat as close to them as she could get, crouched down, then looked up at Aunty Ivy growling quietly but firmly, curling her upper lip. This was so unlike Tessa. Her good, gentle nature meant snarling and growling were, as a rule, foreign to her character. Then we realised the problem. Aunty was standing too close to my bag so Tessa was dutifully and loyally guarding it. What a good girl to watch over her Mum so well. How praised, fussed and patted she was once the light had dawned on we mere humans.

From that time onwards Tessa took it upon herself to staunchly protect anything belonging to me that was placed either on the floor or low on a stool, sofa or similar article of furniture whether at home or elsewhere.

Whenever she was especially good, as when she protected or was very well behaved when it was important, just like Kimmy and Trixie, Tessa was given a "find". The mention of the word itself always brought her running up to see what delightful treat was about to be presented to her. Her reward varied from a doggie choc to, on special occasions, a small tin of carrots – something she loved.

Food was never a problem with Tessie. She loved anything she was given especially fresh fruit. Apples, pears, grapes, melon, oranges, bananas, in fact the only fruit she ever refused was strawberries. Likewise her main meal was always enjoyed though again she had her favourites such as haslet, corned beef, tinned stewed steak, liver, saveloy – which was a special treat when, on the odd occasion during

128

the winter months, I brought chips in for lunch and fried an egg to put on top. Once a week she would have a small tin of Princes ham for supper. This vanished like snow before fire.

Another real favourite proved to be a tin of Waitrose mackerel fillets in tomato sauce. Proving her ability to pick up my thoughts from a distance, she could be under the bed in the spare room fast asleep. Deciding to give her a tin of mackerel, but without saying a word, I would silently open the cupboard door and before I had time to take it down from the shelf Tessa was rushing down the stairs full pelt, into the kitchen sitting there looking up with an expression of expectant delight written all over her face.

She never failed to amaze me. I am aware of the telepathic link between humans and animals. Am aware they are able to both read our thoughts and see the pictures our thoughts transmit however, proof of this ability always – even today – is a source of wonder and joy to me.

I always looked for and tried different foods as a treat for Tessa or indeed any dog who is part of our family, working on the principle that a change is always a welcome experience. One day Waitrose had, on special offer, tins of Princes hot dog sausages. Maybe Tessa would like to try some? That evening her immediate reaction was equal only to that of being given mackerel in tomato sauce. Yes, thank you Mum, these are delicious! Being a life-long vegetarian myself I had to take her word for it. Ever afterwards the occasional tin of hot dogs – if you'll forgive the expression (!) – became part of the menu.

As she grew older and sometimes may not feel like eating, nine times out of ten she would succumb to the temptation of a Princes sausage, munching her way happily through all eight. Maybe this explained why Tessa often wagged her tail in her sleep!

Normal dog food both tinned and fresh from the pet shop did, of course, also feature strongly in her diet, especially Chum which was her definite favourite. I am sure she would have opened the tin herself if she could!

Chapter LXIII

The beginning of July Mother's Cousin Ralph rang me at work on the internal 'phone – he too worked for Kodak but at Swallowdale. His wife Doris had recently died and he wondered whether Mother and I would go up to their bungalow in Hunstanton with him for two weeks as he had booked the time off before Doris had passed. We would travel up on Saturday 10 of July returning on Saturday 24. He would be only too pleased for Tessa to come as well – he loves dogs and knew Tess would enjoy herself on the beach.

Naturally we were only too pleased to accept Ralph's kind offer. His niece's husband Brian would drive Ralph over to us on the Friday so we would be ready for an early start next day.

Our neighbour from Bramley Road, Peggy, kindly agreed to look after James and Joan for the two weeks. I assured her they would be no trouble and was extremely grateful to her for coming to the rescue. Hunstanton would have been a very long journey for two little terrapins to travel and they could not possibly stay at home on their own.

After work on the afternoon of Friday the 9th, I drove round the corner to Peggy carefully balancing James' and Joan's tank on the front seat of the car. A very kindly, compassionate person Peggy was enthralled with them and was thoroughly looking forward to having them with her for a while.

Brain and Ralph arrived that evening as planned. After a meal followed by a relaxing cup of coffee in the drawing room Tessa and I drove down to Tally Ho ahead of Brian to put him on the right road back to Woking. Then returned home to find all the washing up finished!

We left the next morning at 10am full of anticipation. We arrived at Ralph's bungalow 9½ hours later having broken down en route. Unfortunately the radiator kept boiling over. The breakdown service we were still a member of in those days came out twice but were of little help – classic cars not really being their forte. However we eventually arrived in Hunstanton at 7.30 that night very tired but delighted to be there.

The next day before breakfast, Tessa and I went for a walk across the field behind the bungalow then up a steep hill bordered by poppy fields, to the Kings Lynn Road and back. Such new interesting smells for Tessa – she loved every minute of it. Had we walked in the other direction we would have been down on the front in a matter of a few minutes but the poppy fields held more appeal for an inquisitive little dog. The view on the return journey, of the near distant sea was a great delight to me. This pleasurable walk became our regular route each morning for the next fortnight and the memory of it brightened our morning walks back at home long after our holiday was over.

Later we all explored the Sunday market, made one or two purchases then returned home for lunch after which John, the gentleman next door, helped Ralph and myself – ably watched by Tessa – to drain then clean out Rebecca's radiator. A satisfactory job completed it was now Tess's turn for all the attention. To the beach!

We drove down through the quaint little town then out the other side to top of the 60 ft cliffs where rough ground had been made into a car park. Being a nice sunny Sunday afternoon there were naturally a lot of parked cars, presumably most belonging to folk from neighbouring areas who had come out for an after lunch drive or those enjoying their annual holiday.

We drove as near to the cliff edge and beach path as possible to park. Tessa could not have seen the sea or the beach before. What would she make of them?

Clambering out of Rebecca and ensuring she was safely locked and alarmed the three of us, with Tessa trotting along beside, made our way down the gentle slope to the sandy pathway between the dunes which lead straight onto the beach. I kept Tessa on the lead as we crossed the field as cars were constantly coming and going, she was too precious to put at risk.

As the grass became soft golden sand Tessa realised something was different. Her feet were gently sinking into the warm, moving ground beneath her feet. She stopped for a few seconds, looked surprised then decided this new sensation was nice. Off the lead she came, running down the path ahead of us sniffing excitedly here, there and everywhere. This was wonderful!

At the foot of the pathway we turned left along the bottom of the high cliffs which are a striking feature of this part of the Norfolk coastline. A narrow band of red chalk is sandwiched between white and brown sandstone, known locally as "carrstone" and from which many local houses are built.

Tessa was having the time of her life – tail held high she trotted along ahead of us dancing as she went. Always willing to be friendly she ran up to several dogs for a game of chase as we progressed along the beach. She would sleep tonight, no doubt about that!

As the cliffs veered slightly round to the left towards the town, so we came to the rock pools. Here was another new experience, all these lovely rocks to run around. Tess went crazy chasing round and round, up and down, in and out of the pools. What a marvellous game this was!

We let her continue while we rested on the fallen rocks at the foot of the cliffs. Just to watch her enjoying herself so much gave us great pleasure. As usual in those days, I had brought my movie camera along so was delighted to be able to shoot several minutes of Tessa's happy escapade among the weed covered rocks and cool refreshing pools.

Eventually it was time to turn for home. Instead of walking along the upper section of the beach we walked along the shoreline – much to Tessa's continued delight. Paddling along the edge of the sea, daring to run out a few yards before turning, laughing and running back to us. So many new adventures in one day! Fortunately there is always a towel in the car also a bottle of water together with her "travelling" drinking bowl.

We had spent just over an hour on the beach that afternoon. Tomorrow we would take Tessa for a walk along the beach at the other end of the town. Meanwhile, a hearty dinner and good night's sleep were the order of the day.

As arranged, the next morning Mother stayed at home reading her paper and resting while Ralph took Tessa and me, by way of the field behind his bungalow, across the road leading into town, past the grassland which used to be the rail track linking Hunstanton with Kings Lynn then down onto the beach. Refreshed after a good nights sleep Tessa was roaring to go. Sand again – this was going to be fun. Yesterday had been wonderful.

We walked for about an hour along the edge of the shore, crossing over or round the groins which occasionally interrupted our stroll. Once again Tessa had a lovely time running in and out of the sea, trotting along ahead of us taking everything in as she went.

The end of the groins were marked with tall wooden marker-buoys which often stood in pools of sea water left behind after the tide had gone out. These were, for all three of us, great fun to paddle through. The deepest being generally no more than knee high. Naturally where Ralph and Mum went Tessa went to, usually leading the way – though always watched carefully.

Coming up to another pool Tessa rushed on ahead to splash through the water. This was sheer – oh help! The water was much deeper here than expected and suddenly Tessa was swimming like mad to reach the other side. I rushed forward to her as she struggled out onto the beach looking both astonished and startled at her ordeal. What a relief she was safe and sound. Thank heavens dogs swim naturally when the need arises. She had not realised – as indeed neither had Ralph nor I – the water would be any deeper here than round the other buoys and was visibly shaken. From then on she gave the marker pools a wide berth!

All too soon we reluctantly turned to retrace our steps home for lunch. It had been a lovely walk on a warm sunny morning. As we made our way back along the beach Tessa began to tire. Well, it had been a long, exciting walk for all of us. Tessa had four legs as against our two and after all she was not used to such a long walk. We would soon be home when she could have a rest. However, she began to slow down, showing signs of real exhaustion.

When we eventually arrived home, about two hours after setting out, Tessa was really struggling. I quickly put her rug on the sofa then, after giving her a drink, laid her gently down to rest. We spent the rest of the afternoon quietly around the bungalow while Tessa lay sleeping. This was very worrying. Tess was a young dog yet two hours along the beach and back had been too much for her to cope with. She was showing similar signs to those Kimmy had shown in Southwold. I must watch her very carefully, not overtire her. If this reaction was repeated she must see Mr Winwood.

During the remainder of our two weeks I monitored Tessa very carefully. One day Ralph took us all to Sandringham Country Park. Mother and Ralph went into the little church while Tessa and I sat on the grass outside the gates watching the crowds pass through. Then, to Tessa's delight we went for a half-hour walk through the woods where she was able to run free. She trotted along happily nosing around the undergrowth, into the ferns then back onto the path with us.

Another day Ralph took us to Castle Rising, to be found 5 miles north-east of Kings Lynn just off the A149 Hunstanton Road. A charming ruined castle dating back to the days shortly after the Norman Conquest, it has a welcoming, enchanting atmosphere and has always been amongst the most important castles in East Anglia. Controlled now by the Department of the Environment, dogs are allowed to accompany their families into the ruins as well as the grounds.

Castle Rising stands surrounded by man-made earthworks of great banks and ditches covering an area of some 12 acres. Delighted at being able to accompany us Tessa was, as always, impeccably behaved, interested in everything, though the rough stone corridors and passages must have been even more uncomfortable for her to walk on than for us.

Having explored the interior of this fantastic ruin, with Tessa held on a short lead close by my side for safety's sake (the passages are extremely narrow and low ceilinged due to the very small stature of the people who lived in the 11th and 12th centuries), we then walked around the top of the high banks encircling the Castle where we were able to let Tessa run free.

The view from the here is breathtaking – right across the village to the distant farmlands. The banks themselves adorned with wild flowers growing freely amongst the grassy slopes.

All too soon it was time to pack up and go home. Tessa had thoroughly enjoyed her first visit to the seaside and had made our holiday complete. After her exhaustion at the beginning of the first week, I had kept her walks shorter, her rests periods longer with the result she was able to cope well. She had been a very good girl. I could see no problem in taking her anywhere in the future, we would have many happy times together in the years ahead.

Next day after telephoning Peggy, I drove round to collect James and Joan. As Peggy opened the door then led me into the front lounge and they heard my voice the little terrapins went crazy. Scrambling across their tank, clambering up the sides to see their Mum. I was amazed at such a reaction from the little creatures but just as pleased to see them. Apparently they had been very good, no bother at all. In fact Peggy had thoroughly enjoyed having them, she was sorry to see them go.

In no time at all they were back in their own home on their own wide window sill in the sun though they probably enjoyed their holiday with Peggy as much as she did looking after them.

Chapter LXIV

Tessa quickly settled down again into the routine of home life though I am sure she must have dreamt of sandy beaches, warm sea, woodlands and country walks for quite a while after our return. Often while fast asleep her tail would wag furiously while her nose twitched in time with her ears and waggling paws.

Occasionally she would, whether asleep or awake, grind her teeth the sound of which set my teeth on edge! When consulted, Mr Winwood assured me this was merely a habit, nothing to worry about she would probably grow out of it, as indeed she did.

For some reason known only to herself Tessa was terrified whenever she had to go to Wood Street. She had never been hurt or experienced anything unpleasant there – it could only be the atmosphere or smell associated with all medical establishments and personnel. Whenever she had to visit there a treat was always waiting for her in the car when she came out – usually a small piece of Frys Chocolate Cream or Milky Bar for which, like Kimmy, she had developed a strong liking. Kimmy must have taught her to climb up on the back of Rebecca's front seat looking for a treat when Grandma climbed back in after visiting a shop. Neither Mother nor I had encouraged her to imitate this favourite habit of Kimmy's yet she did so every time quite naturally, receiving the looked for small reward for being good.

Chapter LXV

At the beginning of August I decided to visit our friend in Hove then drive on to Pagham to see both Cathy and Ruth. It would be a long day but, hopefully, a happy one. A chance to introduce Tessa to more of our friends. Monday seemed the best day to travel as the roads should not be quite so congested. I had arranged to be at Stuart's by about 12 noon but had not reckoned on the radiator overheating again. Several times it was necessary to stop to allow the water to cool down, which presented an ideal opportunity to take Tessa for a stroll around leaving Mother sitting in the car. This was the second long journey Tessa had made with us, the second time the radiator had given trouble; by now she must be assuming a long car journey automatically meant lots of stops! I must, somehow, get a new radiator as soon as possible.

Eventually, nearly an hour and a half late, we arrived in Hove. The long delay meant we were only able to stay with Stuart for about an hour but never-the-less it was good to see him again.

Before setting off for Bognor, we drove down to the front to look at the sea which, in the face of the strong gusty wind blowing, was whipped up into grey menacing five foot high walls of water which threw themselves in a frenzied state upon the shingle with a deafening crash which eliminated all other sounds – just like it had on our last visit with Kimmy. Conversation was impossible, the mere effort of standing upright took all our concentration. I held Tessa's lead very tightly to keep her safe.

Though she seemed to be enjoying the experience despite the wind giving a good impression of trying to tear the long soft fur from her small, slender body. Her ears too were caught up by the wind and flattened against her head while her tail stood out behind her defiantly. Rather than being frightened by the elements Tessa seemed to become part of them, caught up in the excitement of Nature's test of endurance.

However, time to climb back into Rebecca and eat the picnic lunch we had brought with us. Out came, firstly, Tessa's small red travelling dish into which was emptied a small tin of corned beef. Emm – this was good! While she enjoyed her meal Mother and I consumed our cheese sandwiches and drank from the thermos flask of coffee before pouring Tessa a drink of water – not too much or she would be wanting to keep stopping for wow-woz.

While reluctant to leave the wonder of this exhilarated sea we were anxious to be on our way. Cathy would be waiting for us.

The drive to Pagham took just over an hour by which time the tide had changed and the wind had dropped considerably.

I drove up onto the rough ground behind Cathy's garage as she opened the front/back door of the bungalow. She had been standing at the sink hence spotting us from the kitchen window. Ahead of her down the garden path tumbled one young apricot coloured poodle.

Peppa barked like mad at this intrusion onto his property until Tessa jumped out of the front seat of Rebecca. Human visitors were one thing but what was this? A canine visitor as well! He came up to Tessa who, always willing to be friendly, stood stock still before having a good look, sniff and tail wagging session with her host. Cathy was (naturally) enchanted with Tessa – what a pretty dog, so alert, so friendly.

Once inside Windy Ridge the chattering began in earnest! The latest family news from both sides was exchanged. A shame Rosie could not be there but she was away for a few days at present. Yes, she and Simon were well. The details of Keith's tragic accident were of course discussed together with all the local gossip from the Bognor/Pagham area. After all it had been our second home for so many years. At one time we had known more people down there than back in London.

Being situated between Bognor and Selsey the bay was sheltered. In any case the wind had by now abandoned it's former ferocity in favour of a gentle blow so, there was only one thing to do now – go for a swim! Cathy and I changed into our costumes, grabbed a beach robe apiece and calling Tessa to "come on Tessa, come with us" made our way across the cobbles to the sea's edge before plunging into the briny. Mother stood outside the bungalow on the shingle watching – it was quite a few years since she had ventured in. Tessa did not fancy the look of this sea either – it was not for paddling in – not like the gentle sea flowing and ebbing on the Norfolk coast. She would give this one a miss, thank you. Instead she loyally sat patiently guarding our clothing while Cathy and I wallowed shamelessly in the sheer bliss of bathing in the strongest force on earth.

Peppa wasn't impressed with either our eccentric fascination with all that water or Tessa's guard duties. He wandered about the shingles sniffing around, inspecting various oddments of seaweed or rubbish dropped by lazy folk and blown along the beach by the previous strong wind.

For three quarters of an hour we swam, splashed and chatted thoroughly enjoying the luxury of the warm, caressing water. Eventually we reluctantly clambered out onto the shingle beach to where dear Tessa still sat patiently watching and guarding. Telling her what a good girl she was, we retrieved our robes then made our way up the shingle to Windy Ridge where Peppa sat – equally patiently now – beside Mother who was waiting for us.

Having dried ourselves and dressed again, Cathy made a most welcome pot of tea shared of course by Tessa and Peppa. After all they may not have been for a swim but both being on guard duty and exploring the beach in the fresh air does give one a thirst! Mother too had been inhaling the good sea air standing at the top of the beach then sitting in a deckchair keeping an eye on proceedings – all very thirsty work!

About 4 o'clock we reluctantly took our leave of Cathy and Peppa, thanking them most sincerely for such warm, welcoming hospitality. It had been lovely to see Cathy again and to introduce her to our little Tessa.

The half mile drive round to Ruth in Nyetimber only took a few minutes. As we pulled up outside "Ruthena" Ruth spotted us through the lounge window and came to the front door (at the side of the bungalow) to greet us. A big smile on her face, her hands went up in exclamation "Oh what a lovely little dog – aren't you beautiful"! Drawn by the warmth of Ruth's welcome strengthened by her intense love of dogs, Tessa ran up to her with eyes shining and tail wagging nineteen to the dozen. Another new friend – how thrilling!

Ruth's gardens and verge were always a picture. She worked hard to maintain the lavishly stocked flower beds surrounding neatly trimmed lawns. An interest she knew Mother shared, so we were invited to see the garden before going indoors for tea. The rear of the back garden Ruth had turned into a very productive vegetable plot. All presenting more new smells for Tessa to investigate, what a wonderful day she was having!

The gardens inspected, we all went indoors where I gave Tessa an early evening meal – we would soon have to be on our way home so she would need to digest it before starting off.

Meanwhile Ruth made a pot of tea, produced cake and biscuits then led the way into the lounge in the front of the bungalow. As with Kimmy, Tessa was immediately given the sofa to sit on before being supplied with a hand-held dish of tea accompanied by two chocolate biscuits. She could get used to this!

All too soon the clock struck 5.30pm. Time to be making tracks. The right time to be setting off in order to avoid the heavy evening traffic at Chiswick, Ealing and Hanger Lane. Any earlier and the roads would be horrendous, any later and we would be too late getting home.

Ruth came down the path, across the verge to Rebecca waiting patiently for us on the roadway. Not that she could do anything else in reality but it is nice to think that way. Once again we reluctantly said our goodbyes to a dear friend. As we pulled away Tessa, sitting upright on the front passenger seat, turned to look back at Ruth whom she would not forget in a hurry – nor those chocolate biscuits with tea!

As we speed through the open country towards Bury Hill, the excitement of the day caught up with Tessa as she slipped down on the seat and curled up in a ball to allow a peaceful sleep to take hold.

The roads were fairly clear for that time of night so we made good time arriving home just after 9pm very tired but very contented.

Chapter LXVI

Towards the end of 1982 Tessa began behaving strangely. On two different days she snapped at Mother and at my eldest nephew, Phillip. She became very protective of her toys and bed, so with obvious suspicions I took her up to Mr Winwood. Yes, she was experiencing a phantom pregnancy. In her best interests she should be spayed as soon as the time was right.

So, at 7.30am on the morning of 12 January I took Tessie up to Wood Street for her operation. She had to be in the hospital by 8am. Even though I knew she could not be in better hands and the operation was both desirable and necessary, I hated leaving her there. To have sat in the waiting room all day would not have been practical or sensible but somehow it was what I wanted to do – to be near her. However common sense had to prevail and with a last look round at the hospital I drove down to Finchley and work.

After what seemed like an eternity, 2pm arrived and I telephoned the hospital for a progress report. Wonderful news, the operation had been a success and Tessa was sleeping peacefully – all was well. I should telephone again tomorrow and if all remained well, could collect her later that day.

I had arranged for a day's leave on the Thursday in order to collect Tessa and stay with her. Mr Winwood had suggested purchasing a pair of tights and cutting the legs off to make a thin pair of panties for Tess to go over her bandage. What a good idea. Three pair of tights were duly bought and "doctored" for Tessa's needs.

At last the time came to be off. Putting her bed in front of the fire ready for her, Mother and I drove up to Barnet to collect our girl.

When anxious to arrive somewhere, even driving at 40 mph the car seems to crawl, the journey endless. However at last we pulled up outside the hospital and I went in.

Before the RANAs brought Tessa out I had to settle the account, be brought up to date with her condition and be advised how to look after her. She must not jump up on the furniture nor up or down the stairs. She must be sensible and move gently for a few days allowing the wound time to heal. She had to attend the hospital again on Saturday

22 to have the bandage removed and a check up. Apparently she had been a very good patient – of course she had, she was our Tessa!

The RANA then went out to the wards behind the public area and brought Tessa through. It was wonderful to see her again – she was equally pleased to see me pulling towards me on her lead, tail wagging as usual. Bless her she must be wondering what on earth had been happening the last 36 hours. Why she had been taken there and left, why had she been in a deep sleep only to wake up feeling sore with a bandage round her tummy? Whatever the reason her "mum" was here now and overjoyed to see her so all must be right with the world!

Down the front path, through the tall wrought iron gate to the car where Grandma was waiting for her. Once again she received and gave a truly warm welcome before being helped onto the front seat for the journey home.

Home again Tessa was quickly in her bed snug and warm. She looked so pathetic with her tummy bound up but it was a good job done. No more phantom pregnancies for her, no more worry lest she became pregnant. Her life would be much easier from now on.

Tessa really was an excellent patient. She didn't make a fuss about anything, she seemed to know whatever I did for her was for her own good. She even refrained from jumping on and off the chairs!

Saturday the 22nd arrived and Tessa was virtually back to normal. Her appointment was 10.05am with Mr Winwood so we were all up early and feeling positive about her check up.

We were not disappointed. Mr Winwood was extremely pleased with her and, baring the unexpected, did not need to see her again.

Needless to say Tessa had been on the healing list at our church in Potters Bar where, like Kimmy and Trixie before her, she too was a regular visitor known and loved by all. She also visited our church in Freston Gardens where she followed in her predecessors footsteps once again. Here too she enjoyed a lot of fuss when arriving for or departing from a service.

The Church Fayre also held it's attractions for her, (again as it had for Trix and Kim) here she too spent the day sitting by the stall Mother ran, taking an interest in everyone who came to look or buy, who nearly always spoke to her ensuring a friendly look and wag of the tail. Lunch time she came into the Stuart Room for her share of sandwiches, biscuits and tea accompanied by more fussing especially from her special friend Dorothy Tolfree who regularly visited our home.

When the cold weather began in earnest, James and Joan needed a proper tank with some kind of heating. On Tony's suggestion we went along to Wildwoods in Crewes Hill, about a couple of miles from home. Tessa waited in Rebecca with Grandma while Tony came into the centre with me. What a fantastic place! Every size, shape, description of tank or aquarium it is possible to imagine. Fountains too, in the shape of animals, birds, nymphs or simply futuristic designs. Water playfully tumbling over pebbles, out of urns or pitchers held by maidens or out of the mouth of birds and animals. Fish too of so many different sizes and colours, all swimming around in huge tanks of running water, to say nothing of row upon row of shelves of fish food and supplies.

With the help of an assistant we chose a medium Clear Seal tank with a hood, a light fitment and a model frog to decorate James' and Joan's new home. They already had sufficient rocks in their existing tank to equip this new one.

As always Tessa was anxious to see what had been purchased – what on earth could this thing be? Her nose was trying to penetrate every corner or opening of the glass box and it's contents. When I explained to her that it was a new home for James and Joan she looked at me, looked at the tank on Tony's lap then with an expression of puzzlement settled herself back onto the rear seat next to Grandma. Well, she was obviously not getting very far with her investigations so may as well give up – it did not look all that interesting anyway!

Fortunately James and Joan thought otherwise. The warmest place for their tank was in the kitchen on part of the worksurface. The lamp could be plugged in to the wall socket there.

Before long the tank was set up ready for it's new inhabitants. Gently lifting them in one at a time, the three of us watched while they explored their new surroundings. Em, this was nice. Lots more room, much warmer too. A feed as well, gosh this was super. They seemed really pleased. Let's hope they would live comfortably there throughout the winter months.

Unfortunately this was not to be. Before the winter was over James and Joan died, albeit peacefully, in their sleep. I took them up to Wood Street where Mr Winwood sadly confirmed they were both dead then humanely dealt with their little bodies.

The tears began to trickle down my face even before I left the consulting room. James and Joan had been such great little characters, so endearing. Why had they died? I had done my very best to give them everything they needed.

As I sat in the car outside the hospital the trickle of tears gave way to unashamed, heartfelt sobs before finally subsiding enough to allow me to drive home.

Chapter LXVII

The end of January brought more problems for Rebecca. In addition to those created by the over heating radiator, Beccy developed an oil leak coupled with rapid loss of fluid from the reservoir. Something must be done. How to pay for it that was the question? Only one answer – an insurance policy must be surrendered. So the deed was done. The money obtained. A new radiator bought and the necessary repairs undertaken.

When all bills had been settled there was just £15 left over. Along to the pet shop in Bush Hill Park I went to look for a daytime bed for Tessa. One to keep in the lounge to save carrying her Goddards up and down.

Tessa came in the shop with me although of course she had no idea what it was all about. No matter, the shop was full of delightful smells to be attended to. While she enjoyed herself nosing around, I located the perfect bed for her. A round, 26 inch diameter, golden brown fur fabric beanbag bed with a beige edge. It was just £9 which left £6 for a few extra treats and a small piece of beef to be shared with Grandma. A very satisfying shopping trip.

If ever Tessa was told something was for her she always showed her appreciation by taking a great interest in whatever it happened to be. Sniffing it all over then looking up, wagging her tail, eyes shining. The new bed was no exception – she loved it immediately. On arriving home it was put in front of the coal effect fire in the lounge where she promptly and emphatically sat in the middle of it turning to look at us as if saying "yes, I know it is mine – thank you – I love it".

Chapter LXVIII

Oakwood Park remained our regular exercise area though from time to time we visited other open grounds and parks round about. Saturday morning we got into the habit of going to Grovelands Park just the other side of Southgate, about five minutes drive in Rebecca. We had heard about Grovelands from a friend who used to walk down there to sit watching the ducks on the lake, the people strolling along and the dogs playing. I shall always be grateful to Ann for introducing us to Grovelands. A truly beautiful park, full of character.

Tessa and I usually entered through the tall wrought iron gates at the main entrance in The Bourne, a semi-main road uniting Southgate with Palmers Green. Just inside the gates on the right, the land has been given over to a Pitch and Putt course so, naturally, dogs are not allowed on the green which is partly fenced off. This is a very sensible idea as the players are able to enjoy themselves in peace without interfering with the general public or vice versa.

A well maintained pathway runs right round the park which covers a considerable area incorporating open grassland, tennis courts, football pitch, bowling green, childrens' play area, quaint tea room and wooded area through which a stream runs. So vast is the park itself that none of these facilities are too close to one another. Consequently it provides a marvellous free running area for the many dogs who visit there each day.

Tessa and I made our established route along the edge of the field facing the Pitch and Putt, up over the hill, round the far side of the football pitch then down the other side past the tennis courts into the woodland via one of the several wooden bridges crossing the stream. The walk through the woods was always a great delight, especially in the early morning with the sun shining, the birds singing and the rich smell of the undergrowth. A wooden bench is conveniently sited towards the near end of the woods where, after chasing in and out of the trees, up and down like a lunatic, Tessa would sit by my feet while I enjoyed ten minutes peace and quiet before wending our way up to the lake, round the far side through the rough undergrowth, sparsely populated by huge oak trees, then returning past the Pitch and Putt to the main gates. The average walk lasting about an hour.

There were always other dogs for Tessa to play with in Grovelands which made the walks so much more enjoyable for her. She was never nervous or afraid no matter how large or boisterous the other dog. She would run up to the huge Mastiff, unbelievably almost the size of a Shetland pony, as easily as to a Jack Russell. Yet, when we met a little dog in the woods one morning who was very, very nervous she seemed to sense something was wrong. She ran up to her, gently rubbed noses then, because the other dog was reluctant to walk and kept stopping dead in her tracks, Tessa stayed beside her or stood with her giving the little dog all her attention. The other dog seemed afraid to walk though there did not appear to be anything physically wrong with her. Her dad explained she had sadly experienced what, in human terms, would be called a nervous breakdown. Although she had previously loved her walks, now he had great difficulty in getting her to come out. He had to carry her initially then encourage her every inch of the way. The vet had advised he persevere with her walks as she needed exercise. Bless her. It is bad enough when a human suffers a nervous breakdown but at least they know what is happening to them. When such a fate befalls a little dog it must be terrifying. Only TLC administered with endless patience can really help. This little dog was very lucky – her dad adored her and was willing to devote himself entirely to her recovery.

One friend she chased in Grovelands did not respond. In fact he ran away as fast as he could!

Emerging from the undergrowth near the Pitch and Putt area Tessa was ahead of me when suddenly she stopped, looked up towards the boundary fence then ran full pelt after what she thought was a young dog. Here was someone else to play with – what sport. She didn't realise. Instead of another dog she was chasing after a young brown fox. A truly beautiful creature. The fox was naturally in no mood to play with a dog! He ran like mad along by the fence keeping as close to it as he could.

Realising what was happening I urgently called after Tessa as loudly as I could – terrified the fox may stop and turn on her. She slowed down, stopped, watched the fox still running away before disappearing out of sight, then came running back to me. Oh well, the "dog" did not want to play, he obviously had somewhere to go in a hurry.

Not being quite sure how the fox could have reacted I telephoned Wood Street on my return home to ask their advice should such a happening occur again. The RANA I spoke with was most re-assuring. Apparently a fox will not turn on a dog unless it is cornered which, happily, this one was not. Never-the-less it is always better to be safe than sorry. Tessa can certainly play with as many dogs as she likes but foxes are definitely not for chasing!

Whichever park she was in winter meant, more often than not, she would return from her exercise covered in mud. Usually from head to tail! I always think a muddy dog is a happy dog because it has been allowed to run around freely enjoying itself.

Fortunately Tessa had no objection to having a bath, in fact she seemed to really enjoy it, unlike Trixie or Kimmy before her who both hated it and did their best to run away and hide when they sensed a bath was eminent.

The most convenient place for Tessa to be bathed was in our own bath upstairs. Several inches of warm water, a sponge, dog shampoo, two or three large warm towels and we were ready. On one occasion, Tessa ably demonstrated both her high intelligence and her strong sense of humour by jumping into the bath while I was still preparing her toiletries, turning round and sitting there looking at me with a laughing expression on her face which clearly said "see, I am here. I am ready and waiting for my bath"!

She would stand there as good as gold while she was gently sponged down then had a beaker of clean water poured over her. The bath water rapidly changing from clean to an opaque brown colour. At least twice the water had to be changed before the final rinse. Then with the bath emptied she was told to "shake" while I stood well back shielding myself with a towel. Having joyfully obeyed, out she would jump onto the bath mat before shaking again then being enveloped in her warm towels. Rubbing her dry was always an energetic job. The hairdryer would have been much quicker but unfortunately she hated it, struggling like an eel to escape, she made it impossible to use anything other than the lengthy towel process.

It quickly became obvious it was not the air blowing on her she objected to but the noise the dryer made. Tessa could not bear any loud noises, particularly thunderstorms, fireworks or the television. If a programme was even slightly noisy or the volume too high, Tessa disappeared from the lounge only to be found either in the dining room or upstairs under the bed in the guest room – a favourite place of hers. When downstairs, to relax she would lie on the floor, sideways along the wall with all four feet pressing on it. A position she also took up in the armchairs – her feet resting up the back of the chair.

Chapter LXIX

One evening we all three went over to visit Tony for a couple of hours. Tessa adored Tony and went crazy whenever he visited us. She turned round and round in circles, nose wrinkling, feet dancing. However this evening she was the one paying the visit for a change. As always Tony made a tremendous fuss of her. Tea in her dish, a biscuit then a quiet lie down while the humans chatted for an hour.

At last it was time to go. Tony and Jean have a small, very pretty front garden with a four foot brick wall at the street boundary in which is set a black wrought iron gate. There was no need to put Tessa on her lead, we were only walking down the path, through the gate, across the pavement into the car.

What a silly thing to do. A dog should always be on the lead unless in a secured area.

As she walked down the path Tessie spotted a cat stroll down the pavement and cross the road immediately in front of Rebecca. That was it – CAT! Tess darted down the path like a thing possessed, didn't stop to think whether the gate was open, whether she could get out. No, there is a cat to chase, just carry on straight through the gate!

Oh dear Tessa you may be small but not that small. She darted half way through the gate then stopped abruptly, jammed between the iron railings.

Mother, Tony and I dashed down the path after her. What on earth had she done – was she hurt – could we free her? Tony and I tried very gently to pull her back but she didn't give an inch. She was stuck fast round her middle. Maybe if we could push her right through and out the other side. No. I began to feel panic – maybe we should call the Fire Brigade.

Don't panic just yet – Tony advised calm – before doing anything quite so drastic let's try again. He went indoors to fetch a tub of margarine. Poor Tessa she must be feeling frightened by now and probably experiencing a deal of discomfort to say the least. The railings were digging right into her sides.

Trying desperately to sound re-assuringly confident I stroked her head, talking quietly to her in an attempt to keep her still. Outwardly unruffled Tony proceeded to smear the grease all over Tessa's coat as far as he could reach. This done we once again tried to gently free her from her captive position. Yes, she was moving! Very slightly at first then, with two hands carefully pulling her backwards out of the railings while two more were through the next section of ironwork trying to gently push her from the front she was gradually released. At last she was free. What a relief!

Wanting to hug her but careful not to in case I inadvertently hurt her I checked her little body for outward signs of injury. There wasn't a mark on her. This did not mean however that she was not suffering from internal bruising or worse. She seemed fine if a little shaken up. Never-the-less first thing tomorrow I would telephone Mr Winwood asking him to be kind enough to call in. Meanwhile, home! I lifted her gently into the car, expressed grateful thanks to Tony for all his help then made for home as quickly as safely possible.

Once indoors the grease had to be delicately cleaned from her coat before she went to bed. Hopefully, after her ordeal, she would sleep. No trouble there – she slept peacefully until morning.

Naturally there was no question of my going to work until Mr Winwood had been. Even then I should stay with Tessa – today would have to be a days leave. Tessa came first.

About 11.30am Mr Winwood arrived smiling kindly as he entered the hall. Tessa, curled up on her round bed in the lounge, made no attempt to come out to see who was arriving. Probably a good thing or she would have begun trembling before it was necessary.

Mr Winwood came into the lounge, sat in the armchair and asked what young Tessa had been up to. I related the previous evenings escapade, explaining although there were no outward signs of injury I would be most grateful if he would check her over just to be certain all was well. Gladly.

Efficiently gentle as always, Mr Winwood examined Tessa thoroughly. The conclusion he came to was that though Tessa was not seriously hurt in any way she was probably suffering a certain amount of internal bruising, she would be feeling rather tender for a day or two. He gave her an injection to ease the bruising saying if I was worried about her in the next day or two, to give him a ring.

While Mr Winwood was with us I took the opportunity of emphasizing my certainty there was something wrong with her heart. On a previous occasion I'd expressed this opinion to Mr Winwood siting the trouble Tessa had experienced while in Norfolk – her complete exhaustion after what should have been a normal walk for a young dog. Since then she had, from time to time, stopped when walking out to stand still resting for a while. In all probability it was nothing dramatic but there was *definitely* something wrong.

Mr Winwood sat looking at me for a few moments. He had, so far, rejected the suggestion of heart trouble. To be absolutely fair to him, quite understandably because – though much too kind a person to actually say so – he probably thought I was just being neurotic. Kimmy having suffered from a heart condition I was of course only too familiar with the symptoms. It is so easy to imagine Kimmy's symptoms materialising once more, on Tessa. After all a little knowledge is a dangerous thing. However so adamant was I that he finally agreed to run an ECG just to be on the safe side. To give me peace of mind.

A few days later we took Tessa up to Wood Street for her ECG. Kimmy had had several ECGs so we were au fait with the routine.

Having seen Mr Winwood in the consulting room first, we sat restlessly in the waiting room while the EGG was run. It seemed to take for ever though in reality it could not have been more than about quarter of an hour or so. At last a nurse appeared hanging on to Tessa's lead while Tess pulled towards us. Mr Winwood would call us in a few minutes. Thanking her, I bent to make a fuss of our Tess. She was a good girl. She was glad to be away from the treatment room – hopefully she was on the way home. No such luck. The consulting room door opened and we were called in.

Mr Winwood stood there with the long strip of pink and white paper bearing the tracing of Tessa's heart. Yes. Tessa had a heart condition. Mr Winwood was surprised. Apparently the chances of having two consecutive dogs with a heart condition are a million to one. Tess would need to take tablets for the rest of her life, though providing I was sensible with her, she should be able to lead a fairly good life. As with Kimmy though, I must realise she could be running and suddenly drop. This was hopefully not likely to happen but better to be warned.

Armed with her first supply of millophyline tablets we thanked Mr Winwood and made our way out to Rebecca. Oh dear. Our little Tessa. Kimmy had lived a good, long life despite her heart condition.

Surely there was no reason why Tessa should not do the same. She could not have more love, more TLC. Think positive, that is the answer.

Tessa's heart problem meant I watched her carefully. It was not that long since our dear Kimmy had passed over, the possibility of loosing our Tessie after so short a time with us was daunting. Instead of simply setting off for a walk, wandering where the urge took us, I made a concentrated effort to mentally plan our route in advance avoiding steep gradients. From time to time, when exercising, she would suddenly stand stock still resting. If the rest continued too long I would pick her up, carry her for a little while then gently put her down again. Fortunately, most times, this would give her sufficient breathing space to recover enough to continue her walk. On the odd occasion however, despite a lengthy rest, Tessa failed to rally then she had to be carried home. This naturally created a strong sense of déjà vu.

Chapter LXX

Tessa coped pretty well with her new way of life. She seemed to know instinctively that something was wrong but that she was being looked after properly. She always stopped racing whenever she was called, looking back over her shoulder as if to say "see Mum, I am trying to be sensible. I have stopped when you called". Naturally she was fussed, told she was a good girl then had it explained to her that she must not race around quite so much now, it was not good for her heart.

I am certain she understood as she would rest for a few moments then trot on her way again but at a slower pace.

Proof of her intelligent understand was demonstrated even more profoundly one Saturday morning as we pulled up outside the gates of Grovelands Park. As unfortunately happens periodically, there was a bout of dog stealing in action. All year round dogs are stolen for varying unpleasant reasons. The unscrupulous people who take them do so when the dogs are away from their owners, for example in parks, on the streets or even when running along behind their owners. Every summer dogs left unattended in cars are stolen particularly from seaside resorts though often in the towns and cities also. There had been a spate of dog stealing reported in the North London area. Always a worry, always putting a devoted dog owner on their guard.

Tessa tended to run around where-ever she liked in the parks. Though always in view, she was often quite some distance from me. Being very aware of the current dangers I wanted to warn her – certain she would comprehend what I was saying. After turning off the engine I sat for a moment. Tessa was of course anxious to be out and away – playtime beckoned. However I put a hand on her collar and stopped her. "Now Tessa I want you to listen to me very carefully. There are nasty, bad people out there who could do you harm. Given the chance they would hurt you – do you understand. You MUST stay very close to me today – you can run around and play but you must not go more than a few yards from me".

All the time I was speaking she sat patiently watching me, listening to every word. Consequently it never entered my head but that she understood.

Our walk lasted nearly an hour during which, though she enjoyed herself, Tessa never went more than six or seven feet away from me. Despite knowing she understood what had been said, her behaviour in line with the warning – her unhesitating obedience – amazed me. Bless her, she really *had* understood – it was not just wishful thinking on my part. At this point I began to comprehend a little more clearly just how intelligent Tessa was.

Another occasion when Tessa demonstrated her keen intelligence came during the winter when the snow and ice were on the ground. Whatever the weather a dog must have daily exercise. The snow had been on the ground for several days, much to Tessa's delight. Like Kimmy and Trixie before her, Tessa loved the snow. She would run, tail held high with "feathers" hanging down behind her like a guardsman's plumed helmet, then bury her nose into the snow before bringing her head up again, shaking it and laughing, eyes gleaming.

This particular day the snow had frozen over turning the pavements into an ice rink. Well wrapped up, Tessa wearing her thick red tartan coat, we set off down the road. Because of the treacherous conditions we walked on the frozen grass verge in an attempt to reduce the risk of accident. Excitedly Tessa pulled ahead, eager to make the most of every minute.

About 50 yards along we came to a turning which meant crossing a wide expanse of pavement then roadway or – to be more accurate, a solid sheet of ice. Oblivious to the dangers Tessa continued to pull hard on her lead as I approached the edge of the verge. Realising how easy it was going to be to slip I called her to a halt. Without hesitation she came straight back to where I stood. Bending down I asked her if she would be a good girl and not pull so much or she would pull me over on the ice and if I broke an arm or a leg and was laid up for a while, we would all three be in trouble. Mother was beginning to rely more on my help also she would not be able to take Tessa out if I were incapacitated. It was essential I remained in one piece. So, please be a good girl and don't pull any more.

Once again Tessa amazed me. Not only did she stop pulling on her lead but she made a point of very carefully leading me across the ice. Stepping confidently yet cautiously she picked her way round the more hazardous patches until we reached the other side then onto the verge once more. Even then Tess trotted along without pulling. Content just to be enjoying her walk, knowing she and I were responsible for each others safety.

Chapter LXXI

Though now living in Oakwood I still subscribed to the local paper for Barnet. Having lived in Cockfosters since the War the Barnet paper was of greater interest covering places, people and events that were part of our lives.

Advertised in one summer issue was a photo opportunity. For one week only, a professional photographer would be sited in the Press offices in Barnet to take portraits of pets or children. The sitting, plus first photograph, being provided free of charge.

What an opportunity! Tessa was certainly a *very* pretty girl. Everyone agreed. Of course I had taken many feet of movie as well as a good number of photos of her but a professional photograph would be wonderful.

In order to look her extra-special best Tessa must be groomed well. The morning of the day we chose to take her up for her session, Tessa had a nice warm bath followed by a good brush and comb. Her coat always looked beautiful, smooth and silky so it was not difficult to prepare her. It did not particularly matter what Mother or I wore as the sitting was for Tessa alone. Hopefully she would be good, sit still and pose like a true professional. What a hope!

Having driven up to Barnet, parked the car then made our way along the High Street to the Press offices housed in one of the older style, quaint black and stone buildings of yesteryear, we opened the door which lead straight into the reception area and went in. Totally unaware of what awaited her, Tessa happily trotted in ahead of us.

A backcloth was hung in front of the reception desk and the photographer was just concluding a session with two young children. It was obvious from his reaction to Tessa that most of his clients that morning had been children. "Ah – a little dog, at last". He beamed at our Tess. Whether out of relief at a change of subject matter or because he was an animal lover was not apparent but in any case anyone who smiled at our girl was alright by me.

Preparing his apparatus, the photographer asked me to sit Tessa on the floor against the backcloth. Fine, no problem. The trouble began when I backed away from her. "Hey Mum, where are you going? Surely you are not leaving me sitting here? If you are not staying then I am not either!"

Well never mind, it was only a first attempt. Try again and again – and again. For some reason, the words "Tessa stay" had suddenly lost their meaning. Could it be the lights? Maybe the strange surroundings? Possibly the increasing tension in the atmosphere? After seven or eight attempts the photographer decided his planned pose was not going to succeed. The only alternative was for Tessa to sit on Mum's lap. Gosh, I only had shopping clothes on – a pair of maroon slacks with pale green casual rain jacket. I was certainly not dressed for the camera – this was supposed to be Tessa's portrait. Reluctantly I had to give in as the photographer placed a wooden chair in front of the backcloth, protesting this was going to be the only way he could take the picture. The next clients were already in the reception, waiting their turn.

Sitting down I bent over, picked up Tessa and settled her on my lap facing into the camera with her tail cascading down over my knees. "That's it – hold it just like that". Delighted to be getting somewhere at last the photographer clicked away as fast as the camera would allow.

Much preferring to be behind a camera rather than in front of it, I tried hard to smile naturally while Tessa, contented now to be on my lap and receiving attention, gave a broad doggie grin with pink tongue showing, ears pulled back and eyes sparkling. This was not so bad after all!

Relieved to have achieved his aim, if in a slightly different guise to that originally planned, the photographer relaxed once more, gave us our receipt slip then told us when to expect the proofs. If the truth be known the poor man, although initially pleased to have an animal model for a change was probably only too willing to return once more to child portraiture!

A few days later the proofs arrived. We were delighted with them all so choosing the best was very difficult. However, at last we settled on the photograph which looked the most natural and ordered half a dozen. All in all I was pleased with the venture.

Chapter LXXII

I took a copy of the portrait with us to give to Helene when we visited Eileen in Dorset later that year. Tessa had not been to the West Country before. Both Helene and Eileen had of course heard about Tessa. Now was their chance to meet her. They both loved Kimmy very much but were also enchanted with little Tessa. Both expressed the similarity to Kimmy despite the difference in size and fur colours.

To Tessa the journey had been long – about 5 hours – never-the-less she had been very good. She sat in the front seat next to me and alternated between looking out of the window and curling up for a nap. As always, we had stopped periodically for a cuppa, snack and wow-woz. A little natural pull-in off the road at Stockbridge being the favourite resting place. At this point we feel we are well on the way – whichever way we are travelling!

Tessa received her food and drink first then, needless to say, helped Mother and I eat our sandwiches after which I took Tess for a short walk along the grassy banks.

The main purpose for this visit to Dorset was the replacement of Rebecca's two sills. They were beginning to rust and as the two gentlemen who run the garage at Lulworth Cove are Woleseley enthusiasts, they had agreed to replace both sills at a very reasonable cost. They kindly lent us a navy blue Volvo Estate to use while they worked on Rebecca.

Tessa had no objection to changing cars, as long as Mother and I were there she was quite happy. Little did we dream what fun the Volvo was going to be. As we drove in through Eileen's gate onto her driveway she emerged from the front door with an "oooh what the ... have you got there"?

Well, maybe it did look rather large and perhaps just a little tatty. Some kind of farmyard material or creatures had been carried in the back because apart from the oddments of straw left behind, there was quite a distinctive smell of something in which Tessa had taken a great interest, sniffing around the interior as far as she could reach from her seat. When we stopped she clambered all over the rear of the car, her nose investigating every nook, cranny and fragrance.

Before long we were all laughing ourselves silly examining the car. It transpired that the quarter-lights did not shut properly; the front passenger door did not lock and the knob on the gearlever frequently fell off as did the interior driving mirror. The windows fell open and the inside door handles came off in your hand every time the door was opened or shut. But none of this really mattered as mechanically it was perfect.

We had been warned all the locals knew the car so we should expect to be hooted at, waved at and generally acknowledged by all and sundry. In short, every journey we made in the Volvo was destined to bring with it hoots of laughter and fun, especially when Eileen travelled with us as her strong sense of humour added to the merriment.

Tess had of course seen the beach and sea in Norfolk so this time she knew what it was all about. Weymouth beach is beautiful however we only visited it twice as apart from the fact the country surrounding also demands attention, Lulworth Cove with it's smaller beach is much closer to East Knighton. Wareham and Dorchester also hold strong attractions in the form of the market, shops and auction house.

On the Wednesday, the four of us drove into Dorchester for the market. Mother stayed in the car while Eileen and I took Tessa with us to look around the stalls. So many people. Market Day always draws crowds from miles around consequently the town is packed. This was definitely not for Tessa. She was not used to crowded areas. All those feet and legs bustling around her. Though she tried hard to avoid them it was impossible. So much noise – something she hated at the best of times. There was no way I could carry her as well as the shopping. There was only one answer. Back to the car. She would be safe there with Mother.

Leaving Eileen to continue with her purchases I walked Tessa back to the dis-used rail track which was utilised as a car park, popped her into the car, gave her a drink then re-assured her I would not be long. Mother would look after her.

She certainly seemed relieved to be back in the peace and quite of Topsey as we had named the Volvo, settling down for a much needed snooze.

As compensation for submitting her to such an ordeal, after lunch we drove down to Weymouth where Tessa, accompanied by the strong presence of Kimmy and Trixie, had a lovely long walk along the sands.

Next day, after visiting Wareham in the morning, we again drove to Weymouth and spent a good hour walking along the beach and back. On returning to the car, we doubled up laughing. An elderly man was standing beside Topsey looking her up and down while scratching his head and shaking it from side to side. We knew how he felt but she was temporarily ours and serving us very well!

Henry and Helene had moved into a little house in Cologne Road where we went to visit them one afternoon. My, how Mary had grown since we had last seen her – she was quite a young lady now. Henry no longer had a dog so Tessa was made all the more welcome. One of Helene's favourite descriptive words is "adorable". I lost count of the times she applied it to Tessa who responded with her usual loving warmth to anyone who showed her such devoted attention. When the tea tray arrived Tessa was given her own dish of tea plus chocolate biscuits. This was wonderful – she must have hoped against hope she would see these nice people again!

Eventually we took our leave of our good friends. There would not be time to see them again this visit as we were leaving next day but hopefully it would not be too long before we were able to come down to Dorset again. Of course there is always the telephone as a means of

Blackie always up to something!

Playing with his 'gonk' in the garden at home
Picture by courtesy of Sovereign Photography, New Barnet

Testing the pond water in Oakwood Park!

Our Family

Humans L–R: Tony, Father, Mother, Gillian
Animals L–R: Kimmy, Tessa, Paddy, Billy, Blackie, Trixie
Picture created and reproduced by courtesy of Sovereign Photography, New Barnet

I take Gilbert Anderson for a ride in Rebecca

Beryl arrives with treats for Blackie and Miffy

Tessa enjoys the open air, especially the park

On her fur-fabric day-bed which she loves

Elizabeth in Oakwood Park with her three rescue dogs Max, Blaze and Zia

'Woody', the groundsman, in Oakwood Park with Miffy

1971
Kimmy sits proudly in Rebecca, our new Wolseley 16/60

1999
Blackie and Miffy sit side-by-side in Rebecca at Sandringham

Miffy on the beach at Hunstanton

and at home on the bed

Miffy and Daisy together in the armchair

Audrey with Miffy and Daisy who are wearing the bright blue
woollen body warmers she bought them for Christmas

keeping in touch because though I am a prolific letter writer dear Helene – as she would be the first to admit – is totally uninventive in this department.

Next morning early Tessa came with me to collect Beccy while Mother stayed with Eileen to finish the packing. We eventually left East Knighton, about 10 o'clock heading for Wool, Wareham and home. It was going to be a long journey again, thank heavens Tessa had proved herself a good traveller.

We did not realise just how long the trip was going to be!

Reaching Stockbridge about 12 noon, sandwiches were consumed by us all. Tessa enjoying a round and a half of corned beef in brown bread and butter. Like Kimmy, travelling made her hungry. There were tins of dog food in the boot but this was the last day of our holiday so a last treat before arriving home was in order.

The usual wow-woz walk completed we all bundled back into Beccy and set off.

Five minutes later, at 12.30, Beccy began slowing down then picking up alternately. By this time we were at Sutton Scotney. Finding a telephone box I rang a well known breakdown service for help. What a waste of time!

As the man drew up a few yards ahead of us and walked towards Beccy he declared "Well, I really wouldn't know where to begin looking". He admitted he had only just left the Army and joined the breakdown service by pulling strings – he did not really know a great deal about cars but was hoping to learn. Obviously at the clients expense!

Having failed to find anything under the bonnet he thought did not look right, he suggested we drive on and if the same thing happened again, stop and put in another call.

All this time Tessa had sat as good as gold on the front seat.

A little way down the road, still in Sutton Scotney, the same thing happened again. I managed to pull into the side of the road outside a large country cottage where the owner kindly allowed me to put in another call. The three of us sat in Beccy and waited.

Oh no – the same man had come out to us. What earthly good was he going to be. Mother and I were both sure the fault lay in the petrol pump but no, the "expert" would not listen. After fiddling about for an hour he finally agreed that maybe it was the petrol pump after all.

Still Tessa sat quietly on the front seat, taking all this kerfuffle in her stride.

The next job was to locate the fuel pipe leading from the fuel tank – to check the flow of petrol. Easy, it is in the boot – I'd show him. No, he didn't think it was. Getting more than a little tired of this useless "expert" I emptied the boot and showed him the pipe coming from the tank, through the back board on the left of the boot interior. "Oh no" he declared "that is not it. The handbook says it is on the right-hand side".

He promptly began trying to remove the back board from the right corner in an attempt to locate the fuel pipe. This man was unbelievable. There was the fuel pipe as large as life on the lefthand side – was he blind or stupid. He certainly was not carrying a white stick nor did he have a guide dog with him! Despite increasingly angry protestations from both Mother – who had been driving since the early 1920's – and myself he continued to insist it had to be on the right and must there-fore be behind the back board.

He spent another half an hour trying to prove his point then reluc-tantly relented, admitting it must be the pipe showing on the left.

At last. Eventually he conceded we needed a new petrol pump. Unfortunately he did not have one with him and would have to drive into Basingstoke to buy one. It would take him about an hour to get there and back. Then he would have to fit it.

By now it was beginning to grow dusk.

Poor Tessa had been sitting on the front seat all this time. When we did finally get on the move again we must get home as quickly as possible. Tomorrow was our Church Bazaar and we were all three expected at the hall at 7pm that night to prepare our stall.

While our "expert" drove off into the distance I took Tessa for a walk along the grass verge to allow her to both stretch her legs and do wow-woz. She had been really wonderful. Some dogs would have fid-geted and cried but not our Tessie. She seemed to understand some-thing was wrong but we were doing our best. As long as we were all together everything was alright. Back in the car, though early, she had her evening meal plus a drink. Mother and I ate the remainder of the sandwiches and finished the thermos flask of tea Eileen had made for us. She would be wondering why we had not rung to say we were home safely.

At long last the man returned with the petrol pump and fitted it. By now it was really dark and we had best part of our journey still to travel. We eventually left Sutton Scotney at 5.30pm, exactly 5 hours after I had first called the breakdown service. The annual subscription renewal was due in a few weeks – no way on earth would I renew with them even though my Father had first joined them back in the mid 1920's.

Just after 8 o'clock we finally arrived home. All three of us very tired and looking very scruffy. I telephoned the church to explain what had happened. When we had not shown up the good folk had realised something must be wrong and had erected our stall for us. We could arrive early in the morning to stock it before the Bazaar opened to the public.

Having unpacked the car, taken Tessa's bed out, opened it up for her and put her blankets in, she was curled up fast asleep before Beccy was even in her garage.

As usual the Bazaar was a great success and despite the ordeal of the previous day Tessa thoroughly enjoyed herself. Enjoyed being fussed by everyone, enjoyed the titbits she received at lunch time and the excitement of seeing so many friends old and new. That night she once again slept a deep sleep, but this time as the result of a happy day.

Chapter LXXIII

Much as she loved to go away on holiday Tessa was always pleased to be home again and back in "her" park. The excitement of seeing the old familiar ground, her friends and their owners was duly demonstrated by her exuberance on being let off the lead.

Trotting along the path beside the small spinney one morning a lady, whom I knew slightly, approached us with her sheepdog bitch. A beautiful dog but unfortunately she had not been spayed, the lack of which left her rather temperamental at times. As she drew level with us she suddenly turned on Tessa pinning her to the ground. Poor Tessie was helpless. Apart from the fact the sheepdog was at least two and a half times her size, Tess seemed unable to defend herself. She just lay there unable to move, eyes wide open staring as her tongue began to turn blue. She did not seem to be able to breath properly. Panic stricken I screamed at the lady to get her dog off. This was a completely unprovoked attack.

The lady was genuinely very upset and apologised profusely. However this did not help Tessa. I stoked her head, spoke gently to her and after a few minutes she recovered, though still badly shaken. She was not used to this sort of thing, she was a peaceful, loving girl.

A few days later Tess was running around the field in her usual hare-brained manner when she suddenly stopped, keeled over on the grass and just lay there. Rushing over to her I knelt beside her trying desperately to calm the panic I felt. Feelings and emotions transmit themselves very quickly to animals especially those who are ultra-sensitive like Tessa. She must not pick up waves of adverse emotion. I must try hard to emit a soothing tranquillity with which to envelop her. Stroking her head I spoke gently to her, re-assuring her all would be well. It was alright – I was there with her.

After a few moments she rallied then unsteadily got to her feet, looking a little bewildered. She must be wondering what on earth had

155

happened to her – so was I for that matter. She must see Mr Winwood – he would be able to tell us what caused this.

As soon as we arrived home I telephoned Wood Street to book an early appointment.

Once recovered from her ordeal Tessa seemed fine again – no signs that anything untoward had occurred. Never-the-less something had caused her to keel over.

Mr Winwood was, as always, very sympathetic, understanding and supportive. Apparently because of her heart condition, when she became excited as when she was running too fast or was attacked, the oxygen supply was cut off to the brain creating her inability to react, her tongue to turn blue and her little body to simply keel over as it had done. This kind of thing could very well happen again. I must always keep calm, stroke her head and softly call her name. She will be able to hear and it will help her to recover.

Oh dear, something else for poor Tessa to contend with and for me to worry about but at least we were forewarned and knew what was happening and how to deal with it. We must however be thankful for the lack of lasting affects.

For my own peace of mind I wanted Tessa to have a regular ECG. That way Mr Winwood could be certain what was going on inside and any adjustment to medication or way of life could be made promptly. From then on, for the next few years, Tessa had an ECG every six months. Her condition did worsen a little and Mr Winwood changed her medication to Lanoxin – a tablet often given to humans with a heart condition. Finding the correct dosage took a while but trial and error eventually produced the right daily strength she must have. Thank heavens she took tablets easily, in Frys Cream – she never refused them which was a blessing.

Never-the-less she still enjoyed life. Enjoyed gnawing the largest size chew bone available; playing "tigers" hunting through the long grass in the park; running up to and dancing in front of another dog inviting them to come and play or revelling in a new game she found to play in the garden one summer. As soon as she saw the hose-pipe coming out of the garage, through the side gate and into the back garden she began barking with excitement. Running backwards and forwards between the tap in the garage and the hose-end, waiting impatiently for the water to appear. The instant it came rushing out of the pipe she worried it, darting at it with mouth open trying to bite into it, totally oblivious to the fact she was becoming soaked to the skin!

When the jet was moved around the garden this was even greater fun – not only biting it but chasing it this way and that. Needless to say playtime was always encouraged by my deliberately waving the hose up, down and round the lawn for her to chase. She loved this, never tiring of the fun. It was wonderful to see her playing so happily but her physical condition must never be forgotten. She could play as much as she liked as long as she rested from time to time. Being a sensible, obedient girl she quickly came to know the word "rest" so as soon as she heard it, she would come over to me and sit waiting until told she could continue with what she was doing.

Towards the end of summer each year, when the grass was long and seeded, Tessa would begin scratching like mad. Having experienced a similar condition at a similar time of year with Kimmy, diagnosis was clear. She had grass fever, a canine form of hayfever. Poor girl, she scratched and scratch and scratch with a look of desperation on her face.

Fortunately Mr Winwood had the answer for Tessa as he had Kimmy. One quick injection affected a cure.

Also during the summer months Tessa moulted profusely until her little chest was almost bare of white fur revealing her pink skin underneath. Never before nor since have I seen a dog moult to such an extent. Happily this did not appear to affect her so as long as she stayed out of the hot sun.

Unfortunately summertime also brings storms, often sudden and violent. Very few dogs are not afraid of storms and Tessa was no exception. One Sunday afternoon we walked round the corner into the park. It was a lovely day – warm sunshine, not too hot. As usual there were quite a few doggy friends to be found including Jasper a stocky black and white fellow of mixed breed who had come from the RSPCA at Southridge to live with two brothers and their parents in Oakwood. Jasper was one of Tessa's special friends as he obviously adored her. The instant he spotted her he stopped whatever he was doing to come running over to her to play. Such devotion had it's advantages when he would not return to his master. All I had to do was walk to where his master was standing, Tessa would follow me and Jasper would follow Tessa then before he knew what had happened, Jasper was on the lead. A system which worked very well on a good number of occasions!

This particular afternoon the two dogs had been playing happily for a while before Jasper was taken home. Tessa continued to run about in the lower field – she would play with anyone and everyone. Suddenly there was a terrific crash of violent, rumbling thunder. Before I could stop her Tessa panicked and ran like mad across the field heading for the side gates which lead out onto a busy road.

Terrified of what could happen I ran faster than I thought possible towards the gates to try to catch her before she ran out. She was too fast for me. The screech of car brakes momentarily brought me to a standstill then instigated that extra speed only fear can create. As I tore out of the gates I saw the black taxi standing stock still in the middle of the road. Oh my god – what had happened. Tessa!

There she was crouching on the roadway a matter of inches in front of the taxis' wheels. Thank heavens. Calling to her, I knelt down and picked her up as the driver got out of his cab and came round to the front of the vehicle. He looked thoroughly shaken. He explained she had just shot out of the gates into the roadway in front of him. He thought he was going to hit her. I apologised profoundly explaining the sudden thunder, which was now making a dickens of a row overhead accompanied by lightening flashing across the sky, had frightened her into running wildly in the direction of home. I thanked him most sincerely for stopping so quickly. As he climbed back into his cab and drove away the heavens opened.

Torrential rain was now beating down. A few moments ago it had been a warm sunny afternoon now, without warning, we were in the midst of a violent thunder storm. Having come out of the side gates we were at least three quarters of a mile from home.

Clipping on her lead I put Tessa down and we began running then trotting as fast as we could in the direction of home. Within a few minutes we were both soaked to the skin. Neither the rain nor the thunder or lightening showed any sign of letting up, in fact were getting worse.

Half way home we passed a large church standing in it's own grounds. The porch doors were open so, desperate for shelter, Tessa and I ran round the driveway, up the half a dozen steps into the porch. At least we were out of the rain. We could wait here until the fury had subsided a little. Surely it could not continue with such venom for much longer?

Suddenly a male voice behind us demanded to know what we were doing in their porch. We were ordered to "get out of it – clear off". Open mouthed with amazement I turned to look into the angry face of a middle-aged man neatly dressed in his Sunday best. He had been just inside the church door when he spotted us run into the porch.

Determined Tessie and I were not going out in that deluge of nature until the rains at least had eased a little, I refused to go. We were not doing any harm. We were only sheltering for a few moments. He still insisted we had no right to be there and should be off at once. Having made it abundantly clear to him I had absolutely no intention of leaving our shelter while the rain persisted and informing him this was supposed to be God's house not his, he very grudgingly acknowledged he could not move us without using physical force, so closing the door firmly behind him, he went into the evening service.

After about twenty minutes the rain eased though the thunder still rumbled accompanied by the occasional flash of lightening. All I wanted, and I am sure Tessie felt the same, was to get home.

Chapter LXXIV

We were destined not to visit Dorset again. Mother was growing older and the journey was too long for her.

Never-the-less we continued to visit Norfolk where Cousin Ralph kindly allowed us to use his bungalow. The journey only took about three and a half hours including a stop at the picnic area at Brandon Creek. A lovely spot by the river.

As Rebecca turned off the road into the picnic area Tess, recognising where she was, instantly became excited in anticipation of a rest, drink, meal and good walk. Once the car was safely tucked up in the little car park Tessa eagerly clambered out of the front passenger door, trotted over to the white rail barrier crawled underneath it, up the grassy slope where the picnic tables are scattered, to the path running along the top of the embankment by the water. This being one of the many occasions when a retractable lead is a godsend, allowing a dog to enjoy the freedom of roaming in safety.

In 1984 Cousin Ralph married again and a year later he and his new wife Joan retired and moved into their bungalow. This meant if we wanted to continue visiting Hunstanton we must find somewhere to stay, somewhere where dogs would be welcome. Not only did Mother and I, being of Norfolk origin, love the area but Tessa thoroughly enjoyed the sands, sea and cliff-top walks. We were also very fond of Cousin Ralph so to continue taking a holiday in Hunstanton meant still being able to see him.

Eventually through another Kodak retiree living in the town, we contacted Eileen and Terry Flowerdew who ran a small family hotel only a few minutes walk from the front. They both loved animals and were only too happy to accept Tessa. Rebecca being by now almost a classic car Terry kindly offered to relinquish his parking place in the grassy alleyway between their cottage and the house next door.

The first time we stayed at Kiama Cottage we felt so at home it was almost as though we had been there many times in the past. Eileen and Terry made such a fuss of Tessa who responded with her usual warmth and affection. Her bed was put next to mine in the twin room so she felt secure when she was left during our meal times. After dinner each evening she was allowed into the lounge with us where, having greeted any other guests, she curled up or stretched out on the rug in front of the fire. Her days were always full so she slept soundly both during the evening and at night. Her early morning and her last walk at night took us either down the road to the sea front or up the road, round the block through the deep silence so typical of small Norfolk towns and villages.

One Sunday afternoon towards the end of June, a few weeks prior to a visit to Kiama Cottage, Mother was sitting at home in her armchair by the fireplace, I was on the sofa and Tessa was sitting quietly in the other armchair sleeping. She had enjoyed a busy day and that afternoon had been chasing around in the park with one of her friends a lovable retriever named Fred. They had thoroughly enjoyed themselves. Now she slept peacefully.

Suddenly a screech escaped from Tessa as her eyes opened, her legs shot rigidly straight out in front of her, claws and fingers stretched as she sucked her lips while trying desperately to swallow.

Panic stricken I leapt from the sofa to the floor in front of her, automatically asking her what was wrong. I stroked her head gently, speaking re-assuringly to her while fighting to control the violent urges of fear and alarm rising inside me. Whatever could this be. Keep calm. See what happens.

After what seemed like an eternity but in reality was probably only a minute or two, Tessa quietened. Her legs relaxing, her eyes returning to their normal size though still containing a look of bewildered puzzlement.

Should I call Wood Street or wait till the morning? Tessa, though exhausted appeared to have recovered. I would watch over her carefully during the night and consult Mr Winwood first thing in the morning. She slept soundly the rest of the evening and throughout the night.

Monday morning first thing, I rang the hospital, explained what had happened and asked if Mr Winwood would be kind enough to call – which he did just after 11am. By now Tessa was quite her old self again. Never-the-less Mr Winwood examined her thoroughly, asked numerous questions then lent forward in his chair before giving his opinion. It could have been a mild heart attack or even a very slight stroke. The main thing was that she had recovered seeming none the worse for her experience. Of course there was a strong possibility it could happen again. I had done all the right things. As when she had collapsed in the park it was essential to keep calm, speak softly calling her name while stroking her gently.

After explaining further the various possibilities of what may have physically happened, Mr Winwood prescribed further medication telling me not to hesitate to ring him again should I be still worried.

Two and a half weeks later, on the 9 July, Tessa had another attack as Mr Winwood had predicted. This time she was sitting in the hall. The symptoms were identical to those she had suffered on the previous occasion. I rang Wood Street immediately though I knew there was nothing more at this stage they could do but somehow telling them gave me confidence. If Tessa did not recover as quickly as last time I was to take her up to the hospital. Fortunately she did and, as before, slept soundly the rest of the day and night through till morning.

Between attacks Tess was fine, in fact you would never know there was anything amiss with her. For a while all was well. No more attacks of any kind.

We booked a week with Eileen and Terry in Hunstanton, it would be good to get away for a few days. On a regular check-up visit to Wood Street Mr Winwood kindly looked up the name and address of the veterinary surgeon nearest to Hunstanton, a Mr Haverson who had a surgery a few miles down the road in Heacham. Hopefully we would not require his services but better safe than sorry.

Eileen and Terry were very sorry to hear Tessa had not been well, they had become very fond of her and she of them.

The first few days of the holiday were fine. The weather was kind so Tess was able to enjoy runs on the beach, paddles in the sea and tea and biscuits with Cousin Ralph. An ideal holiday.

The morning of the fourth day I was awoken by strange noises coming from Tessa's bed, which was on the floor next to mine. Oh no – poor Tessie, she was having another attack. At least now I knew how to cope with these fits. If only we were not so far away from home – should I increase her tablets? As soon as Tess had calmed down again I left her in Mother's care, hurriedly dressed, quietly crept downstairs, out of the front door in search of the nearest telephone box. In retrospect it would have been better to ask Eileen if I could ring from Kiama Cottage but it was early and I did not want to disturb anyone.

By the time I had found a 'phone box, spoken with Mr Winwood – who advised increasing Tessa's tablet by half a one a day – and returned to Kiama Cottage Eileen and Terry were preparing the dining room for breakfast. They were both very distressed to hear Tessa had been poorly again and asked if they could do anything for her. It was kind of them but she would be fine again after a good sleep.

Breakfast over, Mother and I took Tessa down to the cliff top in the car so she could rest quietly.

When we eventually returned to our room later in the day there, sitting in the corner of Tessa's bed was a large parcel wrapped in tissue paper with a gift card attached. Whatever could this be?

Tess was instantly interested – this was obviously for her as it was in her bed. The card read "We are so sorry you have been poorly and do hope you will soon be much better – love Eileen and Terry". Tessie's nose was all over the parcel – her tail wagging like mad. So anxious was she to see the contents I could not tear the paper off quickly enough. Her head kept turning up towards my face with big excited eyes that said as clearly as though they spoke "Come on Mum – hurry up".

At last the parcel was unwrapped to reveal the most beautiful, soft white, fluffy 16 inch teddy bear. He was gorgeous! His face round and smiling, the end of his nose and his forelock tinted a soft light sandy colour and two big black eyes nestling amongst the deep white fur. Tessa could not believe her own eyes. She looked from teddy to me, back again then once more at teddy, hardly able to believe this wonderful creature was really for her! She climbed into her bed and lay down putting her paws across teddy to acknowledge possession of him.

How very, very kind, what a generous gift. Mother and I were as overwhelmed as Tess. We would call teddy "Terry". Immediately we went downstairs to thank Eileen and Terry and tell them the name teddy had been given.

From that day onwards Terry went everywhere with Tessa. He was played with, shaken, cuddled, taken out in the car and always taken to bed at night.

Tessa enjoyed the remainder of the holiday without further mishap and when we arrived home I took her for a routine check-up with Mr Winwood. Once again, there were no obvious ill affects as a result of her attack.

Life quickly returned to normal.

Chapter LXXV

In 1985 the computer company I worked for had closed its local branch and I had, once again, taken voluntary severance. The thought of moving right away from everyone and everything I knew did not appeal to me. However I was fortunate in obtaining a new position only a mile from home with a printing firm. It meant taking a drop of £2,500 a year but this was preferable to being unemployed for a long time and was more convenient for looking after Mother.

Shortly after joining the firm and with the kind help and encouragement of Sid Kenton the owner and an outstanding craftsman in the world of artwork, photography and printing, I began my own business in conjunction with my employers. Having purchased my own Word Processor I undertook typing of all kinds including basic artwork. In time this enabled me to work part-time for Sid and part-time at home. Though "part-time" could easily mean working until 2 or 3 in the morning!

Having found and for some years used the services of Enfield Autos and Enfield Garages, Bill Medcalf the proprietor, was kind enough to give me some of his personal work which I undertook on a Saturday morning. This meant no longer being able to take Tessa to Grovelands Park, which was disappointing. However we soon found our way round this obstacle by re-arranging our weekly programme.

On Sunday mornings Tessa and I would drive Mother to the church in Freston Gardens then, having seen her safely into the vestibule where her friend Dorothy took care of her, Tessa and I drove to Grovelands to enjoy an hours run – hopefully in the sunshine! Whether winter or summer the peace and tranquillity of the grounds was breathtaking. That is until, having walked across the fields, through the wood and along beside the lake, listening to the birds singing and the ducks chattering, the peace was shattered by the loud morose clanging of church bells. Never very fond of bells at the best of times my dislike of them intensified as a result of their unwarranted intrusion into the serenity of those Sunday morning walks.

Chapter LXXVI

Sunday afternoons Tessa and I often walked to Oakwood Park taking a gentle stroll across the fields to the far side of the park and back. On one such stroll, as we ambled towards the top field, a little black dog about the same size as Tess, with elegantly feathered soft, silky fur spotted Tess from some 200 yards away and scampered across to greet her. As he drew near Tessa became alert. Eyes laughing, head held high, tail erect she watched his approach with obvious delight. The little dog came to a halt a few feet in front of Tess as the two eyed each other with mutual admiring interest.

Suddenly they bounced into life, chasing each other round in ever increasing circles, up the hill, round the trees then back again. This was wonderful! They had both found a delightful new friend. Both seemed enchanted.

Into view, approaching across the field, came a young man in his early twenties calling to "Mutley". The two new pals being the only dogs in sight he must be referring to the little black dog. Mutley's attention attracted, he turned to look at his master, ran back to him then immediately returned to Tess who watched the whole procedure with an aire of expectancy on her face.

John and I introduced ourselves, both expressing pleasure in the delight Tess and Mutley had obviously found in each other's company. John was thrilled Mutley had at last found a special friend and of his own size. Jenny, Tessa's pal of several years had recently had to move away from the area with her owner, so I was equally pleased Tess had found another playmate with whom she could build a lasting relationship. The foundation had been firmly laid; if further proof were necessary Mutley provided it by licking Tessa's face all over. She loved this and almost glowed with pleasure.

Having stood still watching the pals playing for about a quarter of an hour John and I began to head off towards the entrance Tess and I had come in. John lived at the junction of Prince George and Sherringham Avenues sited only a short distance away. Though he had entered the park via a side gate he was only too willing to walk across the fields to the far entrance. To curtail the friends fun unnecessarily early would be a shame. What were they doing now? Both dogs were standing on their hind legs having a gentle boxing match while their tails wagged nineteen to the dozen!

Apparently John usually took Mutley to Trent Park during the week only coming to Oakwood on a Sunday so we agreed to meet about the same time – 2.15pm – the following week to enable Tessa and Mutley to play together again.

On Monday, having walked through the little copse, down the path, through the hedge and into the top half of the bottom field Tessa stopped, tail up, head erect expectantly looking around obviously wandering if Mutley would be there again today. I noticed with interest she made no attempt to look for him until we passed through the hedge and into the bottom field where we had found him the day before. Naturally there was no sign of Mutley. Realising this, Tessa's ears went down the same time as her tail drooped. She looked up at me with a downcast yet enquiring expression on her face as if trying to ask "Where is he Mum – where is my new friend"? "Tessa dear – Mutley will not be here today – he will be here next week though and you can play together again like you did yesterday. Yes Tessie, I promise you he *will* be here but not today. "Gently I stroked her head while trying to explain to her. She looked up at me with big trusting eyes. However much she had actually understood I could not then tell but my words had undoubtedly reassured her as she perked up and trotted off in search of one of her "everyday" playmates.

The week passed, for me at least, quite quickly. Though she had a quick look around each day when we went to the park Tess appeared to accept Mutley's absence.

Sunday came round again. I had told Mother about last week's encounter explaining Tess had a 2.15 appointment that afternoon in the park.

As we sat down at the table to have our dinner Tessa became unusually restless. She walked backwards and forwards in front of the window, jumped up on her carver, onto the window-sill, back onto the carver, up to me, this way and that. Whatever was the matter with her?

Surely she could not know it was Sunday, the day for her assignation? Perhaps she *did* realise it was Sunday – not of course by name but our routine was different from the rest of the week. Could it be she understood what this meant?

The instant we had finished eating and left the table Tessa dashed into the hall dancing about with excitement – she hardly knew how to contain herself! She *did* know it was the day!

When ready at last to set off for the park Tess pulled on her lead as hard as she could, continuing to do so the whole way there. Something she rarely, if ever, did.

Once through the gate and over the roadbridge I unclipped her lead while she strained to be free. She was away! Through the copse, down the path, through the hedge into "their field". By the time I caught up with her she was tearing headlong across the field, her tail going in circles, while Mutley raced towards her from the far side.

This was amazing. The dogs were like reunited lovers. Their tails wagged crazily while they licked each other's faces all over, laughing and dancing in sheer delight!

Tessa was in love!

John was as surprised and pleased as I was to see how joyfully the two dogs greeted each other. He told me Mutley had behaved very oddly for an hour before they left home. He had been very restless and had driven John mad "asking" to go out for his walk. Like Tessa, once on the lead he had pulled hard all the way to the park. As soon as he was released Mutley had raced full pelt into the field where he'd met Tess last week. Exactly the same extraordinary behaviour as Tess had displayed. We both agreed there was no doubt our two canine wonders had known it was "the day" and could not wait to meet again.

Having allowed Tessa and Mutley to play for best part of an hour, we made our way out of the park and up the road to the junction with Merryvale where our ways parted. John and Mutley went to the right while Tessa and I turned left. All the way along the pavement Tess and Mutley were playing as they walked. When it was time to go our separate ways the two dogs stood still for a moment just looking at each other. Then, as we made tracks for home Tessa kept turning around to look back at Mutley as he and John slowly disappeared. We later heard Mutley had behaved similarly until they eventually rounded the corner and were lost to sight.

Each visit to the park the following week, Tessa glanced round in case Mutley should appear, just as she had the day after they first met. Having established he was not there she ran and played quite happily as usual.

However, come Sunday the previous week's pattern of events was repeated. Tessa's restless behaviour immediately before and during our mealtime; her excited anticipation waiting for me to get ready for our walk then pulling on the lead as hard as she possibly could in her anxiety to reach the park. Following the, now usual, route to the bottom field Tessa stopped and looked around – Mutley had not arrived yet. Anxious to reach the top end of the field and Mutley as quickly as possible, Tess set off at a trot. Before she was halfway across the open space a black image appeared at the far side, running like the wind in our direction. As soon as the two dogs met they danced round and round each other, Mutley licked Tessa's face then off they went chasing and playing as though the interim week had never been.

Once again, at the end of their hour and our walk up the road, they were loathed to leave each other. As had happened the previous week, both dogs kept looking round to watch the other until they were finally hidden from view.

The obvious happiness the two dogs enjoyed as a result of meeting and becoming devoted friends was reflected in the enormous pleasure John and I received from seeing them together.

For best part of two months the four of us met in Oakwood Park every Sunday. Never did the two dogs devotion to each other wane. Each week Tessa displayed the same excited, restless anticipation until she and Mutley were once again playing together. They were wonderful times I shall never forget.

Then one Sunday we arrived in the bottom field and waited and waited and waited but there was no sign of either Mutley or John.

Tessa could not believe they were not going to come – nor could I for that matter. She kept looking across the field then up at me with a pleading look on her face. Where is he Mum? Gradually her ears went down, her tail drooped between her legs and her eyes developed a sad, soulful expression.

We waited until nearly 3 o'clock by which time it was obvious our friends would not be appearing. I tried to comfort Tess by stroking her gently while telling her there must be a good reason why Mutley and John had not come. Maybe something had cropped up at home. Maybe either Mutley or John were unwell. I was sure they would be there next Sunday.

If only Tessa could understand what I was saying but alas she was dreadfully crestfallen and walked slowly all the way home with her tail down. That evening she would not eat her supper nor the next morning would she eat her breakfast. Watching her fret was tearing me to pieces and knowing there was nothing I could do to help her made things worse.

Through the following week Tessa gradually perked up then began eating again. Maybe she was thinking about the coming Sunday and hoping Mutley would be in the park as usual.

Come Sunday, Tess was once again excited and anxious to be off to Oakwood Park. Something untoward must have happened last week – Mutley would be sure to be there this week. All would be well.

Once again we waited in the field in vain. My poor Tessa. She looked so dejected. Nothing I did nor said could change the expression on her face or bring her ears or tail up again. If she could cry she would.

We walked slowly home and Tess laid down on the lounge carpet with her head on her paws, her eyes just staring blindly ahead.

Tess did not eat for several days then only very little. It was heartbreaking to see her. By now I was beginning to wonder whether perhaps John did not want to continue with what had become a routine, instead had taken Mutley elsewhere for his Sunday afternoon walk. As neither of us knew exactly where the other lived there was no way of communicating.

The following Sunday I felt there was little hope of Mutley and John coming to the park. Never-the-less we went along at 2.15pm just in case. Alas, there was no sign of them. Tessa was very down in spirits. I tried to explain Mutley would be here if he could but he could not come on his own and obviously now John had other plans. She must not blame Mutley or think badly of him – it was not his fault he was not able to come to see her. If only I could make her understand but nothing I could do or say would cheer her up.

Six weeks passed before we saw Mutley and John again. It was a warm summer's evening and we had been enjoying a walk round the park. Tessa, as usual willing to play with any dog large or small who would join in the fun. Eventually it was time to go home for dinner.

We walked up through the little copse, along the pathway over the roadbridge towards the gate. Several dogs were just coming in with their owners including a large silky black dog built something like a red setter, named Bruno. Despite his attempts to say "good evening" to Tess, she took no notice, just carried on her way.

I felt sorry for Bruno because he was such a lovely dog with a truly gentle, kindly nature.

Having passed through the gate we made our way homeward. About 50 yards up the road who should be coming towards us but Mutley and John. As soon as Mutley spotted Tessa he could not contain his excitement. He pulled and pulled on the lead until he was level with Tess then licked her face all over. His tail wagging frenziedly while his feet danced this way and that with sheer uncontrollable pleasure at seeing his friend again.

"Oh look Tessa, it's Mutley. It's your friend". Tessa looked but put her head in the air and tried to walk straight past up the road. Astounded I could not believe her reaction. She adored Mutley. She

167

had fretted and pined for him so much – surely she must be overwhelmed at seeing him again? How could she ignore him – ignore his obvious delight; all the attention he was giving her. Poor Mutley he was totally unperturbed by Tessa's indifference to him. He was so delighted to see her. He kept pulling towards her to lick her face – to show how pleased he was to see her again.

As John was on his way into the park I decided to turn around and go back with him. I knew Tess had been very deeply hurt but she must realise it was not Mutley's fault. She would soon come round. Within no time the two would be playing happily together.

As we walked down the road Mutley continued to give Tessa all his attention despite the cold shoulder he was receiving from her. We approached the gate as Bruno was coming through with his dad. To my utter astonishment Tessa ran up to him wriggling, wagging her tail and looking up into his face. She was deliberately flirting with Bruno in front of Mutley! She had always ignored Bruno – never played with him – taken absolutely no notice of him. She had even ignored him five minutes ago on our way out of the park when he had tried to be friendly. Now, she was behaving like a love-sick teenager!

Mutley just stood still and looked. I felt so sorry for him – so embarrassed yet at the same time so completely dumbfounded by Tessa's astonishingly human behaviour. She was punishing Mutley for letting her down. For hurting her so deeply.

Although we never again met Mutley and John in the park we did bump into them once or twice when walking round the roads. Each time Mutley displayed delight at seeing Tessa, wanting to lick her face and play. Tess, on the other hand, would not be won round. She grudgingly acknowledged him, condescendingly giving him a lick but always holding back with her affection and pleasure. Could it be she never forgave him or was it simply that she had been hurt so badly she was not prepared to give way to her true feelings and risk being hurt again? What-ever the reason I am sure she inwardly retained great affection for Mutley.

Chapter LXXVII

The idea gradually came into my mind that perhaps Tessa would like another dog in the house for company. There was no doubt she loved other dogs. In comparison with the sight of two or more dogs going for a walk with their owner, a solitary dog presented rather a sad picture. Surely a dog, no matter how much it may love it's "Mum" or "Dad", must yearn for the companionship of a canine house-mate? After all a human being living, no matter how happily, in a world of alien beings must long for another human. Admittedly there are some dogs who need to be the only dog in a home but generally speaking the company of their own kind must be preferable? I would send the thought out into the ether and let it develop as it will.

The weeks passed by and Tessa's booster became due so up to Mr Winwood we went. Tessa never grew accustomed to the Hospital. Always she would sit either on my lap or at my feet visibly trembling violently from head to tail. There was no logical reason for her fear – it could only be the smell of clinical cleanliness or her sensitivity picking up the suffering of other animals who had passed through the doors.

Whatever the reason, Tessa always commanded a great deal of sympathy from the staff and the owners of other patients waiting to be seen. However, despite the number of kind words and gentle strokes she received, nothing would ever calm her.

Her booster successfully given we drove home again only to find fresh blood on her coat where the needle had entered. After telephoning Wood Street I turned Rebecca round and we once again headed for Barnet. By now the noise and bustle of the rush hour was beginning.

Mr Winwood kindly saw Tessa when we arrived. There was nothing too drastic – a burst blood vessel, it was clearing up nicely already. He cleaned the area then applied a small bandage. All would be well.

I picked Tessa up to carry her out of the surgery while Mr Winwood held the door open but Tess had had enough for today. As we moved into the entrance hall she struggled and wriggled like a tiger. Seeing my predicament, a lady sitting nearby kindly opened the front door for me.

This was an even greater incentive to Tessa to escape! She struggled so hard I was unable to hold her and she shot out of my arms down the front path as fast as she could. The front gate was open! Straight through the gate Tessa went out into the rush hour traffic in Wood Street. Realising what was about to happen I let out an involuntary yell while tearing after her down the path. Two nurses, who had also seen Tessa jump and run towards the open gate, tore down the path behind me.

Fortunately the traffic was so heavy it was virtually at a standstill. There was Tessa, not knowing which way to turn, standing stock still in front of a car!

I made a grab for her as the driver opened his door and got out. He had seen Tessa run out of the gate and, because he was barely moving, had managed to slam the brakes on in the nick of time. His attention was then caught by the three of us running frantically out onto the pavement behind Tessa.

Was ever a girl cuddled so tightly? I thanked both the driver and the nurses profusely before putting Tess into Rebecca. Poor Mother had been sitting in the car and saw Tess run out into the roadway but, the doors being security locked, could do nothing but watch in horror.

Thank heavens Tessa was safe. This was the second time she had run out in front of a vehicle and survived – memories of Oakwood Park when sudden thunder had panicked her into running across the field into the road in front of a taxi, came flooding back. Dad had certainly been looking after her once again.

Another animal had a lucky escape with a car, this time our car. The Morris Marina and a subsequent Riley Elf both having served me well but eventually, having given their all as my "going to work car", had gone to the rest home for tired motor cars in the sky! I was obliged to acquire another second car for travelling to work. Rebecca was much too good to be used as a "workhorse". I had therefore purchased, with the guidance of Bill Medcalf, a 1971 Morris Minor, an ex-police Panda car. She needed quite a lot of work to get her through the MOT but had proved worth the effort and served the purpose well.

Tessa and I would drive into Oakwood Park, over the railbridge then park alongside the wire fencing separating the embankment and land above owned by London Transport from the park owned by Enfield Council. For as long as I can remember cars have parked along this short stretch of road crossing the railway line. There is enough room for about 20 cars though through the winter months and in the early morning or late evening, about half a dozen, at most, are usually to be found and those mainly belonging to dog owners.

One particular morning, there being no other cars parked here, we drove down to the end of the wire, parking Moggie (the accepted nickname for a Morris Minor) at the end of the track where the park itself begins. Making sure she was securely locked, Tessa and I set off towards the copse.

We spent about half an hour walking round the fields, through the spinney then back up the path towards the little copse. As we approached the wooded area a neighbour of ours, who was exercising his German Shepherd, came out from the trees calling excitedly to us and waving his arms. From that distance it was not possible to hear clearly what he was saying – something about our car? Whatever could have happened now? Surely it had not been broken into while we were in the fields? So often this happens when cars are left unattended but surely not so early in the morning – it was still only a quarter to eight.

As Eric drew nearer I could see he was very agitated about something. Apparently a cat had been frightened by a dog and shot up under Moggie's mudguards into the main body of the car. Several people had tried to reach the cat without success so had gone on their way. Eric was worried that if he didn't manage to catch me I would, not knowing about the cat, get into the car and start the engine. Then it would certainly be goodbye pussy!

Hurrying back to Moggie I opened up the bonnet but alas, no sign of puss. Maybe the cat had come down again? Then Eric spotted her curled up at the very back of the works, between the engine and the bodywork, covered in oil. She was only tiny – a beautiful tortoiseshell kitten. She was obviously extremely frightened as each time one of us put a hand round the engine in an attempt to grab her she squeezed further back away from us.

What were we going to do? Maybe one of the Council gardeners or workmen could help. The offices and yard were only a short distance away, the other side of the copse.

While Tessa sat in Moggie and Eric kept watch by her open bonnet I ran through the little copse to find help. One of the men were bound to know how to extract the kitten.

As luck would have it, two or three groundsmen were just coming out of the yard. Once they heard of the kitten's plight they were only too eager to offer whatever help they could give and came with me straight away, back to Moggie.

By this time a lovely lady named Rae who lives, with her sister Lily, just across the road from the park came along. Rae and Lily are very genuine animal lovers not only sharing their home with a motley assortment of dogs, cats, birds, fish, rabbits, guinea pigs, hamsters and, at one time, even a goat but always willing to take in and look after any stray or unwanted animal. At this present time they had five dogs to be walked in the park twice or three times a day hence Rae's appearance at this time of the morning.

Having explained the situation to Rae she joined the groundsmen in their attempts to encourage kitty out of her hideaway. The more everyone tried to move kitty the more securely she became wedged in.

All the groundsmen were big, strong men yet they were so gentle in their approach to the kitten, demonstrating such caring and tenderness for the little creature. On a lighter note, one of the men jokingly remarked "you now have your own catalytic converter fitted!".

After nearly half an hour we were becoming desperate. Whatever were we to do? There was no way I could leave the car there as I had to get to work. I was already nearly three quarters of an hour late. Would Sid believe the excuse "Sorry I am late. A cat ran up under my bonnet!"?

Mother would be getting worried and Tessa was wanting her breakfast. She had sat patiently in the car all this time, without so much as a murmur.

Probably because it had been left alone for several minutes, suddenly the kitten freed itself and crawled out from it's hiding place. One of the men grabbed it before it had a chance to go into rapid reverse. What a relief! Safe at last.

None of us had ever seen her before – had no idea where she had come from. What were we going to do with her? Of course – Rae! With a resigned smile on her face Rae agreed to take the little kitten and, if no one answered the notice she would put up, she and Lily would give her a good home. She would call the kitten Phoebe.

No one came forward to claim Phoebe so the lucky little kitten found an excellent home with Rae, Lily and their many rescued animals where she still lives happily to this day.

Chapter LXXVIII

With increased traffic, finding somewhere to park Moggie behind the shops in Southgate had become quite a problem. The only solution was to use the multi-storey car park just across the road from the rear of the parade. A small open car park had been built behind our shops but this was private property for the sole use of the new offices built on the site of the old cinema on the next block. A low wall surrounded three quarters of the area with short iron posts and chains at the entrance and exit points.

Going home to lunch one February day I passed the private car park and saw a beautiful black dog with a small white blaze down his chest, rather like a labrador but slightly smaller, tied to one of the posts at the car park entrance. Presumably someone had left him there while they popped somewhere for a few minutes. I spoke gently to him, saying hello and telling him how beautiful he was. His coat shone. Personally I could never leave a dog tied up like that but maybe he was used to it. He seemed very good. He was not barking, crying or straining on the rope tied to his collar and connecting him to the post.

Feeling sorry for him I went home to take Tessa for a walk in the park and to have lunch.

An hour later I returned to work only to find the black dog still sitting patiently tied to the post. This was awful. How could anyone leave a dog for so long? Again I went over and spoke to him. "Hello. You are a beautiful boy aren't you. What's your name? You're a real Blackie aren't you?".

Bless him, he lifted his face up to mine and looked up at me with the biggest, gentlest brown eyes I have ever seen. He was adorable. I would keep an eye on him. He was not very far from the rear entrance of the printers where I worked. By opening the back door and standing on the top step I could see him. Surely someone would collect him soon.

An hour later I looked out and there he was – still sitting patiently. He had been there at least two and a half hours now, to my knowledge. For the next hour I looked out at him regularly, once or twice going down to speak with him. I could not leave him there, he must come into the shop with me. Sid was on holiday but he would not mind anyway. Jonathon liked dogs though I wasn't so sure about Trevor. I would keep Blackie close by my side – he would be alright. Naturally the police had to be informed but it did not seem likely anyone would claim him. If his owners loved him they would never have tied him up and left him.

Without saying a word to my two colleagues I went round to the car park, untied Blackie and brought him in through the rear entrance of the shop. Jonathon said hello to him kindly but poor Trevor nearly had a fit but there was no way I was taking Blackie out again, if no one came for him by 6 o'clock Blackie was coming home with me. Tessa would not mind – she loved other dogs.

Having telephoned the police, who made a note of all the details, I kept Blackie with me on his length of blue rope. He sat quietly at my feet while I discussed printing orders with clients; he walked up and down behind the counter with me; sat quietly while I wrote out jobs and enjoyed a biscuit and dish of water when I had a cup of tea.

While he was very good with me and clung to me, he did not seem too sure of other people. The afternoon passed and at the end of the day there had been no word from the police concerning his owners. That was it. He was definitely coming home.

Having packed up my belongings and locked up the shop I walked Blackie over to the multi-storey car park. John, the attendant – a very softly spoken Irish gentleman – was delighted to see Blackie. John loves all animals and was disgusted to hear how Blackie had been tied up and abandoned. He spoke gently to Blackie then tried to stroke him but obviously Blackie was not too sure as, though he wagged his tail, he warned John off with a show of his teeth. Poor boy, he had been through an unhappy experience today – no wonder he was unsure of everyone and everything, though he seemed to trust me.

We walked up to the car and I opened the door for Blackie to jump in. There was no response. He just looked at me, then at the open door then back at me with an enquiring expression on his face. To encourage him I patted the front passenger seat while telling him to "Come on Blackie, up here. Theres a good boy. Come on – up". He understood what was expected of him but had obviously never been in a car before. He jumped in and sat down but facing the wrong way – he had his back to the windscreen and was facing towards the rear window. Laughing, I turned him round, started the engine and moved towards the exit.

Poor Blackie – what was happening to him? Ohhhhhhh the "room" he was in was moving around! He was being tilted to one side! Hang on for dear life – the "room" was gathering speed! Similar "rooms", people, buildings, were all rushing passed the windows. This was a very strange and new experience! In an attempt to calm him I spoke re-assuringly to him all the way home.

As usual Tessa was sitting on the windowsill so, having driven onto the driveway, I quickly shut the car door leaving Blackie inside while I greeted Tessa, then shut her in the dining room while I brought Blackie indoors.

Mother was horrified exclaiming that we could not possibly keep Blackie. Well, I would worry about that later. First things first, give Blackie a good meal.

Shutting him in the lounge I opened a tin of Chum, emptied it into a dish and took it into him with a bowl of water. Before I could blink the whole meal had vanished! He was obviously famished so I gave him another dish full of meat which vanished as quickly as the first. To give him more just now would be foolish and probably make him sick – he should have another helping later. Come to think of it he was rather on the lean side, his ribs could be seen quite clearly.

Mother was still upset. To be fair, she was 85 years of age and regrettably in the early stages of Alzheimers Disease. She was not over anxious to have a second, larger dog in the house. Battersea would take him and find him a really good home.

While I took Tessa for a short walk Mother telephoned the police. As Tessa and I arrived home a police lady was putting Blackie into a panda car and then drove off before I could catch her. My heart sank.

Mother was adamant it was the best for Blackie. Now money was not so plentiful we could not really afford to keep another dog – it would not be fair to Tessa etc. etc. Maybe she was right. Maybe I was being selfish in wanting to keep him.

All that evening he was on my mind. Next morning I telephoned the police station to enquire about him. For some reason the Battersea collection van had not called. They would telephone and re-book the van for the following morning. It usually arrived about 7.30am.

During the course of the day I rang again to ask how Blackie was. Yes, he was fine. He'd had a good meal and was settled in the kennel.

That night I tossed, turned, worried and made a decision. First thing in the morning Tessa and I would be off to the police station to collect Blackie before the Battersea van arrived!

I was up at the crack of dawn, dressed and with Tessa beside me drove through to Southgate. Tessa was excited because of the tension I was generating – something was afoot.

As we drove along I told Tessa she must listen to me carefully. We were going to see a poor dog who needed a good home. I still loved Tessa as much as ever. The decision on whether or not Blackie came home to live with us and be part of our family depended entirely on her. She loved other dogs and it would be nice for her to have a companion and friend of her own but it was up to her. If she liked him then we would bring him home with us. If she did not take to him, he would go in the van to Battersea from where he would be found a good home.

Tessa looked at me the whole time I was speaking, listening attentively. Her extreme intelligence had been manifesting itself more and more so I felt it was very important she understood what I was trying to tell her.

We arrived at the police station, parked outside and rushed into the reception area. It was still not quite 7 o'clock. The officer behind the desk assured us the black dog was still outside in the kennel in the yard. The van was not due for another half an hour or so.

After explaining the situation, I asked if Tessa and I could please see Blackie? We were shown through the station into a concrete yard where there were two large concrete "kennels" with strong metal mesh in front which doubled as a door.

What a dreadful looking place. Cold, damp and miserable with only a water bowl and a mucky piece of what can only be described as "rag" for bedding.

Blackie came to the mesh as soon as he saw us come into the yard. Tessa was on a lead just as a precaution. I need not have worried. The two dogs wagged their tails vigorously while they rubbed noses through the mesh. They took to each other immediately. The feeling was clearly mutual.

Thank heavens – that was it – Blackie was coming home with us. From now on he was part of our family.

Telling Blackie we would be back for him in a few minutes, Tessa and I went through into the station again to complete the paperwork. The date was the 14th February – a very appropriate day for Tessa and I to adopt "our boy".

For ease of access Tess and I then drove round into Crown Lane at the rear entrance of the station. Both of us filled with excited anticipation, we left the car and made our way from the road directly into the police yard where the officer was waiting for us. I had brought Kimmy's old lead in the hope Blackie would be coming home with us.

He was still wearing the unusual metal double chain link collar he had on when I found him, so clipping on the lead was no problem.

I could hardly contain my excitement. I had already begun to love him dearly and knew Tessa was heading in the same direction, if she had not already arrived!

With Tessa trotting along beside, I led Blackie out to the car and popped him onto the back seat while Tessa jumped into the front. Her little face was literally beaming – she was happy so I was happy. Blackie was going to be very happy too.

Rather than drive straight home, I went round to see Rae and Lily in Lakenheath to introduce Blackie to them. They were enchanted, despite his warning them off when they tried to stroke him. The sisters are used to animals who are nervous so understood. While there they kindly let me use their telephone to call Mr Winwood before he began his morning consultations. Would he please call round to examine Blackie, make sure all was well and give his opinion? Surprised at the news, he agreed willingly to call after surgery that morning. I'd have to have a days leave from work – that would be no bother as Trevor was in again today so there was ample staff cover.

Mother opened the front door as we drove onto the driveway. Her face was a picture as she caught sight of Blackie climbing out of the car. I hadn't known her all my life without understanding it takes her a little while to adjust to something or someone new. Tessa and I already loved Blackie and with his enormous, soft appealing eyes Mother would be putty in his paws before very long.

Tessa was quite happy for Blackie to come straight into the house. Once there, he was not quite sure what to do. He stood in the hall looking firstly at me, then at Mother, then at Tessa.

None of us had eaten breakfast so the first thing to do was to feed both dogs, Mother, then myself. Tessa's food and water bowl were on the little ledge beside the sink where Kim's bowls had stood. There was no room for another bowl there so the best place to put Blackie's was on the backdoor mat. I would buy him a large bowl of his own at the first opportunity. Meanwhile here he would have plenty of room without being trodden on.

I showed him where the water bowl was then took down a large tin of Chum. Blackie sat patiently watching while I emptied the contents into the two bowls. Tessa began eating immediately – this had been a busy, exciting morning. Makes a girl hungry!

Placing Blackie's bowl on the mat I called him over, telling him the food was for him – he was a good boy. Bless him, he looked up at me, wagged his tail then plunged his muzzle into the bowl finishing the contents before Tessa was half-way through hers.

176

After we had all breakfasted, Mother had arranged to go shopping so I decided to take Tessa and Blackie round the block before Mr Winwood came. Tess thought this was wonderful. All the way down the road she kept turning to look at Blackie as if unable to believe her luck at finding a such a super companion. Blackie looked straight ahead, pulling hard on the lead, eager to get where-ever we were going. However, when we came to a curb he stopped, sat and waited. Obviously someone, at some time had given him basic training. Anxious to introduce Blackie to the house properly, we only went round the short block. To my amazement Blackie did not need to be told which house was ours. When we reached the front gate, he was still pulling hard and ahead of Tess, he turned straight onto our path without any hesitation. Not just handsome and patient but very intelligent as well!

There was just time, before Mr Winwood was due, to take Blackie over the house then out into the back garden. Naturally Tess came too! Blackie sat patiently at the bottom of the stairs making no attempt to follow us up. Either he had not been allowed upstairs or had lived somewhere without them. He was one of our family now so he could come up and down whenever he liked. He would, of course, sleep upstairs anyway.

Surprised yet delighted at being coaxed up, Blackie stood on the landing waiting to be told what to do next. He looked at Tessa to see what she was going to do. Gently I encouraged him "Come on Blackie – come and have a look round your new home". We went into every room. While Tessa trotted about, Blackie had a very polite sniff here and there as though he were on his best behaviour. He still seemed very nervous.

The garden was next on the agenda. Blackie seemed reluctant to go outside. Once again, he needed to be cajoled into the adventure. Then as soon as I turned round to come back indoors Blackie was there ahead of me.

Just after 11 o'clock the doorbell rang. Both Tessa and Blackie ran out into the hall, Tessa barking loudly while Blackie stood still looking at the door. Mr Winwood said hello to Tess then a kindly hello to Blackie who backed away, turned and ran into the lounge ahead of us. I explained Blackie's story to Mr Winwood who listened intently. Unfortunately, Blackie would not let Mr Winwood too near and showed his teeth when a friendly hand was offered. It was becoming patently obvious Blackie was afraid of hands – the poor boy must have been repeatedly hit by his previous owners to be so afraid.

Never-the-less Mr Winwood was able to give him a visual examination declaring that he was a beautiful dog with a lovely shining coat. He

177

was a little on the thin side as his ribs were showing through. He was probably a mixture of labrador and something. He needed feeding up but apart from that, as far as he could tell, Blackie seemed to be in good condition. Mr Winwood considered Blackie to be about five or six years of age, no more. Standing 21 inches high, his legs measure 16 inches which gives his body the appearance of balancing on top of his legs. His straight black tail, measuring a good 14 inches, looked enormous standing out behind him and woebetide anyone who was too near when Blackie's tail was wagging – which it never seemed to stop doing!

Not knowing anything of Blackie's background it was best to assume he had not been vaccinated so that must be done fairly soon. Mr Winwood chatted for a few moments then was on his way again. I was grateful for his advice and agreed to make an appointment to take Blackie up within the next few days, which I did.

Naturally Tessa came along as well and was clearly relieved she was not the one going into the consulting room! Fortunately Blackie did not seem to mind. He simply waited patiently with us in Reception then, when his turn came, trotted in quite casually.

As a reward for being good, that evening Tessa and Blackie were given a nice warm supper of tinned stewed steak. Tess tucked into hers immediately – she knew the smell and couldn't wait to get started. Blackie however, had apparently not been given a warm meal before. After watching in excited anticipation while his bowl was filled, he made a beeline for it as soon as I placed it on the mat then drew back in puzzlement. What was this? Smoke rising from the food, wafting over his face as he put his muzzle down. What had he been given. He looked up with such a look of ambiguity Mother and I could not help laughing. He needed re-assuring that whatever was in his bowl was definitely all right to eat. He turned to look at Tess. Well, she was eating hers and, by the look of it, thoroughly enjoying it. Maybe he would give it a try. Emmmm yes, this was really good.

Before you could count to 30 the whole lot had disappeared then he looked round to see if there was any more!

Chapter LXXIX

By now Blackie had been introduced to the park. The day after his vaccination I took the two of them to Oakwood during my lunch hour as usual and let them off the lead. They had a lovely run round the top field then on the way back to the car through the little copse. Tess and I were slightly ahead of Blackie when an awful noise of fighting dogs came from behind us. Blackie and another dog, about his own size, were snarling, snapping and tussling with each other. The owner of the other dog came rushing up and eventually we were able to get the two apart but blood was running down Blackie's face from the region of his eye.

Oh dear – I was not used to this sort of thing. Neither Kimmy nor Tessa had ever been in a fight. I hoped this was not going to become a habit with Blackie.

Arriving home Mother was horrified to see the blood on Blackie's face. As I had to return to work Mother telephoned Wood Street, explained the situation and asked if whoever was on duty could possibly call in. Yes, Mr Graham would be along shortly, meanwhile just bathe Blackie's face to clean the area.

Amazingly Blackie allowed this to be done. The injury did not seem as bad as it had at first – still best for Mr Graham to have a look. Eyes are very precious. It would be very unwise to take a chance.

Mother rang me at work as soon as Mr Graham had been. Thank heavens there was no real damage. The other dog's claw had missed the eye itself but caught the flesh immediately beneath the lower lid. All would be well in a couple of days. So our trips to the park could continue without interruption.

I soon began to suspect Blackie may have greyhound in him. Each day the three of us drove to Oakwood Park as usual, leaving the car just over the little bridge. Both Tessa and Blackie were always eager for the car doors to be opened so they could be off and away. While Tessa ran ahead to find her friends, Blackie – the instant he was released – was off like a shot out of a gun. Down the side path next to the copse, out of sight along the bushes, right round the copse and back to me thus making a large circle.

He would repeat this run several times, running so fast it was difficult to keep him in view. The groundsmen came to describe this as "Blackie doing his laps". He ran just as quickly across the fields. Literally like a streak of lightening. It was necessary to actually move your head in order to follow him with your eyes. While the majority of dogs run with alternate legs striding ahead Blackie ran like a greyhound with both front legs moving forward at the same time followed by his two back legs moving in unison. With his lean body, manner of running and terrific speed, when I described this to Mr Winwood he agreed Blackie could well be a mixture of labrador and greyhound – it was quite possible.

Whatever mixture he was his underlying nature proved to be very similar to that of the labrador, loving, gentle, sensitive and, as had shown so clearly when I found him, extremely patient. Unfortunately he was also possessed of a great deal of fear. We quickly realised he must have been shouted at while having something thrown at him. The sound of an irritated or raised voice terrified him. He tail went down and he bolted upstairs under the bed in the guest room. This had always been a favourite place of Tessas but in her kind, understanding way she allowed Blackie to adopted this area as his own.

He adored Tessa and seemed to gather a feeling of security and confidence from being with her or somewhere he associated strongly with her.

The sight of a folded newspaper, black sacks, an umbrella, even a roll of wrapping paper filled him with terror. Each time we returned from a walk as soon as the front door opened and his lead was unclipped he was upstairs under the bed as fast as he could possibly get there. Again I can only assume he was used to being shouted at or hit in some way on arriving home from exercise. Though why this should be I cannot imagine. Admittedly he pulled hard on the lead but he always sat at the kerb waiting to be told when to cross. In this respect he was a good example to Tessa who was bemused by his kerb-drill.

The saddest fear of all that haunted Blackie was that of human hands. To put out a hand to stroke him would immediately provoke a sharp snap accompanied by a display of very large, keen looking teeth. I can only surmise what this poor boy had suffered at the hands of his previous owner. That was all in the past now. I tried to re-assure him that no one would ever be cruel to him again.

Each time he snapped at me or showed his teeth, in return he received countless waves of deepest love. I also told him what beautiful teeth he had and asked him what toothpaste he used!

This was usually greeted with a blank, uncomprehending stare. What was this woman talking about? She was definitely addressing him because she had her face down towards him and was looking at him but the words were totally unfamiliar!

After many weeks he finally accepted I was not going to hurt him. No matter how much he threatened me all he would ever receive back would be lots and lots of love. I understood his defensiveness. I could also see the gentleness behind his aggression and loved him all the more.

Though Tess was making it very clear she was the boss – which was only right as Blackie had come to live in her home – she thought the world of her new pal. Indeed Blackie made our home complete. Mother, Tessa, Blackie and myself – we were a happy family together.

Blackie also proved to be very intelligent. Realising he had a lot to learn he always watched Tessa to see what she was doing then copied her. One way in which Tessa helped Blackie enormously was by going into the garden with him at night. From the first day he came to us Blackie demonstrated a fear of the dark. He simply would not outside to spend his penny unless either Tessa or I went with him. Even then he ran back indoors as fast as he could the instant he had finished. Tessa seemed to understand his fear because if ever he stood hesitating at the patio door she came over from where-ever she was sitting, looked at him, then trotted straight out onto the lawn if only to have a sniff around. Immediately Blackie followed her. Tess always waited until Blackie was indoors again before coming in. Never once did she leave him out there on his own.

Like our other dogs before him Blackie quickly learnt the word wow-woz.

His fear of the dark even extended to being out in the car once daylight had gone. Sometimes the four of us would still be coming home from where-ever, as darkness fell and Blackie would become very sheepish, very restless. His eyes open wide, even the occasional little cry was to be heard. Both Mother and I would speak gently to him, re-assuring him.

As well as adoring Tessa, Blackie respected her. He never took advantage of her or of a situation. Meal time he was always ready for his food. Once his head was in place over his bowl nothing could move it. If I needed to get to the larder I could gently turn his whole body away from the door in order to open it, yet despite his anatomy turning a half circle his nose would not leave the bowl until every last morsel had been consumed! This accomplished he would stand in the centre of the kitchen watching Tessa eating her meal. If by chance she happened to leave any scraps, Blackie made no attempt to touch the remains until he was absolutely certain Tessa was not going back to finish them. He waited until Tess had walked away and settled herself down some-where then he gobbled up what-ever she had left.

Like Tess he also developed a fancy for cheese, spaghetti, vegetables, fruit, hot-dog sausages, mackerel in tomato sauce, lettuce and tinned stewed steak. Unlike Tess though he definitely did not like peppermint of any kind nor was he very fond of chocolate. He would however, make an exception in the case of white chocolate rabbits! Whenever I went to London I always brought Mother home a box of mixed Turkish Delight from Selfridges (her favourite) and from Thorntons, a white chocolate rabbit each for Tessa and Blackie.

In time Blackie gradually came to accept a small piece from a finger of fudge but only after Tess had eaten her share. Although, like Kimmy, hiding tablets inside Frys Cream was the easiest way to ensure Tess accepted all her medication, it was necessary to monitor her chocolate intake very carefully as she was one of lifes natural chocoholics. On one occasion, in playful mood, she actually jumped up and took a piece of chocolate out of my hand. Biscuits, particularly rich tea or digestive are, to this day, Blackies weakness, he is a real biscu-holic.

When one of them decided he or she wanted either a treat, a meal, a walk or perhaps an extra chew stick, the two of them joined forces standing side by side staring at me until I succumbed! It never failed! After all who could possible resist four pleading eyes?

Shortly after Blackie arrived in our home Andy's mum and dad, Bill and Rene, called round one evening to see him. They had heard his story and though they would not contemplate another dog themselves, they thought Blackie a lovely boy. So much so when they left Bill very generously gave me a gift for Blackie towards his keep. Two very kind people who sincerely love animals so were not put off by Blackie's nervousness.

Beryl too was very much taken with Blackie. The first time she saw him I opened the front door as Tess and Black came running to greet her. Of course Blackie had no idea who was coming in but Tessa was excited. She must have good reason so he would join in!

"Hello. Who is this"? Beryl was genuinely pleased to see Blackie and although he would not let her stroke him she was not put off by his show of teeth. Her love and understanding of dogs made her sad rather than annoyed by his reaction. She realised he must be frightened – no dog with such big brown soft eyes set in so gentle a face could be other than scared to react as he did. Bless him, what was the matter? She wasn't going to hurt him. He was a darling.

Blackie quietened down as Beryl spoke softly to him then cautiously took the chew she offered but only after he watched Tessa take one. Maybe this lady was like his new mum – could be trusted. Time would tell.

So touched was Beryl by his story the true warmth of her love for animals manifested itself on the next occasion she came to the house. She not only brought him a soft baby seal doll to play with but bless her, she came armed with a carrier bag of tins of dog food to help with his keep, as she did on several successive visits.

Animal lovers are such kind, compassionate people.

Blackie loved his baby seal, taking it everywhere with him especially to bed where he either put his head on it or his front paws round it. Either way baby seal was his baby.

Though both Blackie and Tessa had very gentle, loving natures Tess would play with her soft toys till they fell to pieces or she tore them into shreds. Blackie on the other hand would shake a soft toy vigorously, play with it endlessly yet never tear it – his teeth not even marking the cloth it was made from. His gentle patience and good manners earned him the title of a "gentleman". He never took, instead he always waited to be offered or given, always allowing Tessa to receive first. He even stood by one evening while Tessa ate all his supper – he simply sat and watched her with a bewildered expression on his face. It was only when she had virtually finished eating that I came into the kitchen and saw what was happening. Heaven knows why Tess suddenly took the notion into her head to eat Black's dinner but he made no attempt to stop her – if she wanted it, she should have it!

An entry in my diary for this period states "Tessa has become the most important member of our household and family. To Mother for essential, loving companionship. To Blackie for example, security and a "mother" image. To me – her intelligence gives me confidence. She is wise and a loyal, true friend at all times."

Chapter LXXX

In May, after discussion with Mr Winwood, it was decided for his own sake Blackie should be neutered. The date for his operation was set for the 16th. He had to be in the hospital between 8 and 9am.

It was a lovely morning, warm bright and sunny. Tess could not understand why she could not come in the car with Blackie. She always came. The three or four of us went everywhere together. Why was she being left at home with Mother while Blackie was taken out in the car? Before actually putting Blackie on the front passenger seat, I had stroked Tessa, trying to explain Blackie had to go on his own this time but would be home before long.

She could not understand and stood at the front door with Mother watching while we drove out through the gates. Poor Tess, she must be terribly bewildered. She and Blackie had not been parted since he came to live with us. Never-the-less the operation had to be undertaken.

To re-assure him, I chatted to Blackie all the way along. Though probably not understanding a word I said, he kept looking at me listening intently. Then, as we drove across Barnet Common I began singing to him. True I may be tone deaf but he pointedly turned his head, gave me a long, hard stare with those enormous soft brown eyes, then promptly stood up on his seat, shifted his whole body round, deliberately turning his back on me he sat down again staring out of the side window!

He had made his feelings known so plainly it was impossible not to burst out laughing. What a character our boy was turning out to be!

It was nearly 8.30am when we arrived at the hospital and I lead him reluctantly into the waiting room. He looked up – why am I here Mum? I am not ill! I feel fine! His expression said it all. "Oh Blackie – it is alright old fellow. You are not being abandoned again PROMISE. You are very much loved. You only have to stay a little while, have a nice sleep then I will be here again to take you home to Tessa".

We only had to wait a few minutes before the nurse came to collect Blackie. All the staff at Wood Street are very nice, very kind gentle and understanding. Never-the-less poor Blackie did not want to leave me. He did not want to go with the nurse. She re-assured me he would be alright. She would look after him, he would soon settle down.

Oh I hated leaving him especially as he kept looking back at me. Was he wondering whether he was being left again, whether he was being taken away from the home and family he had grown to love? If only I could make him understand. No matter how much he loved and trusted me there must be a doubt in his mind because it had happened to him once before. He had been taken away from his home, tied up and left for hours on end.

The day ahead loomed like an eternity. Tearfully I drove home. It was silly to be so upset. He would be fine. He could not be anywhere better than Wood Street. He was in good caring hands. But he was not in *my* hands. I was his Mum, the one who loved him dearly. The one who gave him a cuddle when he wanted it. Who held his paw and squeezed it to feel, in return, his paw clenching up in my hand giving me a "doggie – squeeze".

No matter how hard a kick you give yourself at these times, it does not really make any difference. The herding instinct is strong – the family was split and nothing would be quite right until it was together again.

As soon as the car stopped on the drive, the front door was open and Tessa came rushing out of the house at top speed. She ignored me, nosing into the car to see where Blackie was. She stopped short – where was he? Where was Blackie? She looked up at me stunned. What had I done with him?

I picked her up, gave her a cuddle and tried to re-assure her that he would be coming home very soon. He was with Mr Winwood. Hopefully she would recognise Mr Winwood's name thus knowing as best she could that Blackie was alright – he was with someone she knew. She went to see Mr Winwood and always came home again so Blackie would be home too.

The day seemed to pass so slowly. 2pm I telephoned Wood Street to enquiry about Blacks. He was fine. His operation was over. Would I please ring again that evening about 6.30–7?

That evening in the park, everyone we met wanted to know where Blackie was. Whenever a dog appears in the park without his or her pal, for one reason or another, all the other owners always hold their breath while anxiously asking where the missing canine is. You can almost feel the sigh of relief as the explanation is given.

6.30pm sharp I telephoned the hospital. Blackie was upset – he was getting a little grumpy. Could I please collect him between 8 and 9 in the morning?

The morning could not come quickly enough. Apart from wanting to have him home for my own sake, he would know for sure he had not been abandoned. Tessa would be delighted to see him so would Mother. Despite her early mis-givings she had become fond of Blackie very quickly.

After getting up at the crack of dawn, Tessa went for her first run of the day in the park about 7am. The gates are always open early for the groundsmen, tractor drivers and the like who begin work when most of us are just thinking about breakfast.

It would not be wise to take Tessie with me to collect Blackie, best she wait at home to greet him.

When you are anxious to arrive at a destination quickly the journey seems to take three times as long. This was the case on the 17 May. Another bright clear morning, the roads to Barnet appeared to have grown considerably longer than they were yesterday! Eventually I arrived, parked outside the hospital then went in to settle the account before collecting Blackie.

The paperwork attended to I sat impatiently waiting for the nurse to fetch Black from the ward. Suddenly the door in the corner of the room opened and Blackie came through pulling the nurse behind him. As soon as he caught sight of me his tail wagged furiously. Bless him, the time of uncertainty was over. I was there waiting for him and he knew he had not been abandoned. His eyes and tail said it all. The former shining like large, dark brown diamonds, the latter crashing into nurse's legs as it thrashed from side to side.

He sat quietly all the way home. Tessa would be waiting for him.

Little did I realise just how much she had missed him until, having parked on the drive, I opened the door and got out to greet her. She wasn't interested in me! She shot past, completely ignoring me, straight into the car to see Blackie. Her tail whirled in rapid circles, her nose wrinkled and sneezed with excitement as her body writhed in ecstasy. Her pal had come back to her!!

Blackie was equally delighted to see Tess. What a reunion!

In celebration of Blackie's return they both had a packet of Birds Eye Roast Beef slices for supper. This was a very special treat recently introduced as a result of my giving it to Mother on Sundays. Being a life-long vegetarian I could not face cooking raw meat for her so, having discovered roast beef slices, they were the obvious answer. Naturally Tessa and Blackie had immediately found their way to the table with their noses predominantly sniffing the air. From then on the two of them always had a packet each on very special occasions or when one of them had been ill.

Chapter LXXXI

Blackie was quickly back to his normal self and eager to be off to the park each day. Though Tessa still loved to play with her friends she was also very proud of having her own special pal. She trotted along beside him with her head and tail held high.

Walking along the pathways behind the two of them reminded me of the pictures of the Lady and the Tramp. Not that Blackie was a tramp by any means but Tessa was half Blackie's size, very dainty and trotted along almost on tip-toe while Black, his four gangling legs appearing to go in all directions, kept pace beside her. It was obvious he was as proud to be her escort as she was to have him escort her. They made a very touching scene – one I never tired of seeing.

In the early days they played chase together round the top field but on one or two occasions had collided in mid-air so I called a halt to this particular game. Blackie would never intentionally hurt Tess but being bigger than her, of sturdier build and moving with the speed of lightening, I was afraid she may accidently be injured. There was still plenty of fun to be had though. Like Tess, Blackie found fun in chasing the poor squirrels as they ran for cover. With his tremendous speed it was easy for Blackie to catch them but like Tess, at the last moment he held himself back to allow the squirrel to escape up a tree. One day however, he was so excited he forgot to hang back. To his own astonishment he caught a squirrel in his mouth. He stood stock still for a moment, shook it gently then very carefully put it down on the ground, watching while it made it's escape. It is difficult to say who was the more surprised Blackie or the squirrel!

While Tessa would play with any dog whatever size, shape or breed Blackie seemed to prefer smaller dogs. Almost as though he had paternal feelings towards them. He ran up to them, sniffed, then very gently played chase the way an adult plays with a child. In the case of very small dogs however he thought it great sport to pick them gently up then shake them like a soft toy. He was never rough with them; he would certainly never hurt them but naturally they did not appreciate being played with in this manner. Nor did their owners think very much of this particular game.

When it came to larger dogs though he was more boisterous. He loved to dance up and down in front of them while shaking his head, play-growling. As his head shook, his ears flopped up and down exposing the pink interior creating a most amusing picture. Though he only wanted a rough and tumble play unfortunately not all dogs appreciated this behaviour thus a tussle would ensue, so I had to watch him carefully avoiding the dogs I knew did not recognise his playful intentions.

Suzy, a little grey, white and black mottled mongrel about Tessa's size, came to the park every morning with her master Jack and his great friend Kit. Like most of the dogs in the park Suzy was a rescue dog. She was devoted to both Jack and Kit. Though on the small size, Suzy was rather wary of Blackie because of his boisterousness. Never-the-less the six of us often walked round the park together.

Jack was such an interesting person. He was a retired professional magician and at one time had been a great friend of David Nixon so, as can be imagined, the conversation was never boring.

Despite Suzy's early reticence, the three dogs ran along together happily.

Kit often kept an old hanky in his pocket for Suzy who would jump up, pull it out then run off with it. All good sport. Another favourite trick of hers was to run like mad up to Kit then jump straight up into his arms. Bearing in mind Kit was average height and no longer a young man he proved a very good sport, indulging Suzy whenever she wanted to play. Fortunately neither Tess nor Black attempted to copy her example!

Unfortunately Jack died not long after Blackie joined us and his wife donated a seat in the park to his memory. Though he kept in touch, Kit missed Jack very much and eventually moved away to Somerset where he had good friends he had known for many years.

Among the other four legged characters who enjoyed Oakwood Park was a young boxer who always brought a flower pot with him, carrying it very gently in his mouth. The pot went all round the park with him and was then carried safely home again!

Yet another boxer insisted on splashing around in the pond each morning playing with a large ball, continually pushing it under the water with his paws then moving back as he watched it bob up again before he attacked it once more. If he could find a discarded plastic container to splash around with as well, this was even greater fun!

Buffey was an adorable, gentle natured German Shepherd who went in the pond every day of the year irrespective of the weather. He was not even detered by the presence of thin ice on the surface. As he grew older he ambled across the grass, down onto the path surrounding the pond then waded in, tail wagging genteelly. There he would stand for a few minutes then walk slowly around before coming out again to shake himself free of the excess water.

Other than a bath which she loved, Tess was not over-fond of water so did not bother with the pond. Blackie on the other hand was fascinated. He obviously wanted to go in but was not sure. On his first encounter with the pond he trotted round and round the edge looking down into the water. Occasionally he stopped, looked down intensely then put out a paw and just dabbled the surface. On his second visit he plucked up the courage to jump in.

So popular was the pond, that one dear old golden retriever named Scoobie walked the length of the park most days to enjoy a paddle. Her master was known to all the staff and regular walkers. Jock spent all his mornings often afternoons as well – winter and summer alike – searching the lower fields for stray golf balls for his son. His tam-o-shanter more often folded up in his jacket pocket than where it should be, keeping his head warm. A very cheerful, lovable character he thought the world of Scoobie who frequently accompanied him on his expeditions. She would wander off sniffing here or there then take herself across the fields, through the wooded area, up the field the other side and into the pond. When she'd had enough of paddling around she slowly wandered back to Jock who would still be searching diligently.

Though Scoobie did not take much notice of the other dogs in the park, so gentle and friendly was her nature that even Blackie quietly accepted her.

Sadly Scoobie died of old age in 1995 and Jock followed her not long after. Two young trees, a Hornbeam paid for by their many friends in the park and a Rowan contributed by his family, were planted in their memory at a small ceremony conducted by Tony – better known as "Woody" and Pete, two of the groundsmen.

The planting was attended by Jock's wife, park staff and a large group of Jock and Scoobie's friends both human and canine. A lasting tribute to two much loved characters.

Chapter LXXXII

Blackie's first Christmas with us was sheer delight. Whatever had happened during this festive occasion in his previous home, this was plainly a very different experience. As usual Blackie watched everything Tessa did with intense interest before following her example.

The tree was duly assembled and decorated then the various accrued presents gathered round the base. What was this all about? Tessa was going over to sniff around the parcels. Maybe he should do the same. Gosh what lovely smells! That one definitely contained chicken – no mistaking that wonderful odour emmmmm! Blackie was rapidly becoming a chick-o-holic.

Some of the parcels had no smell at all yet Mum was telling him they were his. Tessa was told the same. All very mysterious. The atmosphere was one of excitement though so something special must be happening.

Next morning after breakfast Mother sat in her armchair by the fire while I dispensed the various presents. One for Grandma, one for Tessa, one for Blackie, one for Mum. Very soon both dogs had a little pile of presents in front of them causing much excitement and tail wagging. Noses pushed their way in amongst the wrapping paper as it was removed. Doggie chews, treats, biscuits, fluffy toys, chicken joints – how wonderful all this was. Tessie wriggled from side to side, nose wrinkling with excitement while Blackie watched her in wonder, before joining in the fun.

One parcel each left to open. What could this possibly be? There was a strange smell but not one that tempted the taste-buds.

Tessa's parcel was opened first while Blackie watched in tense anticipation.

A big red rubber cone shaped toy approximately 4½ inches high and hollow! Tessa looked at hers, sniffed it then picked it up in her mouth tossing her head from side to side with delight.

Blackie looked on eagerly while his present was opened. His eyes transfixed to the parcel in front of him. Could he possibly have the same as Tessie? His ears shot up, his eyes opened wide, his tail stood straight up in the air. Then, as his kong was revealed he pounced on it. What a fantastic object! Never have I seen an animal so totally overwhelmed. His tail could not wag fast enough. The kong was in his mouth in an instant. He shook it, chewed it, tossed it, picked it up and carried it around. All the time his tail continued to wag furiously. Tessa loved hers but Blackie did not know how to contain himself, so ecstatic was his happiness and joy with his new plaything!

Blackie carried his kong – or as I called it, his "gonk" – in his mouth the whole day. Everything else was forgotten. Gonk was only put down just long enough to allow him to eat his food, even then it sat beside his dish ready to be picked up again the instant he had finished eating. When we went out for our walk Blackie took his gonk with him, carrying it in his mouth the whole time we were out. He even managed to spend his penny and sniff various interesting lamp-posts while clinging on to his new wonder toy. Bedtime came and the gonk went upstairs into Blackies bed with him. No way was he going to be parted from it!

Tessa was greatly bemused by her friend's obsession with his toy. She kept looking at him in amazement. Now Blackie had his gonk and Tessa her Terry. Two very contented dogs.

Blackie's enchantment with his gonk was in no way a nine-day wonder. Where-ever Blackie went his gonk went too. To Mother's chagrin he would sit bolt upright beside her on the back seat of Rebecca holding gonk firmly in his mouth until two long slimy strings of dripple hung down either side. If he suddenly turned his head dripple would be thrown all over his Grandma, accompanied by her cry of "Ohhhh Blackie – you dirty little devil". But she still loved him!

One day when we were going to visit my friend Connie (her real name is Ann but Connie is a nick-name that has survived since our school days together) and her husband Don at Park Street, St Albans Mother decided she could not stand Blackie's gonk beside her any more. He would have to leave it at home.

I warned her but she would not listen. The only thing to do was go along with her. By now she was nearly 90 and the Alzheimers was really taking hold. So Blackie's gonk was duly left in the hall. He looked from me to his gonk. He hung back. Very reluctantly he climbed into the car. Sorry Blackie, it has to stay behind this time – Grandma is tired of being soaked.

He clambered onto the back seat behind mine then just sat there while I locked the front door and climbed into Rebecca next to Tessa. Blackie began to cry. "What is the matter with Blackie"? Mother asked. "He wants his gonk" I replied. "Oh", she said "he will soon forget it". Mentally I bet myself he wouldn't. I was right.

We drove a mile down the road, just passed Cockfosters Station while Blackie cried constantly and pitifully for his toy. Tessa kept looking round at him, obviously disturbed by her friend being so upset.

No good, even Mother agreed we would have to turn round, go home and fetch it for him. She hadn't realised just how precious his toy and comforter was – she would willingly put up with being showered to make him happy again.

Back home we went. I opened up the house and collected his gonk. The instant he caught sight of it in my hand his ears and eyebrows shot up, his eyes lit up and his upper lip puffed slightly in relieved joy. His gonk!! Gently he seized the precious object from my hands then sat back ready for anything. He was content – no more crying. He had his gonk so all was well with the world!

Never again did Grandma complain about Blackie spraying her while shaking his head with a mouthful of gonk – instead she always made sure she carried a spare hankie in her handbag!

Blackies love of his gonk did not prevent him from enjoying other games. One warm April afternoon we were sitting in the lounge with the patio door open when in from the garden trots Blackie carrying a very large plastic flower pot in his mouth. He pattered across the carpet, deposited the pot on the floor in front of me then looked up as if to say "Look what I have brought you Mum – aren't I a clever boy"? Yes, of course he was!

On another occasion, while pegging the washing on the line I had laid the prop on the lawn. Made by Father 40 years previously from part of a tree he had cut down in our garden in Cockfosters, the prop was full size and by no means light to carry. Never-the-less Blackie spotted it, with a gleam in wide open eyes, he picked the prop up in his mouth then ran off with it down the garden.

Tessie, sitting in the middle of the lawn with her beautiful tail spread out beside her and looking like an elegant courtier, gave him a nonchalant look as if his crazy behaviour were beneath requiring her attention.

By now Tessie was "middle-aged" and though she still enjoyed a frolic she was beginning to take life a little more sedately.

In April, for the first time, she showed no real interest in the garden hose when I unreeled it. This was a sad day because it signalled the beginning of the decline of her physical youth though she was still mentally very alert, knew exactly what she was doing and what was going on around her. However, it was time to sit back and allow Blackie to chase the hose water. After all he was younger than her – not a lot admittedly, but he was younger.

Chapter LXXXIII

In May 1991 I awoke suddenly at 3am with pains in my arms which suddenly transferred to the middle of the chest with a sharp stabbing sensation then spread out either side. Realising immediately it was heart I woke Mother and telephoned the emergency doctor who confirmed the angina attack, gave me GTN tablets and a letter for the doctor.

Connie's Aunty Lizzy was staying with us at the time and bless her, within minutes of being woken up, she was in to see if she could do any-thing. Her mere presence was a comfort to us all as she looked after Tessa and Blackie who both sensed something was wrong and were agitated.

That night changed our lives for ever.

Eventually, sent for an ECG at Highlands the local hospital, to my horror I was informed the angina was unstable and I was to be admit-ted immediately without being allowed home.

This was totally unacceptable. I could not just walk out on Mother, Tessa and Blackie without letting them know what was happening. Arrangements had to be made for their care; groceries to be purchased to tide the family over until I was home again. Also, Moggie was parked in the hospital grounds. So agitated was I the consultant decided it was more dangerous for me to be in such a distressed state than to allow me home for an hour.

In a state of numbed disbelief I drove home, stopping on the way to visit the little parade of shops at Chaseville – just round the corner from the hospital – and procure as much as possible in the way of supplies to last a couple of weeks.

30 minutes of the hour had passed by the time I reached home. Mother was stunned by the news but relieved when I rang Tony who agreed to stay over each night with her. Poor Tess and Blackie, they would not understand why I had gone away. We had never been apart before. They would not know what was happening. Tessa had been part of the family long enough to feel secure but what about Blackie? He would be so confused. He could well wonder whether he had been abandoned again – this time by me, the person he had come to love and trust. Mother promised to look after them, never-the-less it was my job to look after all three of them.

While packing a case with a few essential items Bill Medcalf arrived to ask me to type an urgent letter for him. He immediately offered to drive me back to the hospital instead of having to order a taxi. He was so kind, re-assuring Mother and offering any help needed.

Ready to go, it was time to say au revoir to Tessa and Blackie. They had taken shelter, from the chaos of rushing feet, in the quiet of the dinning room. Both of them sat perfectly still, looking up at me and listening intently while I stroked each of them in turn trying to gently explain I had to go away for a little while but still loved them very, very much and promised to be home as soon as possible. Blackie was trying to understand but wore a blank expression of non-comprehension. Tessa looked less confused as though she understood the words I was saying but not the meaning behind them. Leaving the two of them was so painful. If only they could properly understand what was happening. I even tried telling them I had to go to Mr Winwood in the hope their minds could connect his name with what had happened to them in the past and that a similar thing was going to happen to me. They knew even if they had to stay a few days, they always came back from the place where they saw Mr Winwood, hopefully this would re-assure them I would be coming back too. The thought I may not, was dismissed the instant it arose. It did not bear thinking about – whatever would happen to the three of them?

I was away from home nearly two weeks, firstly in the local hospital then in The Middlesex Hospital in London. The condition was inoperable but meant living on 15 tablets a day and adjusting life accordingly.

Four or five times a day I telephoned home, anxious about Mother now 90 years of age, and of course about Tessa and Blackie. The first four days I was away Tessa would not eat a thing. She was very quiet, very subdued. Blackie on the other hand gobbled his meals down as eagerly as ever.

Having had to cancel an appointment with Beryl she called in on a number of occasions to make sure the trio were well and was kind enough to bring a supply of tinned dog food in case Mother ran short. There was no way she could leave the house alone and though Tony was staying with her, he was working all day so did not arrive till mid-evening and was away quite early each morning.

After about a week Mother was becoming distressed and declared she could not cope with both dogs any longer. Tessa was quiet but Blackie of course was more boisterous. A combination of his exuberance, the worry of what was happening to me and the strain of being on her own so much was proving too great an ordeal at her age and in her condition. In desperation she telephoned Wood Street. When learning this I was embarrassed she had taken such a step. The problem was really not one Wood Street could be expected to deal with. Never-the-less they were kindness itself and offered, subject to my agreement, to take Blackie and keep him upstairs with the staff under the control of Carol, the Head Nurse.

Being parted from him was stressful enough, the thought of him being taken out of his home only accentuated the situation. At Carol's request I telephoned to discuss the matter with her. She was very sensible, kind and helpful. Though the hospital would not normally make such an undertaking under the circumstances Mr Winwood had very kindly agreed to Blackie going to Wood Street till I was home again. Mother was by now, due to her age and failing condition, in a very distressed state; it was far better for Blackie if he could be looked after in a more relaxed environment.

So it was agreed and Blackie spent two or three days with Carol and her colleagues at the hospital. He would certainly be very well cared for – if he had to be away from home he could not be in better hands.

At last, complete with a large bag of tablets, I was home. Tessa went crazy with excitement. She turned in circles, her nose wrinkled, her tail wagged frantically – she simply did not know how to contain herself. It was wonderful to see her again; to pick her up and hug her, just to be with her. Oh it was so strange without Blackie – Carol had generously offered to bring him home that afternoon. He had not been naughty but had naturally felt insecure and been a little defensive. In fact he had bitten the thumb of Richard, one of the male nurses. Fortunately people who work with animals take this kind of thing in their stride. They understand. Never-the-less Wood Street must have been relieved when Blackie came home.

Carol arrived early afternoon with Blackie on his lead. Tessa was overjoyed to see her pal again. What a marvellous day she was having. First Mum come back then Blackie. We were all together again.

Blackie seemed a little dazed – as though he could not comprehend all these changes in his life. For two or three weeks after our reunion he was very unsettled just as he had been when he first came to us. It was a matter of re-building his confidence, something time alone could achieve. He had all the love and attention Tessa, Mother and I could give him. Eventually he settled down and everything was back to normal.

Chapter LXXXIV

We were not able to take a holiday that year which was disappointing as apart from Tessa's love of the beach, Blackie had probably not been to the seaside. It was a treat to look forward to – maybe next year.

The year passed quite quickly. I had to make regular visits to hospital and take life more slowly but still took Tessa and Blackie to the park each day sometimes by car, sometimes walking.

Blackie overcame his reticence to go into the pond. Having summoned up the courage to jump in, he decided this really was terrific fun. The water was not very deep, only about 18" – but enough to splash around in and jump through from one side of the pond to the other. All the time his precious gonk remained in his mouth. Only very rarely would Tessa venture into the water, instead she preferred to stand on the side path watching her pal enjoying himself. Occasionally, joining in the fun from a safe distance, she would run round and round the edge of the pond barking at him.

However not always did Blackie feel like going for a "swim". If the weather was a little chilly he would stay firmly put on dry land as was the case on an early morning walk that autumn. The three of us had spent a very pleasant half hour strolling around the park, Blackie carrying his gonk as usual. As we approached the pond I took the gonk from his mouth throwing it for him to chase and catch. He chased it alright but let it roll down the slope into the water. "Oh Blackie – go on in, you go and fetch it. Good boy, fetch it." He looked at the pond, realised the water was cold so gave me a look which clearly said "You are joking!". Despite his love for his gonk Blackie made no attempt to go in after it. Obviously he knew his Mum would be daft enough to get it if he didn't!

There was no alternative. Partly because Blackie loved it so much, partly because gonks cost £6 a piece, Mum would have to go in. I took my shoes and stockings off, hitched up my dress and, while Tess and Blackie stood on the bank watching, waded in to retrieve the cherished object.

Isn't it always the way – one minute there was no else in sight then suddenly a little group of dog walkers appeared on the scene as if from no-where.? At least we all had a good laugh and Blackie had his gonk back.

The pond was popular with other visitors too. From time to time powerboat enthusiasts visited the park to run their remote controlled boats on the pond. Though lovely for humans to watch, the canine population were not so keen. Their play area was being invaded by noisy, buzzing things that whizzed around on top of the water. Blackie could not make the intruders out. He would stand watching with his head on one side then bark at the boats while trying to follow them from the sidewalk. After all this was his pond – what right had these noisy things to come and take over his fun area?

Barney was another dog who considered he had priority in the park. He was a super dog – a mongrel with, by the look of it, a certain amount of bull terrier in him. He lived in a house which backed onto the far end of the park. He was such a good natured dog and at one time, a firm friend of Tessa. Unfortunately he gradually became aggressive towards other dogs, chasing them away. As his behaviour grew worse his owner sought advice from an animal psychiatrist. Apparently, because he lived backing onto the park, Barney had developed the idea that the park was an extension of his own garden. Therefore any other dog found in the park was trespassing on his property so had to be chased off.

Fortunately not all dogs had this attitude – most were pretty sociable like Whimper a sweet little black dog similar in size and coat to Tessa. Or Smiler, an elderly red setter whose approach could never be mistaken. He wore two little bells round his neck. Although he belonged to Steve, a professional musician, Steve's elderly mother was blind so to help her keep track of Smiler's whereabouts he wore his bells. Steve took Smiler to the park regularly twice a day and his father took him each lunchtime then sat on a bench enjoying the fresh air while Smiler sniffed around.

Another dog with a very gentle, loving nature was Gemma, an adorable white dog with one or two ginger markings. She was about the size and shape of a Manchester Terrier. Little more than a puppy she had been out in the car with her owners, a young couple. Tragically they had been involved in a serious car accident. When the police arrived on the scene the young couple were dead but they heard a puppy crying. Wood Green Animal Shelter was not too far away so the puppy was taken there and cared for until adopted and given the name Gemma.

Luck certainly stayed with Gemma because a year or so later she sat too close to the electric fire catching her tail alight but fortunately her Mum was on hand so no real damage was done and eventually the fur grew back returning Gemma's tail to it's former glory.

Chapter LXXXV

During the year both Aunty Ivy and Lizzy continued to come regularly and stay for a while which made pleasant company for all of us. Aunty Ivy was kind to both dogs but was a little nervous of Blackies growling and occasional snapping. His fear of hands was as strong as the day he first came to us. Tessa, being quieter, was much easier for her to get along with. Lizzy on the other hand took no notice of his occasional impolite behaviour to which she playfully responded with a confident "Now what's the matter with you? You dafty". Both ladies always either brought Tess and Black a few treats or bought them some during their stay. Needless to say this endeared them even more to the two pals.

About this time Bill introduced us to Forty Hall, a mansion with surrounding parkland open to the public and only a few miles away, the other side of Enfield. Here the dogs could run free across the fields and through the wooded area while Mother sat in the car watching the comings and goings. Here too is a beautiful large lake where many different species of water birds live and beside which disabled drivers are allowed to park. No longer able to walk easily this was ideal for Mother. She could remain in the car yet enjoy the sights.

Still having plenty of energy after their romp across the fields Tessa and Blackie were always willing and eager to clamber out of the car again to stroll, this time on the retractable leads, round the edge of the pond. Though Tess, busy enjoying the many new smells to be found along the wooded path beside the water, was quite indifferent to the noise being generated by the ducks and their companions, Blackie was excited by it all. He pulled on his lead in an attempt to get closer to the squawking birds, his tail and ears up, his eyes open wide and his tongue lolling out of the side of his mouth. Remembering his gentleness with the squirrel he caught in Oakwood Park there was no worry about him harming the birds even if he could catch one. It was just the fun of pretending.

Having once found this idealic spot we visited it on a regular basis.

Chapter LXXXVI

The following year Mother was taken ill one Saturday night while Audrey, our friend from across the road, was visiting us. Realising the best course of action was to take Mother to Casualty, I telephoned Tony asking him to come with us. This created the problem of Tessa and Blackie. They had never been left alone. Mother now being completely housebound she was with them during the day when I was at work. At all other times the four of us were always together.

Very kindly Audrey offered to stay with Tess and Black until we came home. Both dogs knew her well of course. Blackie was becoming particularly fond of Audrey, initially because she always brought them a packet of Schmakos each, then later just because he seemed to adore her. The mere mention of her name and he immediately looked up, ears erect, eye open wide with a questioning look of expectancy on his face. He only had to be in the front garden and spot her coming out of the flats opposite, to begin barking like mad, tail wagging crazily on the end of a wriggling body. This being the case, and knowing Tess would feel safe in her own home, I was grateful to Audrey for her offer.

The three of us were out of the house for three hours. During this time I telephoned Audrey on several occasions to make sure all was well and to update her. Each call I made I could hear Blackie crying in the background. Patients came and went. Eventually Mother was seen by someone. Apparently she had an infection. She was given a couple of tablets then sent home.

How sad it is to be old in this day and age. How much we owe the older generation for all they did for us in 1939–45. For bringing us through the Second World War to Peace. Giving us the chance to be educated to live the lives we do, yet so few of the younger people really appreciate this fact. So many treat the elderly as though they are a nuisance for simply existing.

When we arrived home with Mother, Tessie and Blackie were beside themselves with joy at seeing us. While wriggling and sneezing, tail wagging and barking they looked up lovingly at Mother and myself, relieved we had come home at last. As if to emphasize his joy Blackie was making funny little whimpering noises. Audrey told us they had both been very good. Tessa had sat in the hall waiting for us but Blackie had cried non-stop the whole time we were out. Bless him – once again, if only I could explain to him and make him understand.

In August that year Mother celebrated her 90th birthday. There were so many people to be invited to help her celebrate, we had two dinner parties. The first on the Saturday and the second the following

Thursday when amongst the guests were Aunty Ivy with her daughter Betty and son-in-law Mick.

Though we did not know it then, it was the last time we were to see Aunty Ivy. She died peacefully in her sleep in December. Mother's friend of over 80 years. A good friend to all our dogs from Dad's Paddy in the 1920's to Tessa and Blackie in the present day. She is still sadly missed.

At both parties Tessa and Blackie had the time of their lives. They sat side by side in the kitchen doorway the whole time I was preparing food. The expressions on their faces a mixture of innocence coupled with expectancy. Trying to look nonchalant yet all the while hoping for the occasional off-cut of cold meats, cheese, ham pie or anything tasty that may come their way. Who could refuse two such angelic creatures – especially on such an auspicious occasion? There were of course several slices of cold meat plus a chicken satay for each of them for supper but somehow titbits were an even bigger treat.

Each guest was greeted at the front door with loud barks, dancing feet and excessive tail wagging. Both dogs were in their element but still no one except Tony, Beryl or myself could actually stroke Blackie. He watched Tessa receiving lots of pats and must have longed for the same petting from these old friends but his fear would not relent. Never-the-less everyone spoke kindly to him which, judging by the acceleration of his tail, gave him great pleasure. Mum was always there to give him hugs and strokes so he didn't miss out.

When each party was over both Tessa and Blackie were tired out but very contented. They had enjoyed Grandma's birthday parties as much as she had.

Chapter LXXXVII

By now I had been forced to give up work which, as Mother needed constant care, was a blessing in disguise. Each day we all went out somewhere together in the car, if only for half-an-hour. Sitting in the back of Beccy Mother could see clearly out of the window. She began coming to the park with us. At first she would walk slowly down through the little copse while Tessa and Blackie ran about enjoying themselves. Later, when walking became difficult for her, she was content to sit in Beccy while the three of us went for our walk. This was ideal because not only was Mother safe in the car but she could enjoy watching the happenings all around here. The squirrels hopping around or scampering up the trees when a dog approached; other dogs chasing each other or playing while they made their way round the path;

mothers with prams or toddlers; joggers in all shapes, sizes and ages; elderly people strolling in the sun; birds singing while they flew here, there and everywhere. It was wonderful for Mother to be able to enjoy the park in this way.

Once a week we went to Waitrose in Totteridge where the disabled bays are sited next to the walk-way up to the rear entrance from the car park. Mother, Tessa and Blackie all sat in the car while I went in to do the shopping. From their vantage point they could watch the people coming and going, which was preferable to being left at home. Here again they were safe not only because they were close to the shop but because Malcolm, one of Waitrose doormen who collected the trolleys, kept an eye on them. Being a dog lover and owner himself he always had a few kind words for Tess and Black. Also he would come up to me in the shop with re-assurance "Mother and the dogs are fine – they are watching for you".

The instant they saw me emerge from the automatic door with the trolley, they began to fidget. As I drew nearer the car so the fidgeting increased until, having loaded the boot, returned the trolley then opened the drivers door the squeals of impatience were let forth. On the back seat Blackie sat bolt upright, ears up, eyebrows up over wide open gleaming eyes. On the front seat Tessa began dancing with expectation, her nose foraging amongst the contents of my hands. The two were never disappointed. Always they had half a pound of sliced cold meat between them. This was their treat for being good while I was shopping.

Dainty as always, Tessa would gently take the slice from my hands then elegantly chew before swallowing it. Blackie, eager as ever, took the proffered meat, without stopping to chew, downed the slice in one swallow. It literally did not have time to touch the sides of his mouth! To be fair to him whenever I cried "Blackie – chew it!" he would look me straight in the eye then do exactly as he was told. Admittedly it only amounted to two or three big chews but never-the-less he was doing as he had been told, as is his nature. He is obedient in every way.

Chapter LXXXVIII

Knowing how obedient both Tessa and Blackie were made the decision to take them to Hunstanton easy. For one reason or another it had not been possible to take a holiday since Blackie came to us. Little did he know what wonders were in store for him!

The thought of taking the two of them away together was exciting. Tessa loved to be by the sea but how would Blackie react?

Eileen and Terry were only too pleased to put the four of us up. They were looking forward to seeing us all again.

As soon as Tess saw the suitcases coming down from on top of the wardrobes she realised what was happening. Blackie was totally mystified by her excitement. Why was she so agitated? What were those big bags and why were all sorts of everyday things being put in them? Mum kept saying "Yes, you are both coming", but coming where? Why is that bag in the hall being filled with our food, leads, towels, brush and lots of other things used for us?

That night, despite all the upheaval, we went to bed as usual. That must have puzzled Blackie even more. All this fuss then back to normal. Ah well, never mind a good sleep is called for.

Next morning the kerfuffle began again only this time Tessa and Blackies beds were brought downstairs and loaded in Rebecca's boot with the rest of the bags and paraphernalia. Eventually Mother was helped into the back of the car and wrapped up with a rug while Blackie was told to jump up next to her. Tessa climbed onto the front passenger seat as usual. Whatever was happening it was happening to all of us.

We left home just after 11am. It was a lovely bright sunny day though very windy. Driving through Enfield we turned left onto the A10 which goes all the way to Kings Lynn. On and on we went. Blackie had never been as far as this before but, whatever his thoughts he did not appear to be worried. We were all four together so everything must be alright. He was quite happy to sit looking out of the rear side window.

Eventually we pulled into the picnic area at Brandon Creek to stretch our legs then eat our packed lunch. Tessa knew where she was immediately so became excited again, anxious to get out of the car. Blackie watched her keenly. Well, if she was getting out obviously he would be taken out too.

Mother sat still, watching while I clipped the retractable leads on Tess and Black, locked the car and set off up the slope to the path running parallel with the river.

This was wonderful! Such exciting new smells. The two pals sniffed every tree, bush and picnic bench. When Blackie clapped eyes on the river he stood stock still, ears erect, and looked. Once again his expression was a joy to behold, his thoughts clearly definable in his face. Water! Yet this was nothing like the pond in the park back home – definitely not to be jumped into! But gosh – how incredible, how exciting!

Tessa led the way along the river path with great confidence. She would show Blackie. It was almost as though she were silently instructing him to "just follow me. I have been here before". Blackie needed no second bidding. He pulled after her on his lead, anxious not to miss a thing.

When the path narrowed alongside the bend of the road we retraced our steps back to the car and lunch.

Tess and Black were firstly given a drink of water then a bowl of corned beef each. When they were satisfied, Mother and I ate our sandwiches and drank the tea from our thermos.

Refreshed we set off again for the last 30 odd miles to Hunstanton.

Instead of going straight to Kiama Cottage, we drove onto the cliff top. Mother loved the view from here so much. Throughout the year she visualised herself sitting on the cliff looking out across the wide stretch of golden sands leading gently into a placid sea and backed by the dunes.

Well, the time had come. What would Blackie make of the sand, the sea, the whole environment? Tessa was in no doubt what she thought. The instant the car stopped she began barking with excitement. Dancing up and down on the seat. Looking up, full of expectancy. Were we going down there on the sand? Of course we were.

Ensuring Mother was quite happy then changing into flip-flops, I clipped on the retractable leads. Tessa was out of Rebecca the instant the door was open, she was ready to be off. Blackie was a little uncertain what all the fuss was about but having watched Tessa intently he realised a walk was on the agenda so promptly picked up his gonk then followed her out onto the grass, tail wagging delightedly.

Down the cliff top track to the start of the sand between the dune bordered path onto the beach. Tessa's erect tail was waving from side to side with happiness as once again she led the way.

As Blackie stepped onto the sand he stopped abruptly, looked up at me in amazement. What was happening? His feet had sunk into the ground which was still moving about under his pads! He took another step. The same thing happened again. It felt wonderful! In his excitement he dropped his gonk. He tried to pick it up. As his mouth covered the rubber toy so the sand stuck to the surface. He jerked backwards, his ears and eyebrows up. You could almost hear him think "errr". Out went a paw in an attempt to turn the gonk over so he could bite the clean side. This was not working. As his paw touched the gonk so it rolled over, sand clinging to the other side. Again he stood stock still, legs apart, bottom back, ears up. He couldn't make this out. Again a tentative paw went out. The same thing happened. The gonk rolled in the sand and by now was covered in it.

Alright, one paw was not getting him anywhere. Use both front paws to turn the gonk, to find a clean patch. He couldn't get that stuff in his mouth! This wasn't working either! His face became a picture of intense concentration. He began scratching at the sand immediately round the gonk, faster and faster, dancing in circles round the much loved object, in sheer desperation to release his precious toy.

By now other walkers, who were queuing up behind us waiting to pass, were in fits of laughter watching Blackie's antics. He was utterly oblivious to them though, he was completely absorbed in what he was doing.

All this time Tessa was standing watching him. Whatever was he doing now?

As poor Blackie was getting nowhere very quickly, I picked up his gonk, brushed it down on my slacks then handed it back to him. In an instant it was in his mouth being held very tightly. He would not let go of it again in a hurry – at least not on the sand.

We continued down the pathway to the beach where I let both dogs off the lead. Suddenly my two middle-aged dogs became puppies again. They ran across the sand towards the sea, tails going in circles. They chased each other round and round, up and down. Blackie may not have been to the seaside before but he was very quickly getting the hang of it!

Down to the water's edge where the seagulls were bobbing about on the surface. Gosh, the pair had spotted pigeons! Out they dashed into the shallow sea, barking like mad as, united in their bid to escape, the gulls took to the air with cries of protest.

Despite holding his gonk in his mouth Blackie is still able to bark although the sound emitted is more a loud muffled bark – but just as effective.

After about 20 minutes I decided that was enough for the first day. Time to be off to Kiama Cottage, to Eileen and Terry.

After a good long drink Tess and Black jumped back into Rebecca looking very pleased with themselves.

As we pulled up outside Kiama, Tessa knew where she was immediately. In excitement she began fidgeting and barking. Blackie looked at her, once again not understanding what it was all about. He couldn't see anything worth barking at – wait, the front door had opened and a lady was coming out. Maybe that was it.

Eileen was as pleased to see us as we were to see her. As Terry followed her out more happy greetings were exchanged. Both looked very well. It had been a year or two since we last met so naturally they were introduced to the, now not so new, member of our family. Greetings over, Terry kindly helped carry the baggage up to our room then left us to unpack.

All this time Blackie was very quiet, rather like a shy little boy. He wasn't quite sure what to do and it showed on his face as well as in his behaviour. So as always he watched Tessa then followed her example. This was all very bemusing but, very exciting. Their beds had been brought upstairs and were being made up so obviously we were sleeping here. He was thoroughly enjoying himself – though beginning to feel very hungry. Must have been that lovely run!

Once both dogs had eaten their fill they curled up in their respective beds for a nap, tired but happy.

The week passed quickly but happily for all four of us. Each morning before breakfast I took Tessa and Blackie for a walk down to the front, along the cliff top gardens to the town green, then back to Kiama Cottage through the little town. Though the weather was a mixture of rain and sunshine, the wind persisted.

On Tuesday morning the sea was very rough, lashing the promenade wall, spilling white foam onto the thoroughfare with a crashing roar. As we walked down the pathway through the gardens above the sea front Blackie began to pull on the retractable. He could hear the noise rising from below and was eager to see for himself what it was all about. Anxious to keep up with him, Tessa strained on her lead to stay abreast. When we reached the railings by the steps leading onto the promenade the two dogs stopped to looked through.

Tessa had seen rough seas before so took the whole business in her stride. Blackie, on the other hand, was fascinated. His whole body erect, his nose went through the rails as he stared in wonder at the sea. He danced back a few steps, glanced up at me with a look of bewildered enthralment, then pushed his nose through the rails once more to stare at the seething water below.

For a good ten minutes he stared hypnotized by the sea. All attempts to drag him away were in vain. Eventually I succeeded in pulling him in the opposite direction so the three of us could continue our walk.

However, Blackie could not forget the experience. Each morning as we made our way through the gardens he pulled in the direction of the railings wanting to look down at the sea. Though not as rough as on the Tuesday, the sea remained choppy so continued to draw Blackie's eager attention.

While in the area we drove through to Wells-Next-Sea, parked on the rough ground at the end of the old cockle sheds then ate our picnic lunch. Once finished, Mother stayed in the car to have a nap while I took Tessa and Blackie for a walk along the causeway, across the marshland, beside the sea estuary where a colourful variety of small craft bobbed about on the end of their anchor chains.

It is quite permissible to allow dogs to run free along this stretch of open country, however with so much water and marshland around, though both dogs were well behaved and obedient, I was not risking either of them falling down the steep embankments into the muddy waters. The retractable leads extend to a length of approximately 12 feet but even this was too much for safety so, with thumb on the controls, they had a maximum leeway of about 6 feet. This allowed them to enjoy sufficient freedom to explore the grassy embankments either side of the pathway without danger of falling. And enjoy themselves they did! It was not just the environment they revelled in but each other's company. As soon as one dog found a really interesting smell to sniff, the other would have to come along to see what had been found. Together they nosed around in the same patch of grass or rough ground until, satisfied, they trotted off side by side in search of the next find.

Despite the continuing wind, it was a beautiful day. This had been a favourite walk of Dad's when he lived here for the year in the late 1940's. When Mother had taken Tony and myself up for a holiday to be near him, we all walked along this causeway together of an evening. Now, over 50 years later, walking with my two best pals Tessa and Blackie, with memories of bygone days flooding back, the world seemed a wonderful place.

We could not visit Hunstanton without paying Cousin Ralph a visit. By now he was on his own again, his second wife having recently passed over. He still had Joan's two collie cross dogs, Bill and Ben, but they were getting on in years now so, being aware of Blackie's excitable nature, he kindly shut the brothers in the bedroom while we visited. As usual Blackie hung back until he saw how Tessa was behaving. She was genuinely pleased to see this man so he would be to. This bungalow smelt of other dogs though – em, the carpet, the furniture, the kitchen and especially the bedroom!

Bill and Ben were very good in their temporary confinement – not a peep from either of them when Blackie sniffed at their door. Maybe he shouldn't have done that but Tessa was busy being made a fuss of by the man being called Ralph.

All four dogs were given a bowl of tea and a biscuit when we had ours but Bill and Ben still had to stay in the bedroom – just to be on the safe side.

After about an hour and a half we took our leave and Ralph's "two boys" as he referred to them, were once again free to go as they pleased in their own home.

With her medication adjusted, Tessa was coping very well. She managed to keep up with Blackie and seemed to be thoroughly enjoying herself. In addition to their morning and evening walks they played on the beach whenever possible. As soon as we pulled onto the cliff top Blackie now recognised where he was and competed with Tessa, barking crazily with excitement.

If the tide were out we walked along the bottom of the cliffs to the rock pools formed by the outgoing sea. This was great fun, giving the two dogs the opportunity to chase each other round and round the rocks, splashing this way and that through the pools then out again to chase off to the next group of rocks further along the beach. Blackie may be fast on his legs but Tessa was doing her best to keep up with him. She was never far behind.

They were having the time of their lives. They were soaked to the skin and loving every minute of it.

The last day of the holiday Tessa's eyes began to look rather red and sore. I bathed them several times very gently with wet cotton wool. They would have to be watched carefully.

It had been a lovely holiday. Mother had been a little confused at times but never-the-less she had been away from home, enjoyed the sea air, the views and the company. It must have done her a lot of good, as indeed it had all of us.

Tessa and Blackie had certainly spent a wonderful time. Blackie's gonk had gone everywhere with him, being carried carefully and lovingly in his mouth; tucked up in his bed at night and sitting beside him in the car. Not to be outdone Tessa always had her "Terry" with her in the car or in her bed.

They would miss the beach but were lucky to have the various parks at home.

On Saturday we reluctantly said our goodbyes then set off for Oakwood. As usual we stopped at Brandon Creek for a snack and to exercise Tessa and Blackie. This time Blackie recognised where he was, he began barking as soon as we turned into the picnic area.

We spent nearly 40 minutes at the Creek then everyone fed and water, Tess and Black exercised, it was time to be on our way again.

As we reached the half-way point in our journey Blackie began to get a little grumpy. Once or twice he snapped at me. He was having a job to keep his eyes open and looked a little sorry for himself. He was probably just tired after such a hectic week. Tessa sat quietly beside me as usual but her eyes were no better. They needed bathing regularly. If they were no better tomorrow she must see Mr Winwood on Monday.

That evening a short walk around the block sufficed. Next day, Sunday we went to Oakwood Park. Tessa and Blackie had enjoyed their holiday but there was no doubt they were both very happy to be back on their own ground. They ran into the park tails held high, barking joyfully, down the path through the little copse.

There must be someone here to play with. Tessa looked this way and that to no avail. Oh well she would play with Blackie. As she turned to face him down went her front legs, up went her bottom as she looked up at him barking, inviting him to come and play.

In the absence of other friends, the two chased round and round the balsam poplar tree eventually slowing down to a trot as various interesting scents attracted their attention and, naturally, had to be investigated.

That evening Tessa's eyes were no better. First thing next morning I rang Wood Street to make an appointment for her. Unfortunately Mr Winwood was fully booked but she could see Mr White. Yes please, her eyes needed professional attention and quickly.

We did not stop for a walk on the Common but went straight to the Veterinary Hospital. Never-the-less as we drove across the Common Tessa began to tremble. She knew exactly where she was going.

Blackie sat in the car with Mother while I picked Tess up and took her into the waiting room. Here as usual, her trembling considerably increased attracting the sympathetic attention of everyone in the room. Luckily it was not long before Mr White appeared at the consulting room door calling for "Tessa please".

Once inside he spoke so kindly to her, stroking her head in an attempt to calm her. He spotted at once the reason for her visit. As Mr White tried to examine her Tess wriggled like an eel, making it very difficult for him to keep hold of her. When he attempted to put drops in her eyes she wriggled even more, freeing herself completely from his hands. In the end it took two of us to hold her while the medication was administered.

Mr Winwood was used to Tessa's wriggles which of course were new to Mr White. He was very kind but said he had never come across a dog who wriggled as much as Tessa.

She had contracted conjunctivitis, probably from the beach, and would need to have medication applied to both eyes for several days. There were going to be lots of wriggling sessions ahead!.

Blackie is as good as gold about having anything done to him but Tess always fought like a tiger.

Fortunately Tessa's eye condition cleared quite quickly once the medication began to work though it re-occurred from time to time for the rest of her life.

Chapter LXXXIX

During the following week I noticed, while out on a walk, Blackie began slowing down then stopping for a rest. At first I told myself he was just tired. Surely it could not be his heart. It would be too much of a co-incidence to have three consecutive dogs with a heart condition.

However, he continued to slow, stop then rest while exercising. He was also becoming a little snappy at night when he was tired, just like he had on the return journey from Norfolk. There was no denying the symptoms. Mr Winwood would think I was mad, never-the-less Blackie must go.

Once again I telephoned the Hospital to make an appointment.

I explained Blackie's symptoms to Mr Winwood who stood quite still for a moment just looking at me. What was he thinking? Was he wondering whether advancing years really had turned my mind or was he perhaps remembering my insistence proved right regarding Tessa's heart?

Whatever his thoughts he was, as always, kindness personified. He listened to Blackie's heart then agreed to book an ECG appointment for a few days later.

Until I knew the result of the ECG Blackie must not rush about, even if he wanted to. As with Kimmy and Tessa before him, the period of waiting was stressful.

When the day came, the four of us went up to Wood Street in Rebecca arriving for the last appointment of the morning. This time is was Tessa who waited – trembling – in the car while I took Blackie in, registered our arrival with Madelaine, the receptionist, then took a seat in the waiting room.

Unlike Tess, Blackie would wait patiently for his turn to be seen. Only a slight occasional tremble betraying the nervousness he was feeling.

Since the introduction of the appointments system, the hospital's patients are never kept waiting very long. Within a minute or two Mr Winwood came to the door inviting us into the consulting room. Blackie reluctantly followed me in.

Having updated Mr Winwood on his condition Blackie was then lead away for his ECG while I sat metaphorically biting my nails in the waiting room. If Blackie's heart was affected he would be fine – he must be. Kimmy had led a long, happy life despite her condition and Tessa was doing well all considered.

After what seemed like an age the door in the corner of the room opened and Blackie came through pulling as hard as he could on the lead, a young nurse holding on for dear life behind him.

Back in the consulting room my suspicions were confirmed. Blackie had a slight heart defect. He would have to live on Lanoxin for the rest of his life. Well, at least I knew how to look after him. I'd had plenty of experience. Understanding coupled with TLC works wonders.

This was not the end of Blackie's problems. A few weeks later he cut his paw very badly while in the park and had to have the injury bandaged for about ten days. Gone are the times when a white bandage is used, which turns rapidly to grey then a dirty black. A wide variety of colours are available now so Blackie had a beautiful bright yellow dressing wrapped around his paw and progressing 3–4 inches up his leg. The contrast with his black shiny coat was very impressive.

Despite Mr Winwood's warning that Blackie would probably try to pull the bandage off, not once did he touch it – not even to lick it. He really was extremely good. Of course he received lots of attention from the many people we met while exercising. "Oh, poor boy what have you done?" He loved this, looking up with such an innocent, pathetic expression waiting for the sympathy to continue!

When he was better, as a reward for being so good I bought him a large white and black plastic football. Treating them both alike Tessa had a present too, a soft yellow disney type animal which immediately found its way straight into her mouth to be tossed around and shaken.

The football was a brilliant idea. Blackie was thrilled with it, he knocked it about with his paws, tried to bite it then kept us in fits of laughter back-kicking it through his rear legs with his front paws then turning round to chase it all over the garden. Tessa sat on the lawn watching all this with bemused interest – as a Mother watches a child playing. She loved to play but this was definitely for boy dogs who have not grown up – really whatever would Blackie get up to next? She preferred a soft toy any day – more ladylike!

Now that he could not rush about so much this game of footy was proving very good exercise for Blackie. The first ball lasted less than a week before his teeth penetrated the outer skin. He'd had so much fun with his new toy and given us so much pleasure watching him that another one had to be purchased forthwith. Over the summer he managed to play his way through an average of three balls a month but it was worth it to see him reaping so much enjoyment from it. However, he had not forgotten his gonk. The football was just a diversion when in the garden. Gonk still went everywhere with him. At times he sat moving his jaws up and down around the middle of the rubber cone so the end closed, then releasing his hold to allow it to open afresh before clamping his mouth round the toy again squashing it shut once more. He even chewed into it as he ran along.

Needless to say with such devoted attention, the gonk did not last for ever, so had to be replaced about every six months. To ensure he should not be without his comforter, a spare gonk was always kept in the drawer in readiness to replace his existing one when it eventually split in two.

Chapter XC

As summer drew to a close it seemed a good idea to prepare for winter by acquiring both dogs a new red tartan, fleecy lined coat for the cold weather and a track suit for the wet days. They both had a thinner coat for chilly days but Tessa was getting older so would be feeling the cold more. Now Blackie also had a heart condition he too would need to be kept warm.

Red is a bright cheerful colour and could be easily spotted when they were off the lead running loose in the fields. The pair looked really smart as they walked along side by side in their tartan coats which, to my delight, often brought admiring remarks from passers-by.

On one occasion Blackie's tartan coat saved him from what could have been serious injury. We were walking around the path through the wooded area in Oakwood Park. As we came up to a bend a boxer dog suddenly sprung into view pouncing on our Blackie pinning him to the ground. The boxer began relentlessly biting into Blackies back with a vengeance. Poor Blackie was powerless. Thank heavens he was wearing his tartan coat which, being so thick, protected him from his attacker's teeth. The boxer's owner ran up pulling her dog off. It was obvious from her attitude this was not the first time the dog had made an unprovoked attack.

Tessa did not know what to do – it all happened so quickly. She stood rooted to the spot in shock, helpless. As soon as Blackie was free she ran up to him, sniffed his muzzle then licked his face all over. He looked really dazed – he had done nothing to warrant such behaviour, he had simply been walking along minding his own business.

When we got home Blackie buried his head in my lap to be fussed and have his ears tickled. This was always his way of coming for a little extra TLC and of course he was never refused.

The track suits also proved worth their weight in gold. Dark blue in colour with a white fluorescent stripe the suits proved wonderful protection against the rain or snow. Tessa in particular benefited as it kept the long white feathers on her tail and legs dry. No wonder, all those years ago in Bramley Road, the Afghan had worn her track suit so much. I may have smiled then but how glad I was now to have similar suits for Tessa and Blackie.

Tessa was beginning to eat less, sleep more and not always respond when called. At first, knowing she had a mind of her own, I erroneously assumed she was simply "doing her own thing". When off the lead she trotted along ignoring the fact Blackie and I were turning onto a different path. I could call and call to no avail. It took a little while for the truth to dawn. Tessa was loosing her hearing. If she was facing me there was no problem it was only when she was not looking directly at me the trouble started.

She would not always eat her food, sometimes missing several meals before tucking heartily into a huge bowl full. Mr Winwood told me she was behaving the way dogs do in the wild. Eating as much as she could to last her until she "found" the next meal rather than eating a little and often as the domesticated dog does. It was all part of growing old.

One time however she never refused to eat, was in the car when I had been shopping. Presumably this was because it had, over the years, become an ingrained habit – one I was frequently pleased she had acquired.

At home, in order to tempt her I would open a tin of carrots or hot dog sausages. Neither would ever be refused but be gobbled up with relish.

Tessa may have been slowing down but her mind was still actively working along with her keen spirit as she aptly demonstrated one day when, standing at the front gate, Trina the noisy German Shepherd from next door but one, came rushing up to the gate barking and snarling. Dear old Tess, she remained perfectly calm. Looked at Trina then gave one placid yet firm "woof". Immediately Trina's tail went down between her legs as she shot off back to her own home.

Unless motivated by a third party to bark, as on this encounter with Trina, since developing hearing problems, Tessa usually only barked when she heard Blackie do so.

Chapter XCI

About this time we came in contact again with cousins Eileen and Dennis who were now living in Iver in Buckinghamshire. Sadly Tina, their beautiful tabby cat, had long since died as a result of a road accident outside their house so, much as Eileen and Dennis love animals, they would not put another cat at risk from the ever increasing traffic. However, they were delighted to hear about our Tessa and Blackie, expressing the hope to see them before long.

Because of Mother's age, in the first instance, Eileen and Dennis came to visit us. It was wonderful to see them again, all the more because they were enchanted with Tess and Black who responded immediately to the love and attention they were receiving. Eileen had thoughtfully brought the pair a doggie treat each which endeared her all the more not only to Tessa and Blackie but to me on their behalf. Tessa was stroked and fussed all afternoon but though Blackie looked on longingly he was still too nervous of people and hands to allow anyone to stroke him. Never-the-less he revelled in all the love emitted to him, all the kind words spoken to him to which he rejoined with his very expressive upturned face reaching out towards the giver in appreciative response, his tail constantly wagging from side to side with pleasure.

Eileen kindly invited the four of us to visit them, if it were not too tiring for Mother. On the contrary she would enjoy going to see them and it would be a nice outing for Tessa and Blackie also. A chance to walk along different paths, enjoy new smells.

A few weeks later, with Mother and Blackie ensconced on Rebecca's back seat and, Tessa next to me in the front, we drove over to Iver. Amazingly we only took a wrong turning once! As usual both dogs were very good on the journey which took just over an hour. They had a little present for Eileen by way of thanking her for having them. Though the three of us went out walking and somewhere in the car every day we were, these days, rarely invited to visit. Alice had sadly died in June 1989; Aunty Ivy was also no longer with us and with Mother becoming more frail, the chance to go "out for tea" was a very special treat.

Both Tessa and Blackie remembered their cousins, greeting them as warmly as they themselves were welcomed. Being a warm, pleasant day we all sat in the back garden most of the afternoon allowing Tess and Black to explore this new ground which held great interest as it backed onto open fields. Then, before tea, Eileen suggested taking the pair for a walk down the lane beside the house. The start of the lane being next to Eileen's and Dennis's property, it runs for about ¾ mile between farmland on the left and hedgerows on the right interspersed by the occasional cottage, then up over the M25 Motorway.

Tess and Black were eager for a walk so, leaving Dennis to talk to Mother, we set off. Progress was slow as it seemed every few yards this fascinating lane held something new to be investigated. Tess was happy to trot along, sniffing here there and everywhere. Blackie, on the other hand, was bouncing along like a year old puppy. He didn't know where to look or sniff first. Then he caught sight of Tessa. What was she looking at? Tess was standing very erect by a gap in the hedge staring at something as hard as she could. He must dash over to have a look. Goodness, they were funny looking dogs! They were certainly very big and all that curly fur – what a funny noise they were making, a kind of bleat.

Though we have cows, goats, horses and sheep in our own area at home, Blackie had never been quite as close to them as he was now. He looked, gave a little bark, danced about then looked again. These creatures were wonderful! He couldn't take his eyes off them.

The instant he came to investigate, Tessa decided she had seen enough so began trotting off down the lane. Finally, Blackie realised he was being left behind so, reluctant to leave his new friends, he gave them one parting glance then dashed down the lane after the rest of us. No matter how captivating these creatures were he certainly did not want to be left behind!

In addition to the sheep we passed at close quarters to a horse. This time both dogs had a good look, being stared at equally hard by the equine, before progressing to the motorway bridge. Time to turn back for tea.

The walk down the lane had taken about 45 minutes in total. So filled with wonder was Blackie, so much had he enjoyed himself that there and then Eileen christened it "Blackies Lane", so it remains to this day.

Back indoors, Eileen had prepared a wonderful high tea for all of us. She had not forgotten Tessa and Blackie in her preparation, having thoughtfully bought them a few slices of cold meat each. How kind she and Dennis were. Like all dog owners I was as thrilled for the pair to have been considered, for them to have such a scrumptious treat, as they were to eat it. They both expressed their appreciation in the usual tail wagging manner.

Chapter XCII

The following week we were sitting in the back garden at home when I suddenly noticed something in Blackie's eye. Calling him over I tried, with a clean hanky, to carefully remove the object. Whatever it was that had adhered to his eyeball it was certainly a fair size. As always he was as good as gold, allowing me to pull his lids this way and that without any fuss. Tessa came over to see what was going on and stood watching what was happening. They always took a keen interest in anything that was being done to or for each other. This time though I was not having much luck. The object refused to budge. Fortunately it didn't appear to be worrying him too much. Maybe it would come out of it's own accord while he was asleep. With any luck it would be out by the morning. All would be well.

However, next morning the fragment was still in Blackie's eye. I had failed to remove it; it had not come out naturally, perhaps Mr Winwood would be able to get it out. Fortunately he was in surgery that morning and was able to see us. All would soon be well again.

Blackie stood perfectly still while Mr Winwood tried to remove the scrap. But alas he too failed to move, let alone dislodge it. There was only one thing to be done, Blackie must have an anaesthetic so allowing Mr Winwood greater ease of movement to lift the offending object off the eyeball. An appointment was made for the next morning and, for the second time, Blackie found himself on the operating table. It was all over very quickly and when I picked Blackie up Mr Winwood told me the cause of all the trouble had been a flake of dried paint. It must have been caught up by the wind which then deposited it on Black's eyeball. Where on earth had it come from? The only possible answer could be the workshop or garage side door which, along with the house, were awaiting a re-paint. What were the chances of such a thing happening – it was too incredible to even think about? Fortunately Black was none-the-worse for his ordeal, in fact he appeared to barely be aware that anything unusual had happened.

However this was not the end of Blackie's mishaps. On the 21 February the following year the three of us were in the field at the far end of the park when suddenly Blackie yelped, lifting his back leg. Whatever was the matter? Tess came running over to see what was wrong while I rubbed his leg trying to ease whatever had caused him to cry out.

There, was that better? Could he walk now? No. He could not put any weight on his leg. We were a good way from the car. With Black's weight and my heart condition there was no way I could carry him. Very slowly the three of us made our way back across the fields to the car where, with help, Blackie eventually managed to clamber in. Hopefully rest would soon put the leg right again.

The remainder of the day Blackie struggled around on three legs. He even had to eat his food standing with the back leg held up. The next day he was no better. This was not right – he would need to see Mr Winwood yet again.

The hospital was beginning to feel like a second home – apart from all the surgery visits it was necessary to go up every week or so to replenish our supply of all the tablets both Tessa and Blackie were now taking. In addition to their heart tablets they were both taking Vivitonin, a medication the hospital magazine had featured some months previously which improves the circulation in older dogs increasing the blood flow generally, particularly to the heart and brain. This helps the regularity of the heartbeat and slows down the onset of senility. Both Tessa, who had begun occasionally walking in circles as the result of a possible growth on one side of her brain, and Blackie were noticeably benefiting from this treatment. Both were more alert mentally and physically.

Once more Blackie was up on the consulting table while Tess sat in Rebecca with Mother. Having examined him thoroughly Mr Winwood said he was sure Black had torn a ligament. This could be positively confirmed with x-rays and if necessary operated on but of course there is always the possibility of danger with anaesthetic on an older dog.

After discussion it was agreed Blackie would have the x-rays taken then we could decide the best course of action, though an operation was best avoided if possible.

On Tuesday 27 February Blackie had to be in hospital by 8.30am. He had his gonk with him also Tessa's 'Terry' and a scarf of mine to give him comfort. Once more Black was under anaesthetic.

The x-rays showed he had torn the anterior crucial ligament in his knee. An operation could be performed but it involved major surgery and because of Blackie's age Mr Winwood suggested we try allowing the knee to heal naturally. This would take a long time and success was not guaranteed.

Worried about Black having another anaesthetic I agreed to try letting nature hold the reigns of recovery first. If this was not successful we would have to discuss the matter further.

Over the next three to four months Blackie made very slow but sure progress. At first he was unable to stand on four legs even to eat his food. His early walks were on three legs with frequent stops to rest. Each day I took a notepad and pencil in order to make a note of the number of steps, if any, Blackie was able to make on four legs. The records show notable events such as "stood on four legs for 30 seconds"; "stood on four legs to do wow-woz". "walked from the house to the car on four legs". The number of steps taken each day on four legs were carefully recorded to show Mr Winwood, who saw Blackie at regular intervals. Gradually Black improved from "stood on four legs and took a step" to "4 steps", "22 steps", "56 steps", "103 steps", "167 steps", "250 steps", "335 steps" then "ran on four legs the length of the retractable lead".

Blackie, like Tessa, was on the healing list at Potters Bar church, being remembered at each healing session. With great patience on his part Black was making progress. It was wonderful to watch him improving a little each day, to know each step taken was a step away from the necessity of an operation. There would now be no need to operate, no need to risk another anaesthetic.

Tessa was wonderful with him. Although she ran around playing with other dogs, she never went far away from Black. Always waiting patiently for him, watching him as he endeavoured to overcome his injury.

Eventually the day came when Blackie was able to walk free again. He would never be able to run as fast as he once had but then he was not as young as he used to be. However, every age has it's compensations and Tessa could not run as fast either. They were growing happily old together.

The following spring while walking in Oak Hill Park in East Barnet Village, Blackie tore the ligament in his other back leg so the recovery routine began all over again. This time the recovery did not take quite so long – he was walking free again in about 2–3 months. Also during this time he developed and overcame a canine influenza virus. Tessa strained the ligament in her front left leg and was stung in the mouth by a wasp. Was there no end to the troubles these two would find themselves in? It was reaching the point where, when I rang the hospital, Madelaine would sympathetically say "Hello Gillian. Oh dear, which one is it this time? What have they done now?"

Chapter XCIII

That summer I realised though there were countless photographs of Tessa and Blackie, they were growing older and I did not have a photograph of myself with the pair of them. This had to be remedied.

Not far from home is Flambards, a photographic studio where we could have a group photograph taken. The appointment was made. Both dogs were given a nice bath followed by a good brush. Unfortunately the weather was very hot, much too hot in fact. Mother waited in the reception area while I took Tess and Black into the studio.

Despite the patient understanding of the photographer, the two of them simply would not settle. There were so many interesting objects about the studio to be investigated. No sooner was one dog settled than the other wandered off. Trying to keep the two of them still on the couch was proving the most difficult of tasks. Fortunately the photographer was a loyal Kodak customer so we had a common bond, which I am sure helped the situation!

Eventually several photographs were taken despite Tessa's and Blackie's best endeavours to disrupt the sitting.

The proofs took about a week and the finished prints about the same length of time. Bearing in mind the difficulty the photographer had experienced the end results were very good so, having chosen a favourite, it was framed and hung on the staircase wall. A wonderful momento for the future.

As is often the case, it never rains but it pours. The photographs were no sooner ready than Kodak gave each of their employees and retirees a photographic voucher for a sitting, plus an enlargement, with one of their listed photographers. It would be a shame to waste this opportunity. Gradually an idea dawned. We have two or three family portraits, dating back to the early 19th Century which hang on the walls of our home. Perhaps we could have a family photograph taken of Mother,

Tony, Tessa, Blackie and myself with Dad and our previous dogs superimposed! Not only would it be a wonderful photograph to have, it could be handed down to future generations together with the existing portraits.

From the list of photographers supplied by Kodak I chose Sovereign Photography in East Barnet, just a few minutes drive from home. After visiting their studio and discussing the matter with photographers Paul and Jason, it was decided the basic photograph, which would be covered by the voucher, should be taken in our back garden. This would not only be easier for Mother but Tessa and Blackie would be more settled than in the studio. Also the garden would provide a more natural setting.

The day of the sitting was warm, bright and sunny. As predicted, unlike the studio session at Flambards, now in their own home Tessa and Blackie behaved perfectly. Mother sat on a chair in front of the camellia while Tony and I stood behind her leaving enough room between us for Dad to be superimposed. Tessa and Blackie, as they were told, sat quietly on the grass in front of us.

While we were all together, Paul and Jason took one or two other shots including one indoors with which we were absolutely delighted. Again Tess and Black were on their best behaviour.

I had searched through literally dozens of old photographs to locate the most natural of Paddy, Trixie, Kimmy and our last Billy to give Paul, ready for adding to the final masterpiece. Unfortunately there was not one to be found of my Paddy. The photo of Dad was easy. After his untimely death, Mother and I had chosen a head and shoulders picture taken of him standing next to Aunty Winnie's bungalow in Sussex. Although he was talking with Aunty's neighbour Elsie, my colleagues in Kodak had kindly made a selective transparency of Dad on his own. The slide they produced measures a mere 1" × ¾" but because of it's clarity, enlarges up to A5 without any problem. This would be perfect.

A week of two later Paul and Jason produced the finished work mounted in a gilt and polished wood frame. A real work of art to hung in pride of place in the drawing room.

Chapter XCIV

Come September, we visited Hunstanton again for a five day break. It would be a treat for Tess and Black, it would do Mother good to have a change of scenery and get a breath of fresh sea air. Also I was much in need of a break. No matter how much you love someone, looking after them 24 hours a day seven days a week eventually takes its toil and a break is essential for all concerned.

The local branch of Crossroads kindly agreed to sit with Mother in the car, on the cliff top, for an hour on the Tuesday and Thursday so I could take Tessa and Blackie on the beach. Without the help of this caring organisation it would not have been possible for Tess and Black to have had more than a short walk as Mother could no longer be left alone, even in Rebecca.

The journey up to Norfolk was very cold and windy with heavy showers. Unfortunately far from improving during our stay, the weather grew much worse. Every day we experienced high winds and/or torrential rain. Amazingly this did not deter either Tessie or Blackie from enjoying themselves. As always they were delighted to greet old friends; to enjoy the short walks we were able to take even if they came back soaked despite their raincoats.

At 12.30pm on the Tuesday we parked on the cliff top as pre-arranged with Crossroads. As always Blackie began barking passionately as soon as we turned onto the cliff track.

Rebecca is rather conspicuous due to her shape and age, so the lady who came to stay with Mother had no trouble finding us and was able to park her car next to ours over-looking the sea.

The rain was simply pouring down and the wind blowing so hard it was difficult to stand up. Never-the-less Crossroads had kept their part of the agreement. Their Carer had arrived on time and, other than the hour on Thursday, it was the only chance Tess and Black would have to run on the sand. So, with the pair dressed in their raincoats to give at least some protection, I donned plastic raincoat, hat and red wellies then clambered out of Rebecca with two excited dogs tumbling out after me.

They seemed oblivious to the elements; both pulled hard on their retractable leads anxious to reach the pathway onto the beach where they knew they would be released.

Intrepid though most dog walkers are, they seemed to have more sense than to venture out in this deluge. At the bottom of the pathway I unclipped both dogs setting them free. I half anticipated them standing looking up as though I were mad expecting them to run around in this weather. Not a bit of it! Tess was the first away. The instant she was unclipped she was off down the beach like a puppy, tail going in circles. It was wonderful to see her revelling in the sheer delight of it all. She had found her lost youth if only temporarily and was enjoying it! Blackie was only a few seconds behind her, barking with excitement. Always the overgrown puppy!

Not surprisingly we were the only people on the beach as far as I could see, in either direction. In a way this was an added bonus as

Tessie and Black could ran around without my having to worry about other dogs.

The tide being halfway out Tess and Black spent the hour running up and down the sand, this way and that, round in circles, in and out of the pools left by the retreating sea, chasing the seagulls until they escaped into the wind battered rain. The two of them were having the time of their lives despite the continuing downpour.

Mother and her companion could be seen sitting in Rebecca high up on the top of the cliff. There were only one or two other cars parked along there this day, the occupants looking out over the rain beaten sea, probably thinking we were stark raving mad to be out on such a day.

The hour passed surprisingly quickly. Before we knew it, it was time to return to Beccy where both Tessa and Blackie had a thorough rub down with several dry towels, followed by a long drink and good lunch. Mother had been in good hands and both dogs had spent a fantastic hour playing on the beach.

Unfortunately Thursday brought little let-up in the wind or rain so for a second time the three of us spent our hour on the beach in cold, miserable conditions but enjoying ourselves never-the-less.

We returned home on Friday, the wind by now having eased considerably. The rain still coming down though not quite so heavily. Despite the weather we must all have benefited from the change of air though I had a feeling this would be our last holiday together. Mother was very distressed by the journey and change of environment. Tessie, now 16 and despite her youthful play on the beach, was showing signs of her age. Her mind was still very alert but she was growing thin, doing everything more slowly and generally becoming an old lady.

Blackie was very conscious of his friends needs. He adored her and his gentle, loving nature was always there for her. If ever Tessie needed help, if she was having difficulty trying to get upstairs or onto a chair; if she wanted to go out and I didn't realise; If she was having one of her fits; whatever her needs Blackie always came to me squeaking loudly, wriggling and looking up until I followed him to Tessa and was able to help her. He then looked up giving a wag of his tail as if to say "Thank you Mum – she is alright now".

Chapter XCV

When it was necessary to replace the hall, stair and landing carpet Blackie ran up and down without any trouble but Tessie could not get a grip so it became necessary to carry her up or down whenever she needed to go.

One morning she wandered to the top of the staircase while I was dressing, walked down the first two steps then jumped the next 12 to the bottom landing. Blackie came running to me as I saw what happened and dashed down stairs, heart thumping, to see what Tessie had done to herself. There was no evident injury. I cuddled her gently trying to re-assure her. She must see Mr Winwood to make sure there were no unseen injuries.

As always Madelaine was kindness itself, of course I could bring Tessa up straight away. Mr Winwood was there and under the circumstances would fit her in.

Bungling Mother and Blackie into the car I put Tessa on her front seat and drove up to Barnet as quickly as possible.

Mr Winwood did not keep us waiting long – a patient was late arriving so he called us in to see Tessa before the late-comer arrived.

He examined Tess very thoroughly. Amazingly she had not injured herself in any way. She certainly appeared to have taken the incident in her stride. It seemed barely credible she was totally unscathed after such a fall, yet the news was a tremendous relief prompting me to give her a big hug. Mr Winwood suggested in all probability because of her medical history and age related conditions, including the onset of cataracts, she had misjudged the distance from the top to the bottom of the stairs. From now on she must be watched even more carefully.

There was no question of Tessa suffering as a result of her aging body or Mr Winwood would not have hesitated to suggest ending her plight. She was still taking an interest in everything. Still enjoying her meal even if she did sometimes put a paw in the food bowl. Then she was fussed and told "Tessie dear feet out, nose in". As it was less tiring for her she very sensibly sat down to eat. And if, when bedtime came she was asleep I would pick her up, carry her upstairs then lay her gently in her own bed without waking her. On such occasions Blackie watched closely, following us up the stairs then standing watching her put to bed, ensuring she was alright before trotting round to his own bed the other side of mine, to find his bedtime treat of a Beggin Strip and Doggaroni.

Tess was still using the Goddards bed which had been bought originally for Kimmy though when Blackie had his new round, padded, red tartan bed in March 1996 she had been bought a smaller version of the same one as she had on several occasions clambered into his and curled up contentedly. However she rarely used her new one and slept every night in the Goddards.

Blackie was considerate of Tessa too when it was time for a walk and she was fast asleep. Normally he barked excitedly at the sight of the retractable lead, however a finger to my lips with a gentle "Ssshh

Blackie – Tessa is asleep. Don't disturb her" and he would be as quiet as a mouse. We would tip-toe out of the house, up the front path then out of the gate leaving Tessa resting peacefully. She could not walk as far as Blackie these days so to try to make her do so would be unkind. She enjoyed as much exercise as she wanted and still loved to go out in the car. When the four of us set out I sang the three of them a little ditty "Oh we are off in the car for a lovely ride. Up to the shops through the countryside. Oh how lucky we really are – for from the farms we are not too far". Not that any of them appreciated it – Mother took no notice; Blackie turned to look out of the side window and Tessie stared straight ahead. Their reaction was always the same!

Tessa may have been aging steadily but she was in no way silly. Whenever the pair were given beef sticks as a treat they always had a mixture of soft and hard ones so each dog would be satisfied. However Tess munched her own soft ones then graciously allowed Blackie to chew the hard ones until they were soft when she quietly walked over and took the soggy mass away from him right under his nose. He had done all the work now she could enjoy the results! Bless him he never objected, never tried to stop her.

There was no question, at any other time, of either dog taking food from the other. Together they shared titbits from Mother's breakfast which, due to her increasing age and incapability, she had in bed each morning. The pair sat next to her bed waiting for that tasty morsel of herring roe, fried egg white, buttered bread or whatever goodies where on offer that day.

They shared their treats too on a Saturday evening when "Aunty" Audrey came across to spend the evening with us and always brought them a packet of ham and a packet of Schmackos between them. The soft, flat beef sticks they shared immediately but had to wait until we had our mid-evening snack before the ham was divided equally between them. Needless to say it was cobbled up in an instant!

Chapter XCVI

Though several years younger than Tessa, a touch of arthritis began to develop in Blackie's back legs. As is the case with this disease there would be days when he walked quite easily then there others when, if he walked at all, he would hobble. Mr Winwood prescribed Metacam, a non-steroid anti-inflammatory drug, to help control the pain. Fortunately Blackie never objected to medication and as this one is in liquid form it was easily added to his food.

Then, as a consequence of meeting Bill Medcalf's Aunty Mary, I was introduced to a wonderful means of helping Blackie even further. To give me a short break from 24 hour caring, Tony stayed with Mother and the dogs for a couple of hours while Bill and Gillian took me to Saffron Walden where we had lunch with Bill's aunt and uncle who are local farmers. Mary, herself a ardent dog lover, had details of a Bioflow Magnotherapy collar which combines traditional magnotherapy with modern science for the relief of aches and pains, arthritis, rheumatism and such like afflictions. Though she did not have personal experience of the collar or the wristband, designed for humans, as she said there would be no harm in trying it.

Before ordering the collar I discussed the matter with Mr Winwood who confessed to being open minded on the matter. I should not expect wonder cures but it could not do any harm. He would be interested to hear how Blackie got along with it.

So I telephoned Wendy Hill, the Bioflow agent in Gwent, talked to her about the benefits and ordered a collar for Blackie. She assured me of a full refund after 60 days if the collar did not prove successful though apparently this is rarely the case. The collar – or wristband – has to be worn 24 hours a day with the magnet on the left of the neck or wrist. It is only taken off for bathing*.

Like Mr Winwood I was open minded but willing to try anything within reason to help Black.

In due course the collar arrived and once in place round Blackie's neck I waited patiently for results. I did not have to wait long. Amazingly in a matter of hours Blackie seemed to be walking a little easier – or was it imagination?

As the days passed so Blackie's walking improved, he actually began to run and play again. The collar was certainly working for him. I was not the only one to notice the improvement. Numerous people we met regularly noticed the betterment including Elizabeth, a charming lady who walked her three dogs in the park each day, she could not believe her eyes when she saw Blackie moving so easily. So impressed was she with the change in him, she asked for details of the collar in order to purchase one for her eldest dog, Max. There was no doubt the magnotherapy collar was a great success!

Though Tessie no longer walked very far the four of us still went to the park each day. Unfortunately, Enfield Council had decided to close the entrance in Lakenheath to vehicles so it was now necessary to drive right round to the side entrance in Prince George Avenue. This meant Mother had to stay in the car on the roadway so, like other elderly or

---

* Telephone ECOFLOW on 0175284114 for further information.

221

disabled folk who could not walk, was denied the pleasure of enjoying watching the activities of the various park users at close quarters as had been the case previously. However, the grassy verges and trees are more interesting to dogs than any pavement so we continued to go there.

Tessie walked very slowly with me stopping now and then for a sniff, while Blackie, though obviously not cured but vastly improved, ran around having doggie fun. However, he never went far from his friend, always returning to her side every few minutes to make sure all was well.

Chapter XCVII

As the year progressed so Tessa grew more frail until on Friday 3 October I took her to see Mr Winwood, taking with me a written account of her daily movements. Though she had been gradually aging for some time, of late her aging process seemed to have accelerated. She was now very thin and becoming wobbly on her feet.

Mr Winwood read the notes then examined her carefully. He stepped back from the examination table, looked at me and said gently "You know what I am going to say don't you?" Too choked to speak I just nodded. "It is not fair to keep her alive now. Her quality of life has completely gone – she must be almost 17, it is a good age and she has had a wonderful life with all the love and care you have given her. Now, for her sake, it is time to let her go. Keep her with you the weekend and if you agree, I will come round to your home on Monday morning."

Hard though it was to face facts, Mr Winwood was right. Despite her medical problems, her heart condition, the various fits and attacks she had experienced throughout most of her life, the infections she had picked up, the different things that had happened to her, she had endured them all bravely and she had enjoyed her life to the full. I had always spoken to her of Kimmy, Trixie and the Paddies so she would be with friends.

Having telephoned Joan Norton, President of our church in Potters Bar, the four of us drove up on Saturday afternoon with two bunches of mixed flowers, two of red roses and two of white freesias. They were to be put on the side table next to the rostrum for the Sunday evening service, staying there throughout the coming week, in remembrance of Tessa and for thoughts for her peaceful passing into spirit on the Monday. She would be given thoughts of healing and love throughout the service especially during the healing intercession.

Returning home, Beryl arrived about 4.30pm to give me a much needed back massage to relieve tension. She was very upset but not surprised to hear the news of Tessa and before she left, with tears in her eyes, said a fond au revior to her. She would see Blackie next time she came – oh dear he was going to miss Tess. She gave Black an affectionate stroke along his back, even Beryl could still not stroke his head – this was the prerogative of Tony or myself.

The weekend was the most difficult, emotional time. Loving Tessa; knowing we were going to lose her physical presence very shortly; trying to keep the mental sadness under control so as not to upset either Tess or Black; wandering how Blackie was going to cope when his best friend went to join our other animals; choking back the tears. Having Mother to look after kept me physically busy – she could not fully comprehend what was happening.

Tessa had weakened too much to take her out for a walk so Blackie had to been taken on his own. Just round the block for these couple of days. He would not mind. He knew something was wrong but could not understand what it was.

As we walked along, whenever a wave of sorrow swept over me Blackie stopped, looked up at me with his head on one side and wearing a worried, puzzled expression. That face of his – so extraordinarily expressive.

Monday dawned a beautiful, bright, sunny day. Mother was up earlier this morning and downstairs sitting in her armchair by the fire in the lounge.

I sat on the bottom stair with Tessa on my lap while she ate her breakfast and as usual tried to put her feet in the dish. "No Tessie dear – feet out, nose in!" She enjoyed her food especially the last few days as she had been treated to all her favourite things which, naturally, Blackie had shared.

When she finished eating she walked unsteadily into the kitchen for a drink then asked to go out of the back door into the yard at the side of the house. She loved to stand here looking out between the six foot gate and the posts. The gap just large enough to poke her nose through so as to see what was going on outside the house. This morning though she merely tottered around the yard. She was so frail she could hardly stand today. The right thing was being done for her – she could not live more than a few days so why let her suffer?

The double front gates were open in readiness for Mr Winwood to drive in. Promptly at 11 o'clock he pulled onto the tarmac. As I opened the front door Blackie spotted Mr Winwood and the nurse coming towards the house so bolted upstairs under the bed in the guest room. Tessa was lying on her fur fabric bed next to Mother in the lounge.

As Mr Winwood walked in she merely glanced up at him then looked at me enquiringly. "It's alright Tessie dear" – now was the time to be strong for her. Dad was standing there with us waiting to receive her into his arms. I stroked her head lovingly fighting to remain emotionally calm for her sake. Her face uplifted, then wearily lowered onto her bed again as Mr Winwood knelt beside her. Nurse came behind Tess as Mr Winwood gently put her to sleep. Her long fight against physical weakness was over – she was at peace and in Dad's arms, he was cradling her gently with a love tender and strong. He would take care of her now, help her to settle and adjust. It was ten past eleven and life had changed for all of us.

At 12.15 I became aware that Tessa, still with Dad, was awake though drowsie. Her transition had been peaceful but she needed to rest now, to regain the strength she had lost as a result of her physical condition immediately prior to her passing.

A very subdued Blackie eventually came downstairs. He had not seen Tessa being taken out of the house but somehow he knew she was not there. He didn't look for her, just came into the lounge and lay down. When lunchtime came he refused any food, he would not even look at it. This was worrying but maybe he would eat some dinner.

About half past two we were in the dining room having a cup of tea when suddenly I became very strongly aware of Tessa's love – she was rested, now she was back with us. Then to my utter amazement I clearly and distinctly heard a voice say "I am sorry I made life difficult at times". Choked with emotion my immediate response was "I'm sorry I was not always as patient as I should have been". A fresh wave of love swept between the two of us. Bless her – she must be very highly evolved to be able to communicate so audibly, so clearly. Neither Trixie nor Kimmy had had any difficulty making themselves known to us after their passing but this was completely different. Tessa's voice had been crystal clear. If I had not heard it for myself I would not have believed it. Then I remembered the day we went to Grovelands Park and she had understood my warning to stay close because there were bad people around who would harm her. She had amazed me then by staying within a few feet of me. Again, when we drove to pick up Blackie from the police station – she had sat in the car visibly listening to every word I said and appeared to understand. I remembered also Stan's words of many years before when he had said quietly "That is an extremely intelligent little dog you have got there. She is highly developed".

Gradually I was beginning to realise what an exceptionally intelligent and spiritual dog we had been living with all these years and felt humbled at the privilege of sharing her life.

As the days passed so Blackie was still very withdrawn. He had lost all interest in everything – he just sat staring into space, lost and lonely.

His best friend had gone. He would not eat. I tried everything I could think of to tempt him – without success. Even his number one favourite, chicken, could not arouse his interest. The only sustenance he was receiving was through the glucose in his drinking water. To this day I can not understand why Blackie could not see Tessa. Animals are supposed to be naturally very psychic, so why couldn't Blackie see Tess? Or could he? Did he realise she had passed over and was this why he was grieving so badly – because he could see her in spirit form?

Knowing his deep grieving would worry Tess I mentally asked if she could help him with his problem. Even as the thought went out I was conscious of her moving close to him in an attempt to comfort and reassure him. She came on walks with us and her presence was a great comfort. Her spirituality was, for me at any rate, easing the loss of her physical body.

Although to the physical eye Blackie and I went to the park alone, in actuality we were accompanied by not only Tessie but Kimmy, Trixie and the Paddies, in other words "The Gang".

If only the rush and tear of everyday life did not have to return to rob me of this extra sensitivity – but one has to live in this world while here. It is undesirable to live constantly bridging the gap between our world and the next. There are times for relaxation, for meditation and harmony to unite with those who have passed over but it is essential to maintain a down to earth attitude. Those who visit and help us have lives of their own to live and we must not impose upon their right to do so.

Always happy memories of Tess were with us. Occasionally she had sat next to Blackie on the back seat of the car then she would take up most of the seat while Blackie sat squashed up in the corner, but he didn't mind, he didn't complain. Other times the two sat side by side on the front seat which, judging by his blissful expression, pleased Blackie enormously. Almost as though he were proud to be sitting in the front of the car and next to Tessie!

Memories of being in bed at night with Tess putting her paw up on the bed from one side to be stroked while Blackie put his paw up from the other side. A matter of "we are both here, we both want fussing please".

Or when walking along the pavement together on their leads both vying with each other to keep abreast. They had enjoyed a wonderful friendship which, I am sure, will continue for many, many years to come.

Days went by and still Blackie would not eat. Eventually I took him up to Mr Winwood to ask if he had any suggestions. Unfortunately there was nothing medically that could be done for Blackie. The glucose in his drinking water was giving him some nourishment but obviously not enough. Not just the lack of food was affecting him but his constant fretting was naturally having an adverse affect on his metabolism. By now his ribs were beginning to show through. In fact he was looking worse than when he first came to us.

On Thursday 16 October I could no longer watch poor Blackie suffer like this. Medical treatment could not help so there was only one thing to be done. I sat down and wrote to Gilbert Anderson. If anyone could help, Gilbert could – he was Blackies only chance now.

Giving Mother the laminated sign I had made for her some years previously which read "HAVE GONE FOR A WALK WITH TESSA AND BLACKIE. WILL BE BACK SOON", Blackie and I set off down the road with the all important letter. Fortunately we just caught the last collection at 5.30pm. Being Thursday evening it was unlikely the letter would be delivered before Saturday but I knew Gilbert would send out his healing thoughts as soon as he received the plea for help.

Next morning, Friday 17, Blackie seemed brighter. For the first time since Tess passed he was anxious to go out for a walk, barking and dancing about as soon as he spotted his lead being picked up. It was such a relief to see him excited about going out. During our walk, instead of plodding along without taking any notice of anyone or anything, Black took an interest in everything. He sniffed here, there and everywhere; barked at other dogs and generally seemed to enjoy his walk.

When we got home, for the first time since the 6 October, he ate solid food. He enjoyed a bowl of boiled chicken and blended ham.

There was only one answer. There was no need to ask as I knew what had happened. Never-the-less I telephoned Gilbert before Blackie had finished eating. Yes, he confirmed he had received my letter that very morning! His thoughts had gone out to Blackie as soon as he read of his plight. How could I ever thank him and Dr Paul, Gilbert's control doctor?

I knew Blackie would improve once Gilbert sent out his healing thoughts but did not expect to see a change until Saturday at the earliest, when I had wrongly assumed the letter would arrive.

Later that morning the three of us went in Rebecca to Barnet. This time Blackie sat looking out of his side window taking a real interest in everything and everyone we passed.

Lunch time he ate another bowl of chicken then a third bowl full for dinner at night. The relief and joy of seeing him return to normal was overwhelming.

The following Monday he consumed his first meal of normal dog food for two and a half weeks. As an aid to his recovery I removed his own round, green food bowl replacing it with Tessa's square off-white mottled one. There was no real reason why the change should make a difference, I just thought he may like to have Tessa's bowl – it was something of hers he could use daily. He certainly did not object and still uses it to this day.

By the middle of the week he began playing with his gonk again – chasing it all over the floor like a puppy. He was beginning to settle down.

Blackie now had to adjust to being an only dog. He had always relied on Tessie to lead him, to show him the way – now he must think for himself.

Within three weeks Blackie was proving he could indeed think for himself. On walks he no longer simply trotted along where he was led. Instead he would decide he wanted to take a different route and turning in the direction he fancied, pull hard on the lead ensuring I followed. This was marvellous! Tessa, Kimmy, Trixie – all had been allowed to choose the way they wanted to go now it was Blackie's turn. This was good for him. He was using his brain more positively.

Whereas previously Blackie had been only too anxious to trot upstairs at night ahead of us, allowing Tessa to wait for me, now he began to wait. I would take Mother up, put her to bed then come down to lock up the house. Blackie sat patiently on the second stair waiting, watching all I was doing. He made no attempt to move until he heard the alarm set then he looked up to make sure I was coming and walked up just behind me as Tessie has done.

With everyone tucked up in bed, like the Waltons, I always called out "goodnight Mother", then "goodnight Blackie". While Mother replied "goodnight Gillie" Blackie never failed to respond with a deep "grrrrrrr". His own particular way of saying goodnight.

First thing in the morning he would go straight into Mother's room, look up waiting for her to greet him when he responded with a vigorous wag of his tail. Usually this was followed by a lovely back roll on "Grandma's" bedroom floor for a good two minutes or so.

Later as I made the beds there was nothing Blackie loved more than jumping on and off the mattress having a high old time. More often than not this resulted in a playful rough and tumble culminating in Blackie burying his head in my lap and having his ears tickled!

Then, while I finished the beds, Blackie would lie on the landing with his paws hanging over the top stair waiting patiently.

Lunch time, if the side door was open and Blackie upstairs on the bed in the small front guest room, as soon as I called him down with a loud "Blackie – lunch", if he were in his kitchen our neighbour Mr Singer whose side door faced ours, always responded with a laugh and a "whoof whoof – come on Blackie or I will have it!" Needless to say Blackie never needed a second bidding. In fact, of an evening if he had not been called downstairs by about 5.30, he came trotting down to sit in the kitchen doorway waiting for his meal. One evening he heard me get his bowl down earlier than usual so came running down expectantly only to be greeted with "Oh sorry Blackie, it is not ready yet. It's still hot." He looked at me in disgust, turned and went back upstairs again.

On another occasion he was sitting on the guest bed looking out of the window while I was downstairs preparing his dinner. Suddenly he began barking at something outside. Jokingly I called up "Blackie – be quiet or you wont get any supper!" The barking stopped as suddenly as it had begun! There was dead silence until he was called down to eat.

He was always a pleasure to feed – he enjoyed all his food so much and always gave a wag to signal his appreciation once it was consumed.

Chapter XCVIII

Those first few months after Tessa's passing I was very conscious of her presence on many occasions. Though I only heard her voice once more she was still able to make herself understood, as Kimmy and Trixie did, by thought transference. In this way she was able to help me understand some of Blackies mystifying behaviour.

Apparently the only reason Blackie "fought" off other dogs when he first came to us was purely and simply because of the cruelty he had suffered previously which had made him very defensive. When later he picked up little dogs and shook them gently, he was genuinely unaware of the fact he was frightening them. To him it was just play – he would not have consciously frightened them for the world.

The other explanation which really made me smile was in answer to the question "why doesn't Blackie always come downstairs to do wow-woz at bedtime when I call him?" "Because he is warm and cosy and doesn't want to move!" Very logical really and simple if one stops to think about it!

The only other time I heard Tessa's voice as opposed to thought transference was on Christmas Eve. The tree was in place and looking very pretty, adorned as it was with tinsel, ornaments and coloured lights. Mother was upstairs in bed so, before going up with Blackie I fetched the presents to put round the bottom of the tree. Of course there were the usual gifts of cold chicken, Frys cream, Polos and doggie treats for Kimmy, Trixie and the two Paddys. The counterpart of which they would be able to enjoy. Later Blackie could eat the physical part that was left.

This year Tessa's gifts were among these little parcels. As I put them under the tree with the name "Tessa" on them, the tears began to flow. I knew she was alright, never-the-less this was our first Christmas without her physical presence which was still missed so much. As the tears and the heartache increased I suddenly heard a clear, strong voice say "I will be here and I will be happy", and I felt her presence beside me. There was no sorrow coming from her, only loving peace. My own feelings of grief vanished to be replaced with overwhelming joy knowing she was with us and happy, and heartfelt gratitude for the ability to be so aware of her. This Christmas had changed – it was going to be a happy time after all.

On Monday 12 January Blackie was on Mother's bed when Tessa obviously came in through the door. First Blackie's eyes opened wide as he sat up erect, then his whole head turned slowly as though watching a progressive walk into and across the bedroom floor. Finally he settled back down again but continued to stare at one spot on the carpet.

Two weeks later he was under the bed in the guest room when, for no apparent reason, he began a low key growl. Could it be that at last he was able to actually see Tessie for himself? Hopefully he could and would now feel re-assured so continue happily with his own life.

Chapter XCIX

Tony came over to see us on Thursday 29 January. He came regularly to make sure the three of us were alright even though Mother rarely recognised him these days.

Somehow there was something lacking in the house – another life form was needed but what? Another dog was out of the question just yet. Having discussed the matter with Tony I suddenly hit on the idea of goldfish. They would be something alive yet not too expensive to keep and they are very relaxing to watch. Yes, that was the answer.

Unlike Mother or Tony, when an idea occurs I have to put it into practice straight away. So, with Blackie and Mother in the back of Rebecca and Tony ensconced beside me, we set of for Wildwoods in Crews Hill, a short ten minute drive away.

An hour and a half later we returned home complete with an appropriate sized tank, two packets of shingle, pump, weed, food, a bottle of AquaSafe (to be added to the water to remove harmful chemicals), an ornamental/play bridge and three very small goldfish. Blackie showed a little interest at first then decided sleep was more to his liking!

An hour later the shingle had been thoroughly washed, the tank set in position on Dad's chairside table in the lounge and the fishes new home made ready for them. They really were tiny but hopefully they would like their tank and would grow bigger in time.

When asked, Mother simply said yes the fish were very nice. I was hoping that watching them would give her an interest. No matter how hard one tries, life is very monotonous for an elderly person when they reach their mid-nineties without enjoying the best of health.

I was equally hopeful Blackie would be fascinated by the fish, spending time sitting or lying by their tank watching them. Alas, he showed no interest what-so-ever, in fact he completely ignored them.

Having failed repeatedly to find names for the three fish they simply became "fishes" – appropriate if not very original! Never-the-less they were loved and their steady growth watched enthusiastically by Audrey as much as anyone. Each Saturday evening when she came over, she was convinced they had grown so much since the previous week. She was quite mesmerized by them, turning to look at them frequently throughout the evening. Still Blackie took no notice.

In March Blackie developed a bowel infection which gave him a lot of discomfort. Later the same month he cut his pad quite badly requiring once again a bright yellow bandage to be administered. As always he was an excellent patient both at the hospital and at home. Once again he became a regular visitor to Mr Winwood's surgery for a while until eventually he was back on form once more.

For the next month or so life went on as normal for Blackie. He still went to the park each day while Mother either stayed in bed or sat in the car on the roadway. He even found a new friend to play with, a little terrier about half his own size, named Ossie. Fortunately he didn't try to pick Ossie up so the two became good pals. Much to Ossie's delight Blackie chased him round and round in circles barking. It would be difficult to tell which of the two dogs enjoyed themselves the most. Fortunately the two met quite often and Ossie's Mum – Daphne, a really charming lady, was only too pleased for them to play together.

Occasionally we visited Trent Park, Grovelands or Oak Hill Park, anything for a change of scenery for both Blackie and Mother.

Chapter C

On the morning of Saturday the 8 August, just five days before her 95th birthday Mother was taken ill with a suspected mild stroke. After telephoning Stephen our Community Nurse, who came within ten minutes, then our doctor, Mother was taken to hospital by ambulance. Naturally I went with her, staying by her side until she was settled into the ward. Later Tony picked me up from the hospital and took me home. As soon as the front door was open Blackie went crazy with excitement and presumably relief. Poor Blackie had had to be left at home alone – something he was not used to. I had been out of the house five hours but he had been very good.

During the evening he kept looking at Mother's chair, obviously wondering where she was. She had always been there – ever since he became part of the family she had sat in her chair in the corner every evening and, of late, most of the day. He couldn't make it out.

Blackie stayed very close to me, never leaving my side for a moment. Something was wrong but he did not know what.

Bedtime came and I was glad he was there with me. This was the first time I had slept alone in a house at night and Blackie was a great comfort. When we went upstairs he ran straight into Mother's room and looked up at the bed. "No Blacks, Grandma is not there, she is in hospital – she is with Mr Winwood" Silly though it sounded I hoped the familiar names of "Grandma" and "Mr Winwood" would perhaps convey something to Blackie. He knew he went to Mr Winwood when he needed help and he always came back. Was he capable of understanding that Grandma needed help so was somewhere she could get help until coming home again? It is impossible to tell, at least I had tried to explain to him in his own terms.

The next day Blackie had to stay alone once more. Most dogs have to be left from time to time so are quite used to it but it was a new experience for Blacks. Either we had all gone out together or he had been at home with Grandma and of late, Tony. I hated leaving him but there was no choice. It was much too hot to leave him in the car even though it was possible to park right outside the ward.

So began a routine. Though tests confirmed Mother had not suffered a stroke, she was far from well and by now had to be spoonfed. Each day Tony visited her about midday to give her lunch while I visited each evening to feed her, her evening meal. I would also occasionally pay her an extra visit during the day. The ward was one of two in a separate building at the far end of the hospital grounds, with parking under the trees for about half a dozen cars and, at the end of the short drive, two bays for disabled drivers.

Fortunately Mother was in a four bed ward and next to the end window which looked down on the parked cars thus it was possible to keep an eye on Rebecca.

The first few days the weather was uncomfortably hot which meant Blackie was really in the best place at home. I always told him "I will not be too long Blackie – am just going to see Grandma" so he grew accustomed to the daily routine though of course he was always delighted to see me return.

When one of the nurses overheard me talking to Mother about Blackie, she kindly enquired after him saying if Mother would like to see him I could willingly bring him into the Day Room and she would take Mother along there. How fantastic! Both Mother and Blackie would love that.!

Next day Blackie watched me getting ready to leave for the hospital. Assuming he was going to be left as usual he sat just inside the dining room door with a look of dejection on his face. "No Blacks – you are coming with me today. Yes, you are coming to see Grandma!"

He needed no second bidding. Up he sprang barking with excitement, a wonderful expression of expectation on his upturned face. He wasn't going to be left – he was coming to and the word "Grandma" had been mentioned!

Eagerly he jumped into the back of the car, ready to be away. The journey to the hospital, traffic permitting, only takes about 8 or 9 minutes so almost before he had settled down we had arrived. The disabled bays were vacant so I was able to park Rebecca without any trouble. Sometimes in the afternoon parking is difficult due to the increase in visitors but not so today.

Leaving Blackie in the car, after re-assuring him I would only be a few minutes, I went up to the ward to let nurse know we had arrived. Mother was pleased to see me, listened carefully while I explained Blackie was waiting downstairs to come up and visit her.

Nurse came along to help Mother out of her chair, onto a walking frame for the short trip down the corridor to the Day Room. While she was doing this I went down to collect Blackie taking him first for a short walk across the grass to ensure he was "comfortable" before entering the hospital.

As we entered the building he trotted along eagerly beside me. This was another new experience – how exciting. He stepped back in surprise as the lift doors opened – he'd never seen a lift before let alone been in one. As I walked into this little room so Blacks followed obediently. Then as the doors closed behind us and the lift began ascending to the next floor, he looked up in surprise – what a funny sensation – not a bit frightening though. In fact rather pleasant – a wag of the tail is called for!

The doors opened and we found ourselves on the landing of Willow Ward. How would Blackie react to the smell of hospitalization? Obviously it would remind him of Wood Street. There was no need to worry – he was perfectly happy. There were too many new interesting things to see.

We passed through the swing doors then turned right down the corridor and into the Day Room. There was his Grandma sitting by the window! He pulled hard on the lead to reach her, his tail unable to wag fast enough.

The smile on her face was wonderful to behold. She said "hello Blackie" over and over again.

The greetings over at last Blackie sat at my feet while I stayed with Mother for an hour. We were the only people in the Day Room that afternoon so it was possible to let Blackie off his lead. This visit was definitely a good idea. Both Mother and Blackie had benefited so much.

Halfway through the hour a nurse came in to make sure everything was alright. "Oh what a lovely dog!" She couldn't resist coming over to speak to Blackie. She even put out a hand to stroke him despite my warning he was very nervous and would not let her touch him. At first he enjoyed her touch, accepting it willingly. Then suddenly he seemed to realise what was happening. His nervousness overrode his pleasure as he pulled away giving a warning snap. Full of apologies I had tried to warn nurse again about his nervousness. She was very kind. Rather than becoming annoyed she spoke gently, understandingly to him, sympathizing with him.

The time passed quickly and it was soon time to take Blackie home. It was still too warm to leave him sitting in the car while I fed Mother so he would have to stay indoors while I came back to the hospital at 5.30pm. With any luck he would be tired after his exciting afternoon and sleep while I was out. He would then be ready for the walk he always had when I returned home of an evening.

Friday the 14 August was Mother's 95th birthday. I made two cakes, one plain and one chocolate to take into the ward together with all her flowers and cards and we had a little tea-party round her bed.

On the Sunday the weather was much cooler so I decided to take Blackie with me. He could sit in the car with all the windows and quarter lights open and I could watch him from Mother's window. He would be quite safe and it would be more interesting for him than staying at home alone. At least here he could see all the people coming and going from the wards. No one would touch him as he would never allow anyone near the car. A bark warning anyone passing within a few feet but should someone be foolish enough to come too close or actually touch the car Blackie would not hesitate to let them see his full set of teeth snapping sharply and accompanied by a series of vehement barks.

He was delighted to be coming with me.

Finding both disabled bays vacant I parked in the one nearest the trees, gave Blackie a drink of water, two dogaronis and a piece of dried tripe then went up to see Mother.

I usually stayed about two hours. Eating her meal was a very slow process, then I stayed with her usually until she was put back into bed about 7.30pm.

Looking out at Blackie periodically he seemed quite happy, he was not isolated. Staff and visitors were coming and going and, having attracted his attention from Mother's window, he knew exactly where

I was. In fact he often looked up just as I looked down to wave at him so there was nothing for either of us to worry about. Thank heavens it was summertime and the evenings were light.

Chapter CI

So the weeks passed. August turned to September, October loomed ahead.

I refused to send Mother into a Home, insisting she came back to me. With the help of Care Assistants I could look after her at home and she would be much happier in her own surroundings. However, all the professionals insisted I had a few days away to rest and prepare for Mother's return. Reluctant to leave her yet able to see the sense of their advice, I rang Cousin Ralph to ask whether Blackie and I could visit for a few days from the 21 September. Blackie deserved a change as much as I did. He really had been very good recently and he loved to go on holiday. Audrey and Tony had kindly agreed to keep an eye on the house and feed the fish twice a day.

So with only two days notice Blackie and I set off at 10.30 on the Monday morning for Hunstanton. Black had watched with interest as the car was loaded, running in and out of the house each time I carried a bag, or his bed, to Rebecca. However, it was obvious from his reaction once we were under way, he did not fully understand what was happening. Where were the two of us going? Each time I glanced at him he looked at me with his head on one side, eyebrows raised and a puzzled expression on his face. We had never been on a long journey on our own before. This was another new experience for him – and for me.

The weather was perfect – bright and sunny but not too hot. The A10 was very busy that morning, we travelled just 37 miles in the first hour but made better headway after that. As usual we stopped at Branden Creek for a picnic lunch and a walk along the river bank. Blackie knew where we were as soon as we pulled into the picnic area, yet despite this he still looked puzzled. There was no hurry so we sat for a little while beside the river watching the occasional boat pass by.

After about three quarters of an hour, feeling relaxed and refreshed, we set off on the last leg of the journey. Blackie sat looking out of his side window, leisurely watching the scenery and the traffic, taking it all now in his stride. Whatever was happening he and I were together, that was all that mattered.

It was not until we arrived at Hunstanton about 2 o'clock that afternoon that he seemed to accept the fact we were once again on holiday but this time he and I were alone.

Instead of going straight to Ralph I drove down to the cliff top to give Blackie a run on the beach. I parked Rebecca with her nose pointing out to sea and waited. At first Blackie took no notice – just sat on the back seat looking out of the window as he had done for the last hour. Then suddenly he realised where he was and began barking like mad with excitement. Joy of joys – he was "here" again!

Laughing, I ruffled his head saying "I wondered when you would realise where you are – come on, lets go for a walk on the beach".

Blackie needed no second bidding, he couldn't wait to get out of the car. Pulling on his retractable he led the way down the sandy path and onto the beach. Despite his eagerness he remembered to keep a tight hold on his gonk!

There were not too many folk around so I was able to release Blackie as soon as we reached the beach. This was wonderful! The tide was out so there was a vast expanse of wet sand for Black to run on and he made the most of it. He ran straight down across the sand, through a narrow channel of water, across the far sand, loving every minute of it.

The last time we had walked on this beach Tessa had been with us while Mother waited in the car with the lady from Crossroads. The strong winds had been gusting and the torrential rain simply dropping down. Today was so different. The sun was warm and the breeze gentle. Now Blackie and I were on our own – Tess was probably with us, maybe even Kimmy and Trixie but the strain of the last few months made it impossible for me to relax sufficiently to be aware, for certain, of their presence.

We spent about half an hour on the sand before starting back to Rebecca and the short distance to Ralph. Blackie was happy now – he was in familiar surroundings, he was going to enjoy himself.

That evening Blackie was too tired for another walk so after an early dinner he stretched out on the floor asleep until bedtime at 10.15 when he curled up in his bed next to mine. He was fast asleep again in no time.

The next day was overcast so, instead of taking Blackie on the beach, Ralph took us to Courtyard Farm just a few miles down the road. Covering 750 acres the Farm is owned by Courtyard Farm Limited and a charity Courtyard Farm Trust, which provides three public trails, one of approximately 2 miles and one of 6½ miles. These Farm walks are trekked by thousands of visitors, both human and canine, every year.

Parking Rebecca in one of the tiny grass car parks we began to make our way up the rough track beside a large field of cultivated, beautiful wild flowers. Blackie no longer being young we strolled slowly enjoying the peace and tranquillity while he ambled along sniffing from side to side of the path.

235

We only met one other person on our walk, a young lady with a golden retriever. Fortunately the path was wide enough to allow the pair to pass without coming into close proximity with us as Blackie will always give a few barks when another dog comes too near. In no way is he aggressive, just likes the sound of his own bark!

Slowly we made our way up to the top of the path, passed two more fields then, as Blackie was beginning to tire, turned for home. The downward journey was of course much easier for all of us. We eventually arrived back at Rebecca pleasantly tired, happy and ready for lunch.

The sun came out in the afternoon so, while Ralph competed in an indoors bowls match with his friends, Blackie and I went for a lovely walk along the sand and rockpools at the bottom of the cliffs.

Bearing in mind the morning's walk Blackie was coping extremely well. His more interesting life was stimulating him into greater activity with no ill effects.

The next day the weather was once again perfect, allowing the three of us to enjoy an hour's stroll along the beach towards Brancaster before turning for home along the sand dunes high up above the back of the beach, in front of the mainly deserted and derelict beach chalets built on stilts. These gave Blackie an added interest as he ran up and down the remains of the chalet steps or underneath the structure to have a good sniff around. When tiring of this he trotted in and out of the dunes keeping just ahead of us then waiting for us to catch up.

In complete contrast to the morning stroll we took Blackie to Sandringham Woods in the afternoon, walking the woodland trail for best part of an hour. Though willing to turn back as soon as Black showed signs of tiring he kept going without any trouble. Whenever the trail was clear I let him off the lead so he could forage amongst the undergrowth nose down, tail up relishing every new scent he encountered before rejoining us on the path.

For a 15 year old dog with a heart murmur he was proving a wonder. It was not until we arrived back at Ralph's bungalow that he flaked out exhausted but obviously contented.

The last day of our break we took Blackie along to Wells-Next-Sea to walk once more along the marshes which held so many memories. Tomorrow Blackie and I would be on our way home, back to Mother. What was waiting in the weeks ahead for us? Whatever had to be faced we had spent a few marvellous and for me at any least, mentally relaxing days with Ralph, though I am afraid we may have overwalked our host in our enthusiasm.

Friday morning very little could be seen from Ralph's windows as a thick mist hung densely over land and sea alike. Never-the-less,

Blackie must have one last run on the beach before we set off so, after a good breakfast, the three of us drove to the cliff top, parked Rebecca and made our way down onto the sand. The high tide had left only a narrow stretch of beach for us to walk along. Never-the-less it was enough for Blackie to run, play and chase seagulls along. He ran after his gonk, splashed in and out of the sea edge and generally behaved like a young puppy. It was almost as though he sensed this was the last beach run for a while – he was making the most of every minute he could.

Our walk over we sadly drove back across town to Ralph's bunga-low. Blackie watched while I packed my bags then dismantled his bed, carrying them down the garden path to put in Rebecca's boot. All week his tail had wagged, his eyes laughed and his ears stood up as he thor-oughly enjoyed every minute of his holiday. Now he realised we were leaving. His tail drooped, his ears were down and he wore a crestfallen expression. He really did not want to go! Bless him – I gave him a big hug, speaking softly reminded him he had had a lovely holiday and very soon would be seeing Grandma again. He just looked at me, gave a little wag then dropped his tail again.

Having said thank you to Ralph for having us we set off in the direc-tion of home. The roads being clear it only took us 50 minutes to reach Branden Creek where we stopped for half an hour for lunch. On the way up on Monday I had noticed a field of all black sheep near the picnic area. Never having seen other than black faced sheep before I had decided to walk Blackie along to have a closer look at them. Unfortunately, in the interim period, they had been moved. Still Blackie, now familiar with the territory, was only too eager to climb the embank-ment and sniff his way along the footpath to the bridge and back.

On the road again we continued to make good time, arriving home at 3 o'clock. Blackie was tired but, like me, must have felt better for the change and the rest.

At 4.45pm Blackie came with me to the hospital and sat in Rebecca while I visited Mother to give her, her evening meal. Back in our every day routine Norfolk seemed a long way away.

Chapter CII

The date for Mother's homecoming was altered a number of times until finally fixed for Friday 2 October.

All preparations had been made with the various organisations who were to help, Mother's bed had been brought downstairs for her and I had turned the lounge into a veritable florist shop to welcome her.

Naturally Blackie realised "something" was happening so he followed me around everywhere. I kept telling him over and over again that "Grandma is coming home this morning, Blackie". Whether he actually understood is debatable but he knew, without doubt, the word "grandma" so, being an intelligent boy and seeing all the preparations, it is quite possible his mind grasped what was going to happen.

At 11am the ambulance drew up outside the house, generating a gleeful "here she is Blackie" from me, coupled with an outburst of excited barking from Blacks.

I waited until the crew had lowered Mother's chair onto the roadway and were entering through the gate. Then opening the front door wide Blackie and I went out to greet her. Blackie did not know how to contain himself. He ran up to Mother, his body wriggling, his nose wrinkling, his tail wagging, his feet dancing like a canine Fred Astaire. There was no doubt he was overjoyed to see his Grandma home again!

It took a few minutes for the crew to transfer Mother to the recliner that awaited her, then as soon as she was comfortable Blackie sat down beside her determined not to let her out of his sight.

The next few weeks saw a constant coming and going of nurses and Care Assistants who, by my reckoning, are the most wonderful of people. They are always cheerful, caring and patient. They never let anyone down come rain, storm or shine. Nothing is ever too much trouble for them and without them there is no way Mother could ever have come home again.

Blackie quickly became accustomed to the new routine. Some of the Carers were a little in awe of him so as soon as the doorbell rang at the appointed time I took him into the dining room, told him "nurse is here Blackie – she will not be long. Good boy" then closed the door. The word "nurse" conveyed to Blackie that someone had come to the house to do something and once they had gone life would return to normal.

One or two Carers were happy for Blackie to remain free and on those visits he sat in the lounge watching all that was going on.

So life continued for a few weeks. Once the Carers had made their early morning visit Blackie enjoyed his usual run in the park. Late afternoon meant a stroll round the block before dinner after which he made himself comfortable on Mother's bed until the Carers came again to prepare her for the night. He took a great fancy to sleeping on her bed during the day presumably not only because it was his Grandma's but also it was extremely soft and comfortable and being much higher than his armchair he could survey the world to greater advantage.

Chapter CIII

On Sunday 8 November the Carers, having put Mother to bed, had left for the night. Blackie and I were just about to sit down when suddenly Mother was taken ill, necessitating a 999 call for an ambulance. While awaiting its arrival I telephoned Tony who came up straight away to stay with Blackie while I went to hospital with Mother.

Admitted to the local hospital it was 3am by the time Mother had been settled in a bed and I was able to return home. Tony had stayed with Blackie all this while. Poor Blacks, despite Tony's company he had apparently been very unsettled. So many strange occurrences were taking place in his life these days – it was all very confusing for him.

Once again Tony and I began the routine of visiting Mother each day. Unfortunately, this time Blackie had to wait at home as Mother was in a different ward and there was nowhere to leave Blacks where I could keep an eye on him. He was very good at home though and was always waiting behind the front door to greet me on my return, his nose searching for the dogaroni he knew was hidden in my hand.

On Wednesday the 2 December at 8.35am Mother passed peacefully in her sleep, age 95. She was now with Dad and all the people she loved who had passed before her. The two Paddys, Billy, Trixie, Kimmy and Tessa would be over-joyed to see her again as she would be to see them.

Naturally I no longer went out each day telling Blackie I was "just going to see Grandma – will not be long". Once again there was a change in Black's life. We were together all day, alone together. It was almost as though he knew Mother was no longer "there", just as he had with Tessa. He became very doleful and sat on Mother's bed all evening looking downcast. He eyes lost their sparkle, his ears and tail were down more often than not.

Blackie and I were solely part of each other now. He even came to Mother's funeral at Golders Green Crematorium. It was a nice bright sunny day. Bill attended and kindly put one of his Bentleys at the disposal of the guests.

Others came in their own cars while, in order to take Blackie with me I cleaned, polished and then travelled in Rebecca. Blackie in his usual place on the back seat looking out of the side window. He waited patiently in the car on the forecourt outside the small chapel while the service took place.

Afterwards, the guests adjourned to the Fountain Room, attached to the Garden Restaurant, for a small reception in Mother's honour. As soon as they were settled in, busily eating and chatting, I collected Blackie from the car and brought him in to join with us. We walked across the parking area, through the arch then round to the open french doors where the reception was in progress. Tony was standing outside in the sunshine and once Blackie spotted him he pulled hard on the lead, tail wagging furiously in welcome. His enthusiasm was promptly rewarded with a cheery word, ruffled pat on the head and a piece of turkey sandwich. Emmm, that was delicious!

Then, attracted by the hubbub of chatter, he spotted the guests inside the Room and once again his tail began wagging crazily, this time in sheer delight at the sight of so many friends and all gathered together in one place!

As he trotted in through the doors he was warmly greeted by gleeful calls of "Hello Blackie!" What a welcome he both received and gave. Times were to get even better though as he was then offered numerous titbits from the buffet. Fresh Salmon, smoked salmon, turkey, cheeses – he was treated to them all – needless to say none were refused!

Of course he did not understand what it was all about, never-the-less he was revelling in all the attention to say nothing of the special "lunch" he was being given. Bless him, he was part – a very important part – of the family so it was only right he should be there.

After a while, as the guests gradually began to take their leave Blackie came with me to see them to their respective cars and say a fond au-revoir. He really had been a very good boy though he was tiring now – it had all been rather a lot of excitement for one day. He was not used to being with so many people at one time but he really had enjoyed himself.

Chapter CIV

The next couple of weeks were very busy yet everywhere I went Blackie came too. He even came to the solicitors with me – Mr Wason had kindly agreed to him accompanying me to his office as I did not want to leave Blackie at home alone. The time would come when it was unavoidable but not just yet – life was too confusing for him.

At the end of each hectic day Blackie and I sat alone in the quietness of the lounge. Mother's bed was still downstairs so Blacks continued to prefer this to anywhere else but he looked so dejected. He stretched across the quilt, his nose on his paws which hung over the edge of the bed, his eyes doleful and sad.

This could not go on. Blackie was lonely, the house was empty. It was lacking another life form. The fish were lovely. In fact they had grown tremendously, developing their own characters. The largest of the three had become quite friendly towards me. He, or it could be "she", came swimming up to the side of the tank as soon as anyone walked close. But they were naturally confined to their aquarium.

The answer had to be another little dog, company for Blackie especially when he would have to be left, also that extra company for me. What type of dog should we look for? As the dog was primarily for Blackie and he adored small dogs he or she must not be too big. Blackie loved Ossie the little dog he often played with in the park – perhaps I should try to find a Yorkshire Terrier or one of similar size.

There was only one place to go for our new family member. Over recent years I had become a supporter of the RSPCA Animal Centre at Southridge. Blackie and I would go up there to see if they had a little dog needing a good home.

A few days before Christmas, Blacks and I drove the 12 miles to Southridge. Bill came with us as he felt it may be too soon after Mother's passing for me to be thinking clearly and he didn't want me bringing home a great dane! Great danes are beautiful, gentle dogs but not only was Blackie not very keen on larger dogs but I could no longer afford to feed a dog that size!

Louise and Anna were both on duty and listened understandingly while I explained the situation.

The Centre did not have a Yorkie or even a dog of similar size at the moment but they were expecting one or two arrivals in the New Year, dogs who had been the subject of a prosecution case. They would give me a ring as soon as the little dogs were in their care.

I was disappointed for Blackie's sake as well as my own that we were unable to have our new family member in time for Christmas but hopefully the wait would not be too long.

On the 11 January Louise telephoned to say three or four little Yorkies had just arrived at the Centre. Would I like her to reserve one for us? Confirming we would be most grateful, it was agreed Blackie and the little Yorkie should meet the following morning.

What should we call our little dog? Before the question had finished forming in my mind the name "Miffy" sprung into my thoughts. That was it! We would call her Miffy. An unusual name but in the 1940's the little girl who had lived next door to us had called herself "Miffy", which was rather attractive.

As luck would have it the following day the heavens were open wide, the rain was torrential. Still, not to be deterred we set off once again with Bill accompanying us. He was anxious, now that I lived alone, that we should have a dog who would be a good guard dog. Blackie has always been a wonderful guard dog but a new one must also be so. Somehow I could not see a Yorkie filling that roll but that was not the object of the exercise as far as I was concerned!

Arriving at the Centre Blackie stayed in Rebecca while Bill and I went in to see Louise.

Yes, the little dog was here. She was one of 22 Yorkshire Terriers who had been rescued from a home where they had been kept in boxes. Since the rescue the little dogs had all spent a year in kennels while the prosecution case took its course. Now they were ready to be re-homed so had been sent to various Centres for this purpose. None of the dogs had names so Louise had called the little girl earmarked for us, "Carol". She was five years old having spent the first four years of her life in a box then the year in kennels. If we cared to wait a moment Carol would be brought from her kennel into the Reception Area.

While Carol was collected I brought Blackie into Reception. Though, as far as I knew, he had never been in an animal centre of any kind he was obviously upset by this new experience. He became very nervous and agitated – his eyes opened wide, his tail drooped and his ears flattened against his head.

I was busy trying to soothe him when through the rear entrance came a Care Assistant leading a little soft golden bundle of fur on four legs. How tiny she seemed! She just stood there looking ahead of her. "Hello Carol – look Blackie, say hello". Leading a reluctant Blackie in Carol's direction he looked then snapped at her. Oh dear, this was not like Blackie – he adored small dogs. Maybe his reaction was generated by the surroundings.

After a few words with Louise, despite the pouring rain and while Bill watched through the window, we took Carol and Blackie out into the driveway and walked them together down to the gate and back. This was much better. They walked side by side without any trouble. Blackie was quite happy now he was out of Reception and even gave Carol one or two inquisitive sniffs. He was obviously interested although Carol did not appear to take much notice of anything. She simply walked along on her lead staring straight ahead.

Back in the warm once more Carol was returned to her kennel to be dried off while Louise and I discussed what was to happen next. We agreed that I should come up to the Centre each day this week and take Carol for a walk, with a staff member at first then on my own with Blackie, to make sure the two dogs could get along together. To give them a chance to get to know each other.

Next day it was still raining hard so Wellington boots and waterproofs were a very necessary requirement. Blackie and I drove the 12 miles with the wipers fighting a loosing battle to keep the windscreen clear. Never-the-less we were on a very important errand from which nothing was going to deter us.

Blackie, wearing his thick raincoat, entered the Reception without any repetition of yesterday's nerves. This was a good start. Then, having spoken with Louise, Blackie and I went outside and walked round to the third kennel block, while a member of staff went on ahead to prepare Carol.

As we met up outside the kennel Carol seemed a little reluctant to leave the safety of her "home". Who could blame her not wanting to come out in the cold and rain? However, the sooner she and Blackie became acquainted the sooner she could, hopefully, come to her new home where she would be warm, cosy, well feed and much loved.

The four of us made our way along the path behind the kennels, across a small patch of mud then into the top end of a very large, rain drenched field. Miffy, as I was now beginning to call her, seemed rather nervous of Blackie at first. Maybe she remembered he had snapped at her the previous day. However this morning, despite the appalling weather, Blackie seemed quite happy to trot along beside Miffy without any trouble.

Ten minutes was quite long enough today. Poor Miffy did not have a coat on so would need a really good rub down. On the way back across the patch of mud we passed an alsatian on his way out for his morning exercise. Miffy looked at him and gave a low growl – what a cheeky little dog she was. She only came up to his knee yet had warned him off!

As we approached her kennel block Miffy began to pull hard on her lead. Though she did not appear perturbed by the weather she was now most anxious to return to her own kennel. Clearly she viewed this as a place of safety. Her bad start in life obviously meant the outside world must seem a strange and rather frightening place to her.

There was no let up in the weather next day but our walk around the field proved encouraging. I took Blackie and Miffy on my own for the first time. There were no problems at all today. Blackie looked at Miffy several times and gave her the occasional sniff to which she raised no objections. They even rubbed noses while sniffing the same patch of grass.

At the end of the walk Miffy again pulled hard towards her kennel – she knew exactly which block she was in and although she appeared to have enjoyed the outing was only too eager to get "home".

Louise and Anna were pleased to hear all had gone well and it was arranged Blackie and I should collect Miffy on Saturday. Meanwhile we would come tomorrow for our exercise round the field.

As was by now perfectly normal, on the Friday the weather was once again atrocious. This was the last time we would be returning Miffy to her kennel. The next time we saw her she would be coming home with us.

There was a lot to do in preparation. Tessa's red tartan bed could stay in the lounge as a day-bed but Miffy would need a new bed for upstairs for the nighttime. Jollyes in Crewes Hill was the best place. There were several soft toys and a small pull at home she could have. Food bowls, collar, lead etc. I could purchase from the RSPCA on the Saturday.

Her first meal in her new home should be a special treat – Blackie's favourite – chicken. It would take time to get to know Miffy's likes and dislikes but I was sure she would like chicken.

Saturday dawned dry but very overcast. By midday the rain had begun again. After lunch I put Miffy's new bed containing a soft white fluffy toy lamb, in front of the fire ready for her, then Blackie and I set off for Southridge.

Being the week-end, Reception was very busy so I had to wait nearly half an hour before being seen. Fortunately Blackie was warm and dry in Rebecca – no soaking for him today. He could see me from where the car was parked outside the window so he was quite happy. On the way up there I had told him repeatedly that we were going to fetch Miffy, she was coming to live with us as his friend and companion. She was for Blackie.

Eventually it was my turn to be attended to. Claire and Louise dealt with all the formalities. There was a lot of paperwork to clear before Miffy could be fetched. General information to be given, papers to be signed. The Adoption Form was made out in my name with the description given as BREED Yorkshire Terrier: AGE 5 years: NAME Carol: SEX Female: COLOUR Black and Tan. The name I immediately changed to Miffy, the colour to gold and silver which I considered more accurate. Her booster jab was due in September. Mr Winwood would take care of that for her. She must be introduced to him in the near future.

Meanwhile one or two items of necessity were acquired from the RSPCA site shop. They did not have a food bowl that I liked so we would have to stop on the way home at Universal Pets just down the road from the Centre.

While I was busy sorting out a collar and lead for Miffy, Claire went to fetch her from the kennel.

Miffy came in looking a little nervous of all the people and chattering that was taking place. Again I thought how tiny she was. Not that she was a toy Yorkie – she was a medium sized terrier, she just seemed small amidst the furniture, people and other dogs occupying the room. She was a funny shape too, her body seemed to narrow towards her neck but she was adorable.

All formalities completed I said goodbye to the girls and thanked them for all their help. Miffy and I would keep in touch, letting them know how she was settling down.

The rain was still very heavy as we made a dash for Rebecca. Instead of putting Miffy in straight away I got Blackie out and took the two of them for a walk down to the gate and back. This would give them a chance to meet again on neutral territory before Miffy came into the car and onto Blackie's home ground.

They both trotted along obediently side by side but were relieved when we returned to the car. As I opened the driver's door Blackie jumped straight in, onto the front passenger seat then turned to watch what was happening. Miffy could not be expected to understand she had to jump into the car – apart from RSPCA vans she had probably never been in a car – maybe never seen one at close quarters. I picked her up and put her gently on the back seat then rubbed both dogs down with a towel.

Once dry, Miffy settled down quietly on the back seat lying full length with her head on her paws. Blackie was very good. He looked at Miffy then at me then he too settled himself comfortably for the drive home.

If this weather was going to continue Miffy must have a raincoat – we had to stop at Universal Pets for her food bowl, I would see what Maggie had in the way of outdoor wear in Miffy's size.

Parking the car in the slip road in front of the dozen or so shops at Cranborne Parade the three of us made a beeline through the rain for the pet shop. Even though the dash had only taken a minute or so we were all soaked again and were glad to reach the shelter of the shop, to be out of the elements.

Maggie was, as always, very helpful and pleased to be introduced to Miffy. Being so near Southridge she was regularly called upon to cater for dogs of all shapes and sizes so had a good selection of coats to choose from.

Blackie sat quietly watching while Miffy was firstly fitted for a navy track suit similar to his, then a warm fleecy lined red tartan winter coat. Next, we found the right size food bowl, a doggie toy and various tasty treats to make her feel welcome.

Like most dogs Blackie loves going into a pet shop, there are so many goodies displayed at nose level to present a wonderful array of smells. While he was busy exciting his nose, Miffy stood still looking blank, making no attempt to sniff the delights. It must of course have been her first visit to a pet shop and all these things happening to her in the space of one afternoon were very overwhelming for a little dog.

However once we were back in Beccy I gave both dogs a large piece of dried tripe knowing Blackie loved it, hoping Miffy would enjoy hers. No need to worry. Whether she found her treat irresistible or whether as the result of nervous tension, Miffy settled down immediately to munch her way through this delicious long black object.

Blackie finished his in no time at all. Miffy was making slower, though none the less enthusiastic, progress. She still had quite a length of tripe to eat when we turned onto our driveway. It was 4.55pm and still pouring with rain.

Leaving the pair sitting in the car I made a dash for the front door, opened it, turned off the alarm then returned to the car for Blackie. He was indoors in a flash. He had been pleased to come on the outing but indoors was dry and warm – much nicer!

Picking Miffy up I told her she was home. She was part of our family now and this was where we lived. The words meant nothing to her. I may as well have been telling her the moon was made of cheese. Poor little girl, she had such a lot to learn.

I lifted her gently into her new bed in front of the fireplace giving her the remainder of her dried tripe to finish. Immediately she took it from my hands and began chewing again contentedly. She took absolutely no notice of her surroundings – she could have been back in her kennel for all the interest she showed. Her reaction was obviously a mixture of nerves and insecurity at the changes that had taken place in so short a time. Best to leave her to finish her treat then let her do just as she liked.

I looked in once or twice during the next half an hour to have a little chat with her but she seemed quite content to stay where she was for the time being.

To welcome her to the family she and Blackie had their bowl of chicken. Blackie did not need to be called twice when he heard the words "Blackie – chick-chick", he was into the kitchen and gobbling it down almost before I had carried Miffy's into the lounge. As this was her first day, her first meal with us and she still had not left her bed, she should have her dinner in her bed on this occasion.

As soon as he had finished his food Blackie came into the lounge to see what was happening. For the umpteenth time that week I told him Miffy was a "friend for Blackie – Miffy is Blackie's friend". His reaction this time was to look at Miffy in her bed, look up at me and wag his tail vigorously. The fact Miffy was here with us indicated to him that she was here to stay.

Now both dogs had eaten it was time for me to have my meal. Blackie sat beside me in the dining room while I ate. Half way through the meal a little black nose followed by a small golden head and two tiny brown eyes peeped round the corner of the doorframe. As I called out "hello Miffy – dear – come in", Blackie looked towards the approaching figure, his eyes watching her every movement.

As the rain was finally easing, once dinner was over I washed up then took Blackie and Miffy for a walk. A short stroll round the block would be sufficient for the two of them tonight. They had both had a very busy day. So with Blackie on his retractable and Miffy on her new canvas lead we set off.

Miffy was evidently very excited at being taken out. She turned in circles every few yards along the pavement while Blackie watched her with great curiosity. He had never seen a dog behave in this manner before. She wasn't making any noise just taking a few steps, turning round and round. Then another few steps and turning again and so on all the way round the block. I was pleased she seemed to be enjoying herself. She didn't realise it yet but there would be many, many more walks to come for her.

Being a Saturday Audrey rang the front door bell at a quarter to seven. I had deliberately not told her Miffy was coming to live with us, thinking it would be a nice surprise.

Blackie greeted his friend with his usual enthusiast barking as Miffy came out of the lounge to see what all the fuss was about but again made no attempt to bark.

Taken aback by the unexpected sight of a little dog standing next to Blackie, Audrey was temporarily lost for words. Then she squealed with delight. "Ohhhhh isn't she is darling! – where did you get her from?" Laughing I introduced her. "This is Miffy. She is Blackie's friend and has come to live with him and be his companion."

As soon as the four of us were settled in the lounge Miffy jumped up on the sofa beside Audrey. One could almost hear her thoughts "this lady thinks I am lovely – I must make the most of her and she will fuss me!" She was not wrong.

As Miffy sat in the corner of the sofa on her back legs, her spine resting against the cushion and her front legs pawing at the air Audrey could not resist her. She cooed over her, tickling her tummy and stroking her head while Blackie looked on. He was very good – he had accepted Miffy into his home willingly and seemed pleased for her to be receiving attention. He must not be overlooked though. Always when one of my dogs has received a treat, stroke or just a kind word the other has always received the same. In Blackie's case I gave him the strokes he would not allow other people to give him. Because he was still nervous of people coming near or touching him I loved him all the more, trying to make up for what he was missing.

When eventually bedtime came Blackie, as usual, waited patiently in the hall while I locked up. Miffy sat in the middle of the carpet not knowing what was going on. This was something else new – what a day of new experiences she had had.

The alarm set, I called the two of them to come up to bed. Blackie immediately trotted up the stairs but Miffy continued to sit where she was. No amount of encouragement could induce her to follow. She just looked at me blankly. There was only one thing to do. I picked her up, tucked her under my arm and carried her.

Once upstairs I put her down on the landing and watched as she explored all the rooms. Of course, she had not been up here since she arrived this afternoon.

When she had seen all she wanted to I picked her up again placing her in her nighttime bed. Blackie was ready for the doggaronis and begginstrip he always had. Tonight Miffy was given the same. She looked, sniffed then, ignoring the proffered treats, curled up in a ball and went to sleep.

Looking at her I could not help thinking again how tiny she was. She did not really look like a dog – more a little animal. Tomorrow she must have a bath followed by a good brush. Kimmy and Tessa had both had longish fur especially on their beautiful tails but Miffy had long hair all over. This was a new experience for *me*! Hopefully Miffy would not mind the hairdryer because without it heaven alone knew how I was to get all that fur dry!

Miffy slept soundly right through the night. If she got up I had not heard her. Blackie always wandered about to a certain extent – he always began the night on the bed in the front room then ambled between his own bed, the landing and Mother's bed, which was once again upstairs.

Chapter CV

Next morning Blackie was up as soon as I moved but Miffy did not stir. By the time Blacks and I were ready to go downstairs for breakfast Miffy had still not moved. Best to leave her a little longer – she was obviously tired.

Breakfast over there was still no sign of Miffy. Going upstairs I walked towards her bed as she lifted her head, looked up and wagged her tail. This was the first time she had given anyone a wag since leaving Southridge. It was a good sign.

Calling her to follow me down for some breakfast I headed towards the staircase. Miffy came out onto the landing but then stopped. She made no attempt to walk down the stairs. She just stood there. Suddenly the light dawned. She had never seen stairs before! She had spent four years in a box – no stairs. A year in kennels – no stairs. But surely most animals would automatically walk up or down stairs if confronted with them? They would instinctively know what to do. The answer had to be because of the monotony of her existence to date, her brain had not had a chance to develop. She had never had to think about things in any great detail. Presumably she had spent her days sitting or sleeping, waking only to eat the food that was put down for her then gone back to sleep.

The only thing to do for now was to pick her up and carry her downstairs. Maybe she would get the idea of what to do when she saw Blackie running up and down.

The next discovery – which of course should have been obvious – was that she was not house-trained! Training in this area must and did begin without any delay. She must learn the meaning of the word wowwoz, that would be easiest for her as with all our previous dogs. Once again I hoped in vain she would be encouraged by seeing Blackie's excellent behaviour and follow his example. No such luck. Perseverance was going to be the order of the day.

Taking the pair out for a walk after lunch on the Sunday proved a mixed blessing. It was grand to be out with two dogs on leads again. The two certainly looked cute trotting along side by side. Blackie much larger and basically jet black and little Miffy a fraction of his size and light golden in colour. Blackie enjoyed a good sniff or a munch on the long grass but Miffy had not yet discovered these simple joys. She walked along, still turning in circles from time to time otherwise taking no notice of natural doggy things.

As we strolled down the road we passed Alan, a retired police inspector, cleaning his car. Looking up he smiled to say "hello". When he spotted Miffy his jaw dropped open and in a broad Scottish accent he said "Wot on errth have ye gowt theere?" Then as his smile broadened – "Why its a wee rat!" This was all in good fun as Alan and Christine are great animal lovers and pet owners. Unfortunately they had recently lost their delightful old black labrador Caska and were, as yet, to adopt another black lab called Poppy. To Alan Miffy appeared even smaller than she did to me but he spoke kindly to her and wished us well as we continued on our way.

Ten minutes later as we began turning a corner to come home Miffy suddenly tugged on her lead, slipped her collar and dashed into the middle of the road. Fortunately Lakenheath is a quiet street and was, at that time, empty. Panic stricken I called her and, trying not to actually emit alarm, followed her into the roadway – taking Blackie with me – in an attempt to catch her.

Miffy did not want to be caught. Being so small she was very nifty on her feet, dodging my hand each time it came near to grabbing her. As she had shown no signs of wanting to play, it was unlikely this escapism was a game. For some reason she was suddenly objecting to wearing a collar or being on a lead.

After what seemed like an eternity but in fact was probably only a few minutes, she was finally caught and the collar put back round her neck. Another hole was needed in the collar to ensure she could not slip it again! Meanwhile, for safety's sake she must be carried.

Home once more it was time to give her a bath. Anxious not to be left out, or curious to see what was happening, Blackie followed closely as I picked Miffy up, carried her upstairs and into the bathroom, closing the door behind the three of us.

Standing just 12" high Miffy only needed five or six inches of warm water. Lifting her gently down into the bath she raised no objections, just stood where she had been put, stock still. Speaking softly to her as she was washed thoroughly all over with baby shampoo, she accepted without question everything that was happening to her.

After the first wash the colour of the water was amazing – she must have been much grubbier than she looked. The water had to be changed twice before she was finally rinsed. Now came the crucial stage – how would she react to the hairdryer? Tessie would never allow it near her, hopefully Miffy was going to co-operate.

Watched constantly by Blackie and after giving her a good rub down with two warm towels I took her into the bedroom, put her on my lap then picked up the dryer. No adverse reaction – so far so good. Tessa would have been out of the room and down the stairs by now! Miffy sat there as good as gold. Brushing her fur as the warm air ranged over her little body, it was about 20 minutes before I was satisfied she was as dry as it was possible to make her. She really looked beautiful now she was clean. Her coat a soft, warm silvery gold. Not once had she complained. Obviously she would have been bathed at the RSPCA kennels on more than one occasion so presumably she was accustomed to this kind of treatment. This was one less hurdle to have to climb.

Chapter CVI

On Monday Miffy was introduced to Mr Winwood. She had of course left the RSPCA in good health so it was simply a matter of Mr Winwood giving her the "once over". Not wishing to leave Blackie alone in the car now Mother was no longer there to wait with him, he came into the surgery with us.

The hospital had recently been refurbished and lead hooks placed in strategic places throughout the public areas. These proved a wonderful addition as, instead of trying to cope with two dogs on two leads, Blackie's lead was simply looped over the hooks keeping him safely in one place while Miffy was attended to.

Mr Winwood checked Miffy over, read her RSPCA notes and stroked her head. Yes, she was a nice little dog. The house-training could be a problem because of her background but after discussion he agreed I was doing all the right things. It would probably take her a little time to learn.

Unfortunately Miffy was proving very slow to learn but it was not her fault. She had still not learned that stairs were for climbing up or down. It was not until the Wednesday – five days after her arrival – that with Blackies help, the light suddenly dawned for her. I had tried unsuccessfully several times each day to demonstrate the art of walking upstairs, even taken her little legs and shown her how it is done – all to no avail. Then after yet another failed exercise, watched closely by Blackie, he looked straight at her and gave a loud bark. Like a shot out of a gun she ran upstairs as fast as her legs could carry her – turned round and ran down again. She had made it!

From then on Miffy found running up and downstairs great fun. She was certainly nimble on her feet, running from the bottom to the top so quickly and lightly she appeared to float up rather than actually touch the stairs as she passed. So another obstacle was surmounted but there were more to come.

Blackie was so patient with Miffy. He looked much happier too. He watched her carefully as she walked about, jumped up or climbed over things, whatever she did he sat or lay with his head still, but his eyes following her. She was fascinated by him too. Watching him as he moved about frequently climbing all over him, even giving him a playful nip. He didn't mind in the least what she did to him.

Miffy had been a brilliant idea which was working well for all three of us.

The day after she discovered the stairs I walked into the dining room in the afternoon and there standing in the middle of the table, very sure of herself, was Miffy! I did not know whether to burst out laughing or scold her. The 80 year old oak table Aunty Winnie's husband, a very talented and renowned craftsman, made when they were first married, had never been treated like this in it's life! Aunty Winnie would have had a fit if she could have seen this little Yorkshire Terrier lording it from her pinnacle of distinction.

Trying to smother a smile I gently but firmly lifted her down to the ground telling her "No! Miffy – down. Your place is on the floor *not* on the furniture."

This was the first of Miffy's antics. Running around the lounge floor one evening she spotted the fish food carton in a box under their tank. Almost as soon as her eyes caught sight of it her teeth were closing over it as she picked it up then proceeded to run round and round the room with it in her mouth. She may not know how to play with doggie things but she was discovering the excitement of other "toys" – some of which were for consuming!

In an attempt to give up the weight producing mid-evening "snack" I had acquired of late, I had taken to sucking one or two boiled mints. These were kept in a dish on the small table beside the sofa.

I began to notice sweet papers appearing all over the carpet in the lounge and in the hall. Where could they be coming from? Then one day I caught the culprit. Miffy was sitting in the middle of the floor tearing the wrapper off a mint! She had climbed onto the sofa, walked across the arm and helped herself to a sweet from the dish. She was now busily unwrapping it prior to enjoying crunching it between her tiny teeth.

Many years previously Hilda, an elderly friend of Stans and consequently of ours, had an adorable sandy coloured mongrel who loved sweets. However, they must be wrapped. Offer him an unwrapped sweet and he was not interested. Wrap it up before giving it to him and he would have the time of his life tearing the paper off before eating the goodie inside. Miffy reminded me of Ruffles, the only other dog I'd known to behave like this.

Not content with eating stolen mints Miffy took a fancy to the leaves of plants or flowers placed on the floor, at just the right height for her, or the green plants growing low in the garden. In retrospect this must have been the result of some of her basic instincts struggling to escape. At that time she had made no attempt to eat grass, not even when Blackie munched away on this natural medicine. It was several weeks before she realised grass was good for her then, having discovered this, she left the various plants alone.

Though she began eating grass, still she did not bark. Trixie had not barked for several months after coming to us from Battersea so hopefully Miffy would find her voice in her own time. In early March she attempted to give a little bark in her sleep but that was the extent of her vocal performance.

March also brought Miffy's first attempt at asking to go out in the garden. Walking to the backdoor she looked at me then looked up at the door. Maybe we were getting somewhere at last. Alas no – it was just one of a few isolated incidents. It was impossible to be cross with her, though at times the effort to keep cool was very difficult. I must just try harder with her.

Trying to get her into the garden at all was a major effort. As the weather improved a little and Blackie came outside while I did some gardening I tried to encourage Miffy to join us. No, she did not want to know. Picking her up I took her out onto the lawn and put her down only to see her dash indoors again as fast as she could. All summer I tried without success. She would rather curl up on a cushion on the footstool or in one of the armchairs and sleep.

Sleep was a main occupation for her – which, having spent four years in a box, is quite understandable as there could not have been anything else to do. So much does Miffy still like to sleep that even today it is sometimes difficult to get her up in the morning. Blackie comes downstairs with me when I open up the house; goes out to do wow-woz; comes back and sits in the kitchen doorway while I prepare his breakfast. He has a love of sitting in doorways, presumably so he can watch whatever is going on around the house while I am moving from one room to another. When I sit down he settles himself near me. Once he has eaten his meal he sits beside me in the dining room while I enjoy my toast and a pot of tea. Then it is time to wash up, make the beds and get the two of them ready for their walk.

Blackie is groomed first then has his collar put on. Miffy is next for grooming, which she loves. She then stands still on the bed waiting while her collar and harness are put on. However, many is the time Blackie and I have gone downstairs ready for our walk assuming – having called her to come – Miffy is following, only to find she has gone back to bed and curled up! I have even carried her downstairs, put her down on the hall carpet, turned round to pick up the front door keys and found she has disappeared once again upstairs to bed.

Chapter CVII

When Tony first saw Miffy he burst out laughing and said "Oh – you've got a rug rat!". It seemed a funny name to call her but if it was how he saw her – well that was fine because he loves animals and made a great fuss of her. It was only recently I discovered he was referring to a childrens' cartoon character!

Beryl also thought Miffy was adorable and though disappointed she did not accept her proffered treats, was – and still is – only too willing for Miffy to curl up on my bed while she was working on my hands and face. Apparently a great many of Beryl's clients have dogs who also insist on lying beside their owners while Beryl works. Blackie, however, is always content to either stretch out in his own bed next to mine or on the rug by Beryl's bags. As long as he is close to us he is happy.

Tony, nicknamed Woody, the groundsman in Oakwood Park, is another admirer who finds Miffy irresistible. As soon as he sees the three of us coming towards him, he holds out his arms calling Miffy to come to him. While Blackie and I follow slowly behind, she runs up to him for a cuddle. He picks her up, cradling her like a baby while he tickles her tummy and tells her how gorgeous she is. Woody knows all the dogs and their owners who use the park regularly and himself has an RSPCA rescue mongrel named Shep whom he adores.

Chapter CVIII

Very soon after Miffy came to us she gave me the shock of my life one day when she calmly walked up the front garden path through the middle of the wrought iron gate. Fortunately there is a wide verge between our boundary and the busy roadway so I was able to catch her before she put herself into real danger. It had not occurred to me she was small enough to simply walk between the railings but now something must be done as a matter of urgency.

Without further delay I got Rebecca out of the garage and the three of us drove to Jollyes for plastic coated netting to cover all the boundary gates. Until this was done Miffy must be watched very carefully if outside the front door.

Tony came over next morning to give a hand and within an hour we had all three gates securely covered. There was no way Miffy could escape now.

Or so I thought.

It was the May Bank Holiday and Blackie and Miffy were wandering round the front garden while I cut the lawns and tidied up. After a while Blackie laid down on the mat in the open doorway as Miffy continued to sniff around the garden. She liked being in the front because, although she could no longer walk through the gates she could see through them. I had made sure the garden was now a safe place for her to be. In any case I kept an eye on both of them just to make sure all was well.

Although the verge belongs to the council and is their responsibility I like to keep mine looking nice, the grass cut and edged and the flower bed neat. Having carefully closed the gate behind me I began giving my attention to the chickweed trying to creep up between the iceplants.

Along the pavement came a lady with a little dog on a lead. As she looked towards me I smiled and said hello. She obviously wanted to exchange a few words as she stopped and came up the short path to the single gate. Miffy and Blackie spotted her at the same time. Blacks came running up to give a "whoof" at the dog while Miffy came trotting up to have a look. She was fascinated by the little dog and even tried to give a funny kind of little bark – her first ever, while awake. She was – and still is always interested to see other dogs, staring at them as though they were something from another planet.

I had never seen the lady before but she seemed at a loose end and was killing time by talking. A few words would have been pleasant but I could not get rid of her. Eventually she went and I returned to the job in hand. About five minutes later I looked round to check on Blackie and Miffy. Blacks was sitting on the drive but there was no sign of Miffy. She must have wandered round the side of the house into the back garden. Asking Blackie where she was I went round the back to make sure she was there. Again no sign of her.

I was beginning to worry. Maybe she had tired of being outside and gone indoors for a nap. I searched the house, calling to her all the time. No response.

Panic was mounting now – where could she be? She must be here somewhere – look again. She wasn't in the front garden; she wasn't in the back garden; she wasn't downstairs in the house; she wasn't upstairs. She couldn't possibly have got out, both the gardens were secure.

In desperation I telephoned Audrey to come and help me look. Without hesitation she came straight over. Together we searched the house and grounds again. Miffy was definitely not here.

I must telephone the police at once. How could she have got out? After what seemed like an age, the police answered and put me through to the Control Room. As soon as I began explaining that I had lost one of my dogs, the policewoman interrupted. "Is she a little golden Yorkshire Terrier?" "Yes! you've found her?"

Apparently a lady had just reported finding a small tan dog running about in the middle of the main road as she was driving home. She had stopped the car, picked Miffy up and as she was not wearing a collar, had taken her home and called the police. Relief flooded over me. She was safe!

Miffy had not been wearing a collar because I thought she was safe in the garden and anyway – like Blackie – she has a microchip in her neck. Never again would I take her collar off until she was indoors for the night. How grateful I was to the lady who had found her.

Could I go and collect Miffy? The lady lived in Cockfosters and had left her telephone number. Thanking the police most sincerely, I rang the number they had given and the lady the other end confirmed she had Miffy safe and sound. She was apparently in the back garden with the children.

Immediately she put the telephone down I dashed round the house locking everything up. Got Rebecca out, put Blackie on the back seat and, thanking Dad, drove round to collect Miffy. Having grown up in Cockfosters, finding the house was no problem.

At first I could not make anyone hear the bell so looked through a side gate. A child came to see who was there and I explained I had come for the little dog his mother had found. A few minutes later the front door opened to reveal a pleasant young woman holding a very frightened looking Miffy.

It was wonderful to see her again! She seemed mesmerized by her experience and did not respond in any way when she saw me. Not even a little wag.

Apparently she had been with the lady and her family in their back garden. They were having a barbecue and Miffy had been given and eaten three sausages! As she has only a very small appetite it was obviously nerves that made her accept and gobble down the food she was offered.

Only four months out of the Centre and still very new to the outside world Miffy was very bewildered and shocked by everything that was happening to her. As I took her from the lady's arms she simply stared ahead showing no reaction or recognition. The sooner she was back in her own home the better it would be for her. She would feel secure again.

Thanking the lady for her kindness and for taking such good care of Miffy, I carried our adventuress out to Rebecca where Blackie was watching out of the window for our return. As I placed Miffy on the seat beside me Blackie stood up, looking down on her wagging his tail with pleasure.

The drive home only took five minutes and Miffy lay very still and quiet. Before long she was back in the armchair in our own lounge being made a fuss of. Blackie was delighted to have her back and sniffed her all over. She did not want any supper and slept an exhausted sleep all evening and right through the night. Still not even a wag.

While Miffy was sleeping I went into the front garden to try to discover where she had got out. The only place I could see was a tiny, concealed gap between the hedge and fencing next to the house where she must have squeezed through – obviously looking for the little dog she had been so fascinated with. That must be blocked up straight away before she found it again!

Fortunately next morning she was back to normal but being watched very carefully.

Chapter CIX

As time went on Miffy gradually began to come out of her shell a little. Though she still did not bark she began making funny little noises like a hamster or guinea pig, particularly when picked up for any reason. Several times she jumped onto a dining room chair only to be told firmly "down" as a finger pointed to the floor. So she was given one of the carvers to sit in. In fact the carver Tessa had used as a jumping off point when she sat on the windowsill.

This pleased Miffy, she had a place of her own and being so small she could either lie down on the seat or sit up and look through the vertical bars in the back of the chair. Also it meant she was in close proximity to me while I was eating. Standing on the seat with her front paws on the carver arms, making her hamster noise, she looks from my plate up to my face then back down again to the plate in the vain hope of being given something. The only titbits she ever receives from my meal are tiny corners of bread crusts or toast, which she adores. Her tiny mouth opens wide as she makes a grab for the offering then munches vigorously until the morsel has been swallowed, when the ritual begins all over again. She has to wait though until the quarter slice has been all but consumed before her fragment is forthcoming.

Now his Grandma is no longer here to give him titbits from the table when I am ostentatiously not looking, unlike Miffy Blackie never asks for anything – just waits patiently to see if he is going to be offered whatever Miffy has. Which of course he always is.

When dinner time comes Miffy is a little slow to begin eating. Blackie as always enjoys his, then watches Miffy while she wanders about trying to decide whether or not to begin her meal. Presumably when she lived in her box the food was put inside it for her and she ate as and when she was ready. Thus it proves very difficult to encourage her to eat at regular times. Never-the-less Blackie will make no attempt to touch Miffy's food. When she eventually attacks the contents of her bowl, if she doesn't clear it all Blackie – without moving from his place in the hall – looks up to see what I am going to do. Of course whatever Miffy has left is immediately given to Blackie. Being now quite elderly there is no worry of him putting on weight. He is, if anything, becoming a little thinner.

In June of her first year with us Tony, Cousin Bill and myself arranged to visit Eileen and Dennis in Iver. They both love Blackie dearly and having heard so much of Miffy were anxious to meet her.

Unfortunately the 16th turned out to be very hot. Fortunately Rebecca is roomy and in addition to the usual four side windows, has four quarter lights to help with ventilation. Tony sat on the back seat with Miffy and Blackie as, being a five seater car, there is plenty of room. Never-the-less it was still a very warm journey but both dogs were extremely good.

This was to be Miffy's first visit out. How would she behave? Despite my very best endeavours she was still not completely house-trained. Eileen is very kind and understanding but it would be terrible if Miffy let herself – and me – down. To be on the safe side she must go out into the garden at regular intervals.

There was no need to worry. She behaved perfectly and, unlike on her unexpected visit to the lady who rescued her from the main road, she was not a bit shy. Once again she was greatly admired but only in turn with Blackie. I must admit, after having a bath the previous day, Miffy looked really beautiful but so did Blackie, his black velvet coat gleaming.

After sitting in the cool of the garden for a while we all adjourned to the dining room for a super high tea. Once again Eileen had kindly not forgotten Blackie and Miffy who were treated to a small dish of ham each. Miffy may not have been visiting before but she was certainly enjoying herself today. While we ate and chatted she stretched out happily under the table. Then as we moved around she scampered about the house as though she were in her own home.

Leaving Dennis to his special chore of washing up, Eileen and I went upstairs for a "girly time", rousting through her wardrobe, nick-nacks and photographs. Naturally Blackie and Miffy came too. They both followed us into the front bedroom and settled down while Eileen and I chattered. Suddenly I looked up to find Miffy missing. Where had she gone? What was she up to? Heavens, no mischief please!?

Our combined search brought us to the doorway of the back bedroom, which had been their son David's bedroom before he left first for university, then his own flat and finally marriage to Jennifer.

We drew up suddenly, simultaneously falling silent as we witnessed the pantomime unfolding before our eyes.

Facing outwards, built into a wardrobe door is a full length mirror. There, standing in front of it was Miffy. She had found another little dog! She was looking with her head first on one side, then on the other. She danced around, backwards and forwards, from left to right trying to get round behind the back of the mirror to the little dog. She wanted to be friends with it. Her ears up, her tail wagging furiously – she was fascinated by the presence of her new pal.

As we stood there watching she became aware of us and looked round but only briefly. The dog in the mirror was far more interesting! She had seen us before!

As she was perfectly happy and not doing any harm Eileen and I left her to her own devices while we returned to our important matters.

Twelve months later when visiting Eileen and Dennis again, Blackie – no longer climbing stairs unnecessarily, waited patiently in the hall while Eileen and I went up to look at a new dress she had bought. Flying up the stairs from behind to overtake us came Miffy, straight into the back bedroom looking for her pal! She had not forgotten nor was she any less intrigued by the image she once again found there.

Chapter CX

On the 6 July, having returned from an eight month tour of the Far East with his wife Gillian, Bill Medcalf called in to see us. As Blackie ran barking excitedly to the front door Miffy gave her first proper bark – in fact she gave three little barks. It had taken nearly seven months but she had made it!

Hopefully she would now continue to bark whenever she was given cause. But alas this did not happen and it was several weeks before she barked again. This time it was a Saturday evening. As usual Blackie went crazy in his welcome of Audrey so Miffy decided to join in. From then on whenever Blackie ran to the front door barking Miffy accompanied him in her own inimical way.

About the same time she began to give an excited little bark when she saw me take their short car leads down from the hook in the kitchen. This meant an outing in Rebecca, something they both loved. While Blackie can sit comfortably looking out of the window watching everything that passes, Miffy is much too small to see anything.

For several months she contented herself curling up next to Blackie. Then one day, after making a few local purchases, as I walked back to Rebecca there was Miffy standing on top of the back of the front seats looking out of the window! She had suddenly realised if the car was not in motion she could jump up, walk to and fro along the top of the seats and see everything that was going out outside. In fact, from her vantage point she could probably see even more than Blackie. She now does this every time the car is stationary. If she gets tired of walking or standing she sits astride the seat top, horseback fashion. Needless to say she often attracts the attention of passers by who cannot resist a smile.

It did not take her long either to learn that a trip to the shops means a meaty treat when I return. While Blackie will eat a whole slice of thin ham or whatever the treat happens to be, in one go, Miffy's share has to be split into smaller pieces which she promptly pushes around with her nose for a few minutes before deciding whether or not to indulge. This repeated nodding of her head while her nose scrapes backwards and forwards along the rug or sheet, rubs the tip of her nose literally red raw yet it never seems to bother her. No amount of finger wagging and "No Miffy. Stop it you will hurt yourself" makes a scrap of difference.

Neither, at times, does calling her. Though she learnt her name quickly, often she failed to respond especially when in the park.

On one particular occasion in the early days the three of us were strolling up the middle of the big field along the natural path worn down and kept clear by numerous dog walkers. At one time a line of trees had stood beside the path but age and storms have reduced the numbers to a handful of elderly trees and bushes.

Having sniffed along one side of the pathway for a while, Blackie decided he would wander across the bush line and sniff along the opposite track. I followed him over, watching carefully to ensure Miffy came with us. Though several feet apart both dogs were enjoying a good nose amongst the undergrowth.

Having completed his inspection of his patch Blackie walked on ahead for about 10 yards.

Not wanting her to be left behind I turned, calling to Miffy. There was no reaction. I called again, then again. Still no reaction. The grass must be extremely interesting where she was ferreting around! Suddenly her head came up and she looked around her. Again I called but instead of running towards me she began running as fast as she could in the opposite direction, towards another lady with a dog on the other side of the field.

The more I called after her the faster Miffy ran towards the stranger. Whatever was Miffy doing? Blackie and I hurried after her as fast as we could but of course Blackie's running days are over so it was impossible to catch up with her.

Luckily the lady saw what was happening and stood still waiting for Miffy to reach her, pointing in our direction. Within a few feet of her target Miffy stopped, looked, then turned around and around, searching this way and that in sheer panic. She had realised the lady was not me and had no idea where Blackie or I were. As we drew nearer I continued calling until eventually, when only a few yards away, Miffy spotted us. She almost leapt into the air as she sprinted across the remaining field towards us.

Reunited, I thanked the lady for her kindness and help as Blackie sniffed Miffy all over. Why had Miffy ignored my calls – could it be she had not heard?

Over the next few days I watched Miffy carefully, noting how she responded to sound. It appeared that if she was facing me when I spoke to her she reacted immediately but should she be looking in another direction there was no response. A dog who can hear well will turn its head when a clicking noise is made behind its ears. Miffy responded only to a sound behind her right ear, from behind her left ear brought no reaction what-so-ever. There was no doubt about it. Miffy was deaf in one ear.

The following week when she had to visit Mr Winwood for a tummy upset, he confirmed my findings.

From now on an extra careful eye was needed when she was out of doors. In the house she needed watching too – she developed a habit of put her nose into any cup or mug left on or near the floor and helping herself to the contents! Tessie had done exactly the same when she first came but after being verbally corrected a couple of times she soon stopped doing it. Thankfully Miffy was cured just as quickly.

As her confidence grew Miffy began jumping up onto one armchair, spending a while curled up asleep then getting up and walking across from one chair to another. After a spell in the second chair she decided to try the sofa then the rocker – the lounge furniture became her playground. After being confined in so small a space for so long she must have thought herself in heaven having so much room to move around.

Chapter CXI

August bank holiday Cousin Ralph came to stay for a week. Naturally he already knew Blackie but this was his first introduction to Miffy. Both Ralph and his son John, who drove him down, were enchanted with Miffy and very quickly nick-named her "Tiddler".

Like Woody in the park Ralph loves to pick Miffy up, cradling her in his arms while tickling her tummy. The expression on her face clearly says "Ohhhhh – this is heaven!" Blackie, never jealous, watches out of the corner of his eye to make sure his friend is not being hurt. He is very protective towards her. In the park one day he even warned off his old friend, Ossie when Ossie got too close to Miffy for too long. Not that Blackie would hurt anyone, he just likes them to know he is watching.

The week Ralph was here the four of us got out and about as much as possible but, remembering our visit of last September, I took great care not to overtire our cousin. On the Sunday Tony joined us and the five of us travelled up to Hunstanton. This was to be Miffy's first holiday – how would she react? She would probably be shy at first – unsure of herself in a strange place.

Not at all – she lapped up every new experience.

The thick early morning mist turned to hot summer sun before we had gone very far. The open windows providing cool relief as we speed along the A10.

At Brandon Creek Miffy was as anxious as Blackie to get out of the car and explore. He had been here before of course so began barking with excitement as soon as we pulled into the picnic area. To Miffy everything was new – such exciting smells to be investigated and what was that? She had never seen a river before nor little boats that passed slowly along. As for the ducks and swans – they were bewitching! She stood on the path mesmerized by all she could see. There was no moving her – she could not take her eyes away from the water.

Blacks was very patient with her. As they were both on their retractables he could not wander more than a few yards until Miffy moved. Eventually she allowed herself to be led away but continued to look back until, walking along the track a little further we came across two men sitting at the water's edge fishing. Again Miffy stopped to stare. She was probably unsure whether, being so close to the river's edge, they were another kind of water bird or simply human beings imitating them! Whatever they were, they were fascinating her.

We stayed 40 minutes at the Creek before travelling on to Hunstanton, stopping on the way to shop in Kings Lynn. This may all be new to Miffy but she remembered what shopping meant – a meaty treat. No sooner was I back in the car than the friends were pushing their noses forward to find what I had for them.

Once again Miffy showed no signs of shyness even when we reached Ralph's bungalow. She marched straight up the path behind Blackie, in through the back door. As we settled ourselves in Miffy made herself completely at home. How she had changed in the last few months. At the beginning of the year she would have been completely traumatised by all these happenings. Now she was perfectly relaxed and enjoying herself.

Next morning the mist was thick again so it was not until about mid-day that we drove onto the cliff top. Even before the car came to a standstill Blackie recognised his favourite place and began barking like mad. Miffy did not as yet understand what all the excitement was about. She looked at Blackie in bewilderment.

What would she make of the sea? How would she react? Being so small she would probably be rather nervous of it.

I could not have been more wrong. As the five of us wandered down onto the beach I let Blacks and Miff off their leads. Tony, Ralph and I stood still for a moment to see what Miffy was going to do. She didn't hesitate. Down the beach she ran, straight into the sea up to her neck! She turned in circles, jumped up and down and splashed about as though she had been used to the sea all her life. The three of us were absolutely amazed by her.

Blackie followed her down straight into the sea, but only up to his knees. Never-the-less he had a whale of a time paddling along the edge of the water, his tail wagging nineteen to the dozen.

As we walked along the beach the two played in and out of the sea, chasing each other as Blackie had done years before with Tessie. For an elderly dog he really had been rejuvenated. It was wonderful to see the pair of them so happy especially as they had both had a very bad beginning to life.

The next few days were spent either in the garden or on the beach. Where-ever we were Blackie and Miffy were quite happy. On the

Thursday we all went for a beach walk the other end of the town where groins are spaced strategically. Once more I was reminded of Tessie as Miffy ran on ahead of us running in and out of the pools that had formed around the groins and breakwaters.

Splashing through what she assumed was a shallow pool she suddenly disappeared from view. The water being two to three feet deep Miffy had suddenly found herself out of her depth and her whole body, including her head, under the water. As I dashed across the sand to her, a tiny face popped up through the surface of the pool and she began to swim for the sand. There was no sign of panic – she had taken the whole episode in her stride.

Friday we all went to Sandringham Woods where we spent a relaxing hour wandering through the trees, along the paths between the undergrowth. It was much cooler here than on the beach and the two dogs thoroughly enjoyed themselves rummaging amongst the bushes, along the pathways and round the tree roots.

Arriving back at the car Blackie was tired and ready for his lunch. Miffy on the other hand was as fresh as when she started out. The morning had been a pleasant change for them. They could go along the beach again for their evening walk.

Before setting off for home on the Sunday, Blackie and Miffy enjoyed a last jaunt along the sand, playing in the sea like a couple of puppies. They were going to miss the beach but they had the park to run in at home.

Saying au revoir to Ralph we made the journey home without incident. It had been a lovely holiday for all of us.

We had been very lucky with the weather while in Norfolk because the first week of our return proved dull, overcast and very wet.

Chapter CXII

The beginning of October Blackie began to look rather sorry for himself and was unusually quiet. When, on the Saturday and Sunday he was very sick it was time to telephone Wood Street for an appointment with Mr Winwood. Fortunately he was able to see us at 3.30pm on the Monday. After examination it was revealed Blackie had a very high temperature in addition to an extremely high protein level in his system.

Remembering that a very high protein count had been the start of Kimmy's last illness I was desperately worried. Blackie was no longer young. Mr Winwood understood exactly my concerns. I knew he would do all he could for Blackie who was given an injection to bring his temperature down. Mr Winwood wanted to see him again next morning at 10.30am.

Blackie was, of course, already on my healing list and with Mr Winwood's help he was improved a little next day when he again visited the hospital. Both his temperature and his protein level were down a little and he seemed brighter in himself. By the Friday his temperature was back to normal but the protein was still on the high side even for an old dog. Mr Winwood advised the lowest possible protein intake from now on.

Fortunately Blackie loves vegetables of any kind so henceforth he was going to have plenty. On the way home from the hospital we stopped to buy him broccoli, cauliflower and sprouts. That evening 25% of his meal was made up of vegetables, all of which he gobbled up hungrily. Since then I read the "typical analysis" on tinned food very carefully, watching even more diligently everything he eats in an attempt to keep him healthy.

As autumn progressed so the deluge of dead leaves began to fall from the many beautiful trees which grace the verges along our road. We are lucky enough to have two trees outside our home, both half again as tall as the house. Facing us across the road are three Japanese cherry trees which wear breathtaking gowns of pink in the spring but whose leaves have a tendency to blow in our direction come autumn. Everyday it is necessary to spend at least an hour sweeping the driveway and paths in a fruitless attempt to keep them clear.

To Blackie and Miffy this is joy as it means they are able to spend time each day in the front garden. During the remainder of the year they are only allowed out there when I am gardening which usually amounts to one half day a week. Now the pair can mooch around to their hearts content before finding a favourite spot to settle down in. Miffy sits herself next to the double gates where she can see everyone passing by, watching everything that happens in the immediate vicinity within her vision. Her interest and curiosity in everything that moves, in no way abates with the passing of time – if anything it is heightened with all she sees. Blackie sits next to her for a while then settles either on the pathway or just inside the open front door.

Amazingly though, Miffy rarely stays in the back garden for more than a few minutes yet Blackie loves to sit out there with me for as long as I am working – or as time occasionally allows – relaxing. Presumably Miffy considers there is very little of interest there, only the same lawn and plants growing. Nothing actually passes the back garden!

The next few weeks were peaceful. Then on Monday the 15 November Blackie was taken ill again. During the evening he was very poorly. Hopefully a good nights sleep would make him feel better. Alas no. Next morning he again was poorly and looked utterly dejected; he would not eat anything and had a badly upset stomach. There must be no delay – I must get him to Wood Street. Unfortunately Mr Winwood was not there but Julie Turner, a lady vet, would see him at 5.20pm.

During the course of the day Blackie slowly deteriorated until by the time we drew up outside the hospital he could hardly walk up the path. Being too heavy for me to carry, it was necessary to coax him every inch of the way. Blackie needed my complete attention so Miffy stayed locked in the car with the windows slightly open and the safety grids in place.

As we reached the outer door of the hospital I had to virtually lift Blackie over the threshold. Once inside he just collapsed on the floor in a heap. Within a couple of minutes Miss Turner came out of the consulting room. By this time Blackie was barely conscious. It took three of us to carry him into the surgery where he lay on the floor lifeless. Miss Turner quickly established Blackie had a temperature of 106° – it should have been 102°, and he was dehydrated. He was desperately ill. His only chance of survival was to stay in hospital overnight where he would be put on a drip and watched over constantly. If I took him home he would not make it through till morning.

There was no alternative – he had to stay. I couldn't bear the thought of being separated from him but he needed the professional nursing I could not give him or he would die. He was still unconscious so was unaware what was happening – he did not know I was going and leaving him there.

Back in the car, Miffy looked for Blackie – her face worried she looked up at me then all around to see where he was. They had only been together ten months but she was obviously devoted to him.

Choking back emotion I tried to explain "poor Blackie not very well – he will be home again soon". Silently saying to myself "PLEASE, PLEASE let him come home again".

As Miss Turner had told me to do, I telephoned the hospital at 9pm to see how Blackie was responding. His temperature had gone up to 107°. The nurse looking after him had given him a cold bath in an attempt to bring his temperature down. I had to ring again at 8.15 in the morning.

Overwhelmed by a feeling of helplessness, there was no way I could eat. That night I begged Dad and the healers to help him, to make him better. Finally, exhausted, I fell asleep but was awake again early.

On the dot of 8.15 I telephoned the hospital to be answered by Carol who kindly went immediately to get an update on Blackies condition.

She returned to the telephone to tell me he "looked comfortable". Miss Turner would be in shortly, if I rang at 8.45 she would speak with me.

He was alive! Memories of another early morning call many years ago when Mr Winwood told me Kimmy had passed during the night, came flooding back. This was not going to be a repeat of that experience. Blackie was going to make it – he had to.

At 8.45am Miss Turner gave me the wonderful news that Blackie's temperature was normal and he was barking! I had to telephone again at 2 o'clock. If he continued to make good progress he could come home with a course of antibiotics.

As relief flooded over me I could hardly believe it – the news was wonderful. A complete turn-around in his condition in so short a space of time.

Relaxed, knowing Blackie was on the road to recovery and in the best of hands, it was a chance to give Miffy a good long walk.

We set off on foot for the park. It was a lovely day and Miffy trotted along quite happily. She was beginning to take more interest in her daily exercise now. She no longer walked along on the lead like a robot. She had discovered the joy of sniffing here, there and everywhere; of eating grass; of looking at what was going on in the streets – in other words behaving like a normal dog.

It was delightful to see her beginning to blossom into a happy, natural little creature enjoying life the way she should. There was no doubt Blackie had helped her tremendously in this respect, both by example and inspiring in her the confidence she needed to face the world.

Walking around the park we met several other dogs enjoying their morning run. To this day, presumably because she had not met many other dogs face to face in her former years, Miffy always shows keen interest and intrigue when she catches sight of another canine. She stops dead in her tracks head, body and ears erect, oblivious to all except the object of her attention. Trotting slowly at first she sets off in the direction of the dog, pausing periodically to stare questioningly at it. If feeling courageous she will trot up to her quarry to investigate. As she still has not learnt to play, the confrontation leads to no more than a few inquisitive sniffs with perhaps a wag thrown in for good measure. Brief though the encounter may be Miffy is very happy with herself. Pleased with her adventure, she turns and runs joyfully back to me.

Our walk lasted and hour and a half yet, as we returned home, Miffy was as fresh as when we started out. Given the opportunity she could probably have continued walking a lot longer.

As is always the case when two dogs of widely differing ages live together, the duration of each walk is determined by the ability of the elder. Latterly Tessa's walking ability governed Blackie's exercise so now in turn Blackie's aging ability controls Miffy's walk. She never complains if Blackie cannot go far so I feel, having presumably been denied perambulations for such a large part of her life, Miffy views all walks – irrespective of length – as a pleasurable outing.

Anxious to know whether Blackie was well enough to come home I telephoned Wood Street promptly at 2 o'clock. Yes – he would be ready for collection anytime after 2.30pm.

Without further ado Miffy and I set off for Barnet calling at Ferny Farm on the way to buy cauliflower, carrots, broccoli and courgettes to add to Blackie's dinner that night. Though Miss Turner had referred to the cause of his sudden collapse and illness as an "infection", his protein levels must be kept under control.

No matter how short a journey, at times like this it seems interminable. I could not wait to see Blackie. To give him a big gentle hug. Twenty four hours previously he had been in danger of leaving us to join Tessa and Grandma – now he was coming home again.

Arriving at Wood Street Miffy came into Reception with me while I settled the account then waited, full of anticipation, while the nurse went to collect Blackie from the ward. A few minutes later the communicating door opened as nurse led Blackie through. The instant he spotted us his tail began to wag. He was as pleased to see us as we were to see him. Miffy pulled towards him as I gave him a hug. He would soon be in his own home again surrounded by all things familiar.

Nurse explained he was much better though still a little weak and needed medication for a further few days. Also, he would have to see Mr Winwood on Friday for a check up.

Thanking everyone most sincerely for all they had done, the three of us made our way slowly out to Rebecca.

Next day, after a good nights sleep, Blackie seemed much brighter in himself. To my utter delight he had a lovely roll on his back on Grandma's bedroom floor. He really was almost back to normal.

The following day his appointment with Mr Winwood was for 10.10am. We left home about 9.15am so Blackie and Miffy could have their walk around Barnet Common before heading for the hospital. It was a cold, brisk morning necessitating the wearing of their thick tartan coats. The pair trotted round the pathway, Blackie in the lead with Miffy trailing along behind as usual – her nose ferreting into the undergrowth every few yards. To see Blackie now it seemed unbelievable he had been so ill only a few days previously. Hopefully Mr Winwood would be pleased with him too.

Mr Winwood certainly was pleased with Blackie's progress. Apparently he had returned to the hospital on the evening Blacks had been admitted and was amazed to see him lying there in the cage so ill.

He had only seen Blackie a few days previously when we had called in to collect a new harness for Miffy. He had looked the picture of health then – it had all happened so suddenly.

After an examination Mr Winwood was really very pleased with Blackie. He would like to see him again in two to three weeks for a final check-up, unless of course I was worried in the meantime.

When Blackie attended for his check-up on the 17 December Mr Winwood was again delighted with him and he was discharged with a clean bill of health. Another crisis safely overcome.

Chapter CXIII

This was to be Miffy's first Christmas with us – hopefully she was going to have a wonderful time.

On the 22 December the little Christmas tree bought last year for Mother and Dad, which had produced new growth during the year, was brought in from the garden and decorated. Miffy wandered over to have a look at what was going on, sniffed for a few minutes then returned nonchalantly to the armchair, curled up and went back to sleep.

Maybe she would take more interest when the parcels were arranged under the tree on Christmas Eve. No. Despite Blackie's excitement, trotting around sniffing, wriggling his body from side to side, wagging his tail non-stop and my attempts to draw her into the fun of things, Miffy remained totally indifferent. Perhaps she would be attracted by the opening of presents on Christmas Day.

Next morning, though her curiosity was aroused by the aroma of sliced ham and turkey wafting from several little parcels, having sniffed the exposed contents she again trotted off in the direction of the armchair to slumber.

It was such a shame – she was missing so much fun but the Christmas spirit was definitely not transmitting to our Miffy.

To Blackie's delight, Audrey spent three days with us then on Monday December the 27, John brought his father – cousin Ralph – over to dinner and Tony and Audrey joined with us to make a happy occasion. Their arrival, greeted by an excited Blackie, encouraged Miffy to join the fun at last. She was finally beginning to get the idea of the festive season. All these people she had come to know over the last eleven months. All folk who loved to make a fuss of her; stroke her; tickle her tummy; tell her how adorable she is. Maybe Blackie was on to a good thing after all. There were certainly lots of tasty tit-bits coming their way. Sausage, ham, turkey, chicken satays – even a mini Melton Mowbry pie each! Dinner that night was a treat to be remembered. Miffy was "letting her fur down" – Christmas had arrived for her.

All too soon Christmas was over. Now it was time to welcome the New Year.

Once again we had the pleasure of Audrey's company, this time it was New Years Eve. Blackie and Miffy enjoyed Birds Eye Roast Beef in gravy for their special dinner after which they curled up or stretched out in their favourite places in the lounge to sleep the contented sleep.

At the stroke of midnight we raised our glasses of Melba peach liqueur in memory of all our loved ones, human and animal now in spirit, hopefully sharing this momentous occasion with us. A toast too to Blackie and Miffy, representatives of the animal kingdom and dearly loved members of this family.

Chapter CXIV

As winter turned to spring so Miffy continued to emerge more from her shell. One day in January she gave her first bark of excitement, not directed at the front door but when she saw me take the car leads down from their hook in the kitchen. She was now confident enough to jump up into Rebecca, without bidding, the instant the door was open. Her curb drill was slowly progressing too. She learnt from Blackie to stand patiently when reaching the traffic lights. Being quick to learn, I had taught him to wait at the lights until he hears the pips which accompany the illuminated green man walking. He knows this is his signal to move so pulls eagerly across the road the instant the sound is emitted, tail wagging furiously.

While Blackie is tall enough for me to stroke his head as I pass, Miffy is too low on the ground to be reached without kneeling on the floor. While therefore it is easy to slip Blackie's chain collar over his head, to dress Miffy in her harness she has to stand on the third stair up while I kneel on the bottom step. However, she no longer needs to be lifted up there, as soon as she sees the harness she runs ahead, leaps up the lower stairs then stands waiting ready to be prepared for her walk.

It is this same stair on which Blackie now lies full length waiting and watching for me if I am temporarily upstairs and he does not want to climb all the way. Being on the bend, the stair is wide enough to take his whole body comfortably. He will stay there for an hour if necessary, waiting patiently. This is also the step he likes to sit on sometimes when I am in the kitchen as he can peep round the banisters and watch me. When on the same level he literally follows me everywhere – from room to room and back again. Miffy, on the other hand, is quite content most of the time, to find somewhere to sleep. I have never known a dog sleep as much as she does but then that is probably all she had to do the five years she was in her box then in a kennel.

Her past still haunts her to a certain extent. On a number of occasions I have found her curled up in the bottom of the broom cupboard or, once or twice, in a cardboard box that has been impermanently left on the floor for one reason of another. Such moments pull tightly on the heartstrings.

When on the move however, Miffy has to be watched carefully. Being so small she manages to walk behind, under and into the most amazingly tiny spaces. She has found her way behind the freezer; behind the television amongst the wires and cables; under the tea trolley; tucked into a corner out of sight behind a chair; even behind the sofa which is supposedly pushed hard against the wall! On the rare occasions the pair are left for a little while it is imperative all danger spots are made secure with a tray, pouffe or similar obstruction.

This need is reminiscent of Tessa in her older days. She developed a fascination for squeezing behind the toilet bowl or bathroom washstand amongst the plumbing; behind the television or any bowl of flowers placed at ground level. Even though it is nearly three years since Tessa passed, closing the bathroom and upstairs toilet door at night to keep her safe became so much of a habit I still do it automatically.

Blackie sits patiently near to me, usually sleeping, as I chronicle these events. Should the written word cause a tear to fall or emotion to be emitted, he is awake in an instant, looks over and immediately comes to me, nuzzles his head into my side then looks up with his big brown eyes full of anxiety and love. Reassured by a gentle word that all is well he wags his tail then returns to his place of rest and drifts once more into a peaceful sleep.

Blackie's tail can only be described as constantly in motion when he is awake. Every word spoken to him or smile given him is always acknowledged with an enthusiast wag. When on exercise his tail wags continually; when strolling down the garden it wags; when climbing the stairs it wags; when barking a greeting it wags. Cousin Eileen once said to him "Blackie you are such a lovely boy – you are *always* wagging your tail – bless you". She was quite right – just about everything in life seems to give him pleasure.

Miffy did not wag her tail for many months after she first came to us – in fact it was some while before she even raised her tail with pleasure. Then gradually she began to twitch the end of it. Just a tiny twitch at first until now she responds to even a kind word with a magical wave of her tiny feathered extremity.

By mid-summer her coat grows so long it is necessary both for her own comfort and my deliverance from constantly bathing her, for her to have a good trim. The first year we took her in the car to Barnet, left her for two hours then went back to collect her beautifully clipped, bathed and groomed.

Miffy had been very nervous both on arrival and when leaving the salon. The lady was extremely kind to her but to Miffy the experience was new and unsettling.

The following year, being unable to contact the lady who had undertaken the work previously, another canine beautician this time came to the house to attend to Miffy's needs. Blackie and I left the two of them in the kitchen and withdrew to the dining room.

All sounds indicated the clipping was proceeding well. Miff did not have to endure a bath this time as she'd had one the day before. A good brush when the work was complete would put the finishing touches.

Blackie was asleep as I sat reading when suddenly the door burst open wide to reveal the new look Miffy as she came trotting in as fast as her little legs would bring her. Head erect, tail held high she ran straight up to me looking up with an air of pride, pleasure and confidence. She was so very pleased with herself, she wanted Blackie and I to see how beautiful she now looked. What a contrast to last summer when she had been so apprehensive and unsure of herself.

Her confidence has also developed sufficiently to enable her to go into the garden at will. During her early days, nothing could entice her into the gardens. Even picking her up, taking her onto the lawn then attempting to stay with her had no effect. The instant her feet touched the ground she bounded indoors again as fast as she could move. One year later, as soon as a door is open Miffy is out like a shot, down the back garden or up the front drive. She will happily stay outside wandering around long after Blackie and I have come indoors. While Blackie, on the other hand will amble around or sit on the patio or lawn constantly to keep me company, but still comes in as soon as he realises I am no longer there.

Given a nice sunny day Miffy will curl up in any pool of sunlight she can find whether it be on the door mat inside the open kitchen door or a carpet somewhere. Needless to say, because she is so small, it is easy to trip over her so it's very necessary to constantly take extra care. As long as she is catching the sun Miffy is happy.

Chapter CXV

In March, despite the cool weather, Blackie began panting more than usual. After a while I became concerned so took him up to see Mr Winwood. Apart from this excessive panting Black seemed to be in good health for his age but I had to know the cause of this new development.

Mr Winwood examined him carefully then revealed that in addition to his existing heart condition, Blackie has a slight heart arrhythmia – an abnormal heart rhythm. As he correctly predicated my flying into a state of panic, he quickly explained that at Blackie's age – in the region of 17–17½ such a condition is not unusual. He is really doing remarkably well – it is all the TLC he has!

Realising Blackie is no longer young, knowing how much he loves the seaside, Tony and I asked Cousin Ralph if we could visit for a few days before the season began and a date in early June was arranged.

Remembering Miffy's love of the sea it seemed logical to buy her a spare harness in case she managed to get her everyday one soaked. Yes, Wood Street had one or two in stock. So, up we went again this time for nothing more serious than to fit Miffy with her spare holiday harness.

This was nowhere near as easy as I thought it was going to be. Certainly there were plenty of harnesses on display but to find one Miffy's size then actually put it on her proved an hilariously difficult task. Needless to say, the style was entirely different to the one she already wears.

Having secured Blackie to the wall hook then lifted Miffy onto the top of the reception desk Madelaine, the Receptionist and I attempted to fit the new harness around Miff. Madelaine was very helpful but had no more success than I did in trying to fathom the correct way to put the garment on.

In desperation Madelaine went in search of Maddy, a nurse who would certainly know the right way to put Miffy into the harness. Well, that was the idea.

Unfortunately, Maddy had no more success than we had. With five thin black straps, one large ring, one small ring, three fasteners and a buckle the object became more and more complicated with each attempt we made. Surely this piece must go over her head? No – that meant the clip for her lead was under her tummy. Well, maybe the small ring should go on the top of her neck – that cannot be right, the rest of it will not fit around her body properly!

Miffy stood there as good as gold while the three of us turned her this way and that in an attempt to achieve our aim. So ludicrous was the whole episode that we could not help laughing at our own inadequacy. The more we laughed the funnier it all seemed.

For nearly a quarter of an hour we stood there laughing and struggling with this gangling length of tape – then suddenly Maddy cried out. "That's it – I have done it! Look this piece goes here then this piece goes round here, up here then through there".

None of us knew exactly how Maddy had managed it but managed it she had. Miffy was standing there proudly wearing the new harness.

I would certainly have to practise at home – hopefully Miffy would keep her old harness dry!

On Sunday the 4 June, Tony, Blackie, Miffy and I set off once more for Hunstanton. The weather was just right, in fact we could not have asked for nicer weather the whole four days we were there, it was bright, sunny and warm without being too hot.

On the Monday the five of us set off to walk the short distance into town but, as I knew would be the case, it was too far for Blackie. The three of us walked slowly behind Tony and Ralph, who periodically stopped to wait for us to catch up, until Blackie decided he had walked far enough and wanted to go back. He enjoys his walk but has the sense to know when he cannot go further if he is to walk home again so he stands perfectly still waiting for me to turn and see him rooted to the spot. Giving him a gentle word of understanding, a stroke of the head and a call to Miffy to follow, the three of us turn around heading back in the direction we have come. Amazingly Blackie always manages to walk quicker on the way home!

Despite his slowness when out walking, Blackie once again returned to his puppyhood as soon as we drove onto the cliff top and made our way down onto the sand. With the tide out the pair enjoyed the wide expanse of beach to run and play on as we made our way to the water's edge. As soon as we were within about 20 feet of the sea Blackie burst into a quick scamper across the remaining sand straight into the water. Was he really 17 or more years of age – he was behaving like a six month old puppy?! He splashed this way and that along the shallow water having the time of his life – it was wonderful to see him enjoying himself so much.

Miffy was having a grand time too. Ralph and Tony were the slow walkers now we were on the beach and were some little distance behind us. This gave Miffy the chance to run backwards and forwards between us. This time she was not as keen to have a paddle as she had been on her first visit. Never-the-less she seemed to be enjoying herself. While Blackie and I splashed about at the edge of the sea she ran along the sand beside the two men.

With the weather holding fine and few holiday makers to be found as yet, we were able to make the most of the beach and sea each day. Even on the morning we were due to come home the five of us spent a most delightful hour strolling along the sand at the bottom of the cliffs. In and out of the channels created by the turning tide.

Almost as though they knew this was our last walk along the seashore for a while, both dogs seemed to make the most of every minute. Blackie and I waded into the sea up to our knees splashing along the shoreline, through the channels chasing each other round in circles.

Despite my best efforts Miffy had not ventured right into the sea this holiday – that is not until this last morning. We were not returning to Ralph's bungalow after our walk. Instead we were taking Ralph into town to keep an appointment then setting straight off on our journey home. So Miffy decided not only to paddle but fully immerse herself repeatedly up to her neck in seawater! The channels were deep enough for her to swim along so swim along she did! Fortunately I had put two towels inside Rebecca just in case they were needed, as indeed they were.

Warm and dry once more we said a fond farewell to the sand, the sea and Ralph. Not goodbye just au-revoir as we set off once more for our own home 130 miles down the A10.

Appendage

As 'From Head to Tail with Love' goes to print five years have past since that last visit to Hunstanton with Blackie and Miffy. During that time the staff, clients and indeed many, many of the local residents were deeply saddened by the sudden passing on the 7th February 2001, in his sleep, of Mark Winwood at the young age of 53. Mark was greatly admired and respected by all who knew him as well as those who, though they never actually met him, knew **of** him. In 1971 Mark qualified from Liverpool University with distinction and joined the team at Wood Street the same year.

Later that year, on Sunday the 10 June dear Blackie had become so weak it was necessary for him too to leave this sphere and join Tessa. He was already in a coma by the time he was gently laid on the examination table. Although the loss of his physical presence was, and is, very painful I was privileged to 'observe' his reunion with Tess and their overwhelming joy and happiness at being together again brought tears of deep emotion, creating a most cherished and wonderful memory.

Miffy could not understand at first where Blackie had gone but as the ability to see beyond the physical is second nature to all animals it was obvious she was very soon aware of him and comforted by his presence. For quite a while after his transition Blackie continued to sleep in his own bed at night and could clearly be heard breathing heavily, wagging his tail and changing his position.

Miffy continued to progress slowly due to her early experiences of life, which had deprived her of mental stimulation. Through no fault of her own, it took two and a half years to house-train her. She was still learning what it meant to actually be a dog, to do all the things dogs do naturally. For example, despite having watched Blackie enjoying his daily Dogaronis and chew stick treats, it was a long, long time before she could be enticed to eat them and longer still before they really became a cherished part of her regular routine. Now she will not eat her dinner until she has munched her way through several pieces of her favourite goodie – puffed jerky! In addition, each evening, she puts her nose into my mug, which is left on the floor beside my chair for her, and drinks the ¼ inch of chocolate Horlicks left there. Needless to say the mug is cleaned thoroughly and never given to anyone else! If I don't finish the drink quickly enough she sits in front of me looking up, staring at me with those beautiful brown eyes, wearing an expression which clearly says "come on – hurry up, I'm waiting for mine!"

She enjoys socialising with other dogs she meets but only when she feels so inclined! Unfortunately, despite all efforts, she has never learnt to play either with other dogs or with toys. The closest she comes is to chase round and round with excitement when I return home after having been forced to leave her for a short while.

Since Blackie passed over Miffy sadly no longer barks at all, except in her sleep, additionally during the night she frequently wakes me up – often with quite a shock – with her loud snoring, grunts and numerous weird noises. During the daytime she still squeaks like a hamster when eventually wanting to jump down after being picked up for a cuddle. Never-the-less she is a very happy, much loved little dog. Very endearing, especially when she sits on the carpet holding one of her front paws just a few inches off the floor or offering it to you – what a beautiful picture! Whenever she learns something new it is a wonderful achievement which brings great joy. Now, after six years of completely ignoring them, she has learnt she is not supposed to like cats, so pulls hard on the lead, with ears erect and eyes wide, in an attempt to give chase whenever she sees one!

In 2002 it was Miffy's turn to be hospitalised as she needed an operation to extract a number of unhealthy teeth, she was at the time and still is, under the care of Mr Mark Antcliffe who joined Wood Street Hospital a few years ago.

On the 4 March 2003 Miffy and I moved from our house in Chase Road to a lovely pseudo Georgian ground floor maisonette, only half a mile away, which backs onto five miles of woods, country park and farmland.

At first, when walking close to our old home Miffy pulled hard in an attempt to 'go home'. However, in time, she settled down in the maisonette and surrounded by familiar things, happily accepted it as home.

She quickly made friends with Carol and Kevin our immediate neighbours, again animals lovers, who adore her and whose love is reciprocated. However, Carol was surprised to discover Miffy was the only dog I had. When Tony, Bill and I had driven up in Rebecca to view the prospective new home, Carol had seen Blackie sitting in the back of the car. Naturally she was astonished when it was explained to her Blackie had passed over some time previously.

Two or three times a year Miffy has a little friend come to stay with us while her family are away. Daisy, who belongs to Paula, the daughter of a friend of Audrey's, is an adorable little Yorkshire Terrier, half Miffy's size and a bungle of energy. As soon as Daisy enters the front door, she dashes into the drawing room, jumps up into the armchair next to Miffy then looks up at her as if to say "hello, it's me – I'm here again".

The two are the very best of friends, even when Daisy clambers into Miffy's bed next to her, pushing her out or curling up beside her or, after eating her own treat snatches Miffy's from under her nose! All of which Miff takes good naturedly in her stride – after all that is what friends do!

As time has progressed Miffy's deafness has become more pronounced so I have taught her our own special sign language, which she has learnt to understand very quickly. If unsure of what is going on around her she looks up for reassurance and of course, thankfully, is not perturbed by thunder storms or fireworks. She really is to be admired for the way she copes with her lack of hearing. My friend Connie, who once had a deaf cat, gave me an excellent piece of advice. If Miff is asleep and needs to be woken up, instead of touching her which will only make her jump, blow on her gently so she wakes up quietly.

Not as a result of putting on weight but because she has grown in length, Miffy has over the years, twice needed a larger size coat. Her early years living in a box had obviously stunted her growth. Since Blackie and I brought her home from Southridge she has grown approximately 5½–6 inches in the body, which is wonderful and all the more to love!

At the end of 2003 I once again experienced a severe angina attack was taken, by ambulance, to hospital and kept there for three days. Both Gillian and Bill looked after and helped me so much during this time, they were really wonderful. Naturally Miffy was my greatest concern. However, Carol and Kevin not only looked after Miffy, taking her into their own home but the first night, because she was whimpering, Carol curled up with her on their sofa and cuddled her all night. Their two cats, Jet and Archie also kindly accepted Miffy into their home, curling with her during the day, licking her face with affection as though they under-stood her anxiety.

Since then Carol kindly looks after Miffy when I go to Waitrose for a 'big shop' once a month with the result, if Carol's door is open (our back doors are only three feet apart) Miffy walks in, makes herself at home and, given the opportunity, curls up with Jet and Archie. Even though she has recently realised cats are for chasing, this definitely does not apply to her friends next door!

Among the other homes she looks on as her own are those of Tony, Eileen and Dennis and Gillian and Bill, all of whom she adores and who show her unconditional love and consideration. She is such lucky girl, yet so deserving of all the love she receives.

Being a Kodak retiree, in December 2003 I was privileged to be accepted by the Cinema and Television Benevolent Fund to spend two weeks convalescence at Glebelands, their beautiful Home in Wokingham, of course Miffy came too! Bill very kindly drove us down and brought us back again at the end of the fortnight.

What a difference those two weeks made to Miffy. Without exception, all the staff and residents made the two of us truly **very** welcome. With so many kind people making a fuss of her, talking to her, stroking her and with so much going on around her to watch all day, everyday, Miffy's intellect was fully activated for the first time. She had the time of her life. She took a keen interest in everything, constantly watching, determined not to miss a thing. Her sharp, alert eyes followed everyone, with her ears erect her head moved in every conceivable direction. Never before in her world, had there been so much activity.

Since then Miffy has gone from strength to strength. She has become much more aware of her surroundings and continues to take a very keen interest in life – her own and everyone else's!

Recommended reading – Animals in the Spirit World by Harold Sharp Available from The Coachhouse, Stansted Hall, Stansted, Essex CM24 8UD. Tel: 01279 817050